The Voyage and Shipwreck of St. Paul

You are holding a reproduction of an original work that is in the public domain in the United States of America, and possibly other countries. You may freely copy and distribute this work as no entity (individual or corporate) has a copyright on the body of the work. This book may contain prior copyright references, and library stamps (as most of these works were scanned from library copies). These have been scanned and retained as part of the historical artifact.

This book may have occasional imperfections such as missing or blurred pages, poor pictures, errant marks, etc. that were either part of the original artifact, or were introduced by the scanning process. We believe this work is culturally important, and despite the imperfections, have elected to bring it back into print as part of our continuing commitment to the preservation of printed works worldwide. We appreciate your understanding of the imperfections in the preservation process, and hope you enjoy this valuable book.

THE

VOYAGE AND SHIPWRECK

OF

ST. PAUL.

LONDON:
Printed by SPOTTISWOODE & Co.,
New-street-Square.

Painted by H Smartly. Jersey. Engraved by H M'ard

The situation of the ship on the fifteenth morning.

THE
VOYAGE AND SHIPWRECK

OF

ST. PAUL:

WITH

Dissertations

ON

THE LIFE AND WRITINGS OF ST. LUKE,

AND THE

SHIPS AND NAVIGATION OF THE ANTIENTS.

BY

JAMES SMITH, ESQ., OF JORDANHILL, F.R.S., &c.

SECOND EDITION,
WITH ADDITIONAL PROOFS AND ILLUSTRATIONS.

LONDON:
LONGMAN, BROWN, GREEN, LONGMANS, & ROBERTS.
1856.

HARVARD COLLEGE LIBRARY

PREFACE

TO

THE SECOND EDITION.

SINCE the publication of the first edition, new and important light has been thrown upon that portion of St. Luke's narrative which records the events in Crete, (the only portion of the voyage in which the evidence was deficient,) by the observations of subsequent visitors.

In conformity with the plan I have adopted of putting my readers in possession of the proofs upon which my conclusions rest, I have included in the Appendix the communications on the subject with which I have been favoured, which are as follows:—

No. 1. A letter which David Urquhart, Esq., M.P., kindly wrote to me, upon observing in my account of the voyage a difficulty respecting the identity of Lutro with the antient Phenice, caused by an impression, which I found to prevail amongst naval officers, that there were no shipharbours on the south coast of Crete; assuring me, from his own knowledge, that Lutro was " an admirable harbour."

No. 2. Extracts from letters from Captain Spratt R. N., author of Travels in Lycia, who visited this part of Crete in 1853, giving an account of his observations there.

No. 3. Extract from the Journal of the St. Ursula, the yacht of Hugh Tennent, Esq., of Wellpark, Glasgow, from the graphic pen of my friend and relative, the Rev. George Brown, who accompanied him.

In his late cruise in the Mediterranean, Mr. Tennent devoted several days to the exploration of that portion of the Cretan coast which was visited by St. Paul. It is only necessary to refer to the journal of the proceedings of himself and his friends to see with what complete success their researches have been crowned.*

---

* The Appendix having been printed before Mr. Tennent's return, I have to add the following information, which I have received from him and Mr. Brown.

After visiting Egypt, the yacht returned to Crete, encountered the Euroclydon a second time, on the 19th of Feb., and took shelter in Lutro (Port Phenice), which Mr. Brown describes as smooth as a mill pond. The master of the yacht remarks: "The east winds never blow home in the port of Lutro. We were twice caught with the Tramontana, or north

THE SECOND EDITION.

It will be observed that in 1853, Captain Spratt discovered an antient causeway and ruins, which

wind, which blows off in fearful squalls, but on arriving close under the high land, a good half mile to the east of the port, it fell calm, and continued so to the harbour." At this visit Mr. Brown took an accurate copy of the inscription mentioned in page 256. It is as follows: —

JOVI . SOLI . OPTIMO . MAXIMO .
SERAPIDI . ET. OMNIBVS . DIIS . ET .
IMPERATORI . CAESARI. NERVAE .
TRAJANO . AVG . GERMANICO . DACICO.
EPICTETVS . LIBERTVS . TABVLARIVS
CVRAM . AGENTE . OPERIS . DIONYSIO .
SOSTRATI. FILIO . ALEXANDRINO . GVBERNATORE
NAVIS . PARASEMO . ISOPHARIA . CL . THEONIS.

This interesting and important inscription may be translated thus: —

"Epictetus the freedman and Recorder (Notary) to Jupiter O. M., to Serapis, and all the Gods, and to the Emp. Cæsar, Nerva, Trajan, Augustus, Germanicus, Dacicus. The work was superintended by Dionysius of Alexandria, the son of Sostratus, and master of the ship whose sign is Isopharia — of the fleet of Theon."

It proves, in the first place, the prolonged stay of a ship of Alexandria at Port Phenice, otherwise the master of the Isopharia could not have had time to superintend "the work" whatever it was,—clearly pointing to a case of wintering in this harbour ; and, in the next place, it proves the accuracy with which St. Luke employs the nautical terminology of Alexandrian seamen in his designations of the master $\tau\hat{\varphi}$ $\kappa\upsilon\beta\epsilon\rho\nu\dot{\eta}\tau\eta$ (xxvii. 11.), Gubernatore (Inscr.), and of the ship $\pi\alpha\rho\alpha\sigma\dot{\eta}\mu\dot{\varphi}$ (xxviii. 11.), parasemo (Inscr.). The Tabularius was an officer of importance in the fleets of the antients, as appears from the inscription given in the Lexicon Antiquitatum Romanorum Petisci, i. 458.

CINCIO . L . F . SABINIANO . TABULARIO . CLASS . RAVENN.

We can now understand the reasons for the anxiety of the master and owner of St. Paul's ship to move to what appears to have been one of the winter stations between Alexandria and Italy. On the other hand, we can now see that the advice given by St. Paul to remain at Fair Havens was in every point of view sound and judicious: we must remember that the situation of a ship unprovided with a compass was, when blown out to sea at a season when neither sun nor stars could be seen, all but desperate. Now

he concluded to be, I have no doubt truly, the port of Lasea; on the other hand, the evidence acquired on the spot, that the ruins discovered by Mr. Tennent and his friends still bore the name of Lasea leaves no doubt but that they were those of the city of Lasea, the situation of which has been hitherto unknown. Both sites are "nigh unto" Fair Havens, and neither of them could have escaped the notice of St. Luke. It is not necessary to suppose that they were ever continuous; neither Phenice nor Myra were immediately adjoining their harbours, yet St. Luke in mentioning them makes no distinction.

There is, however, another difficulty to be removed before this can be fully admitted. Modern map-makers have placed Lebena exactly where the ruins in question stand. The reason of their having done so is obvious; they have followed the generally received reading of Ptolemy, which places Lebena

---

the experience of Messrs. Urquhart, Spratt, and Tennent shows the great probability of such a casualty in crossing the Gulf of Messara, from Fair Havens to Phenice. The reasons for removing from Fair Havens are by no means so strong as I formerly supposed: a certain degree of shelter is afforded by Anchorage Island, to which hawsers could be carried, whilst the stiff clay of the bottom to a ship well provided with anchors and cables, rendered the chance of being driven either on shore or the island very small.

The subject was, as may be supposed, discussed by the "master and owner" of the schooner, whose sign is St. Ursula, whilst anchored at Fair Havens, and the conclusion arrived at was, that a ship might winter there without much danger.

immediately to the east of the promontory of Leon, Λεῶν ακρα; but, in the first place, the reading is a doubtful one; in the latest critical edition (Tauchnitz, 1843) the alternative reading Leia (Λεία) is given, which may well be a clerical error for Lasea (lib. iii. chap. 17.); and in the next place, Strabo lays down the position of Lebena so clearly as to admit of no doubt that it was situated in the Gulf of Messara, considerably to the west of Fair Havens. Dr. Pococke, who visited this part of Crete, pointed out what he considered to be the error of Ptolemy*, but which was probably the error of his transcribers. But in any case, Strabo must be held to be the higher authority in Cretan geography. He was himself of a Cretan family, and his own notices of the places in this part of Crete indicate that he had visited them. According to him, "Lebena was the seaport of Gortyna, which was distant from it, and the Libyan sea, ninety stades" (nine geographical miles†). It was, therefore, at the nearest point of the sea-coast to the city of Gortyna, that is, in the Gulf of Messara. The alleged position assigned to it by modern geo-

* Description of the East vol. ii. p. 250. note.

† In Pashley's map, the nearest point of the sea coast is exactly nine geographical miles. The passage in Strabo is as follows: Ἀίεχει (Γόρτυνα) δὲ τῆς Λιβυκῆς θαλάττης καὶ Λεβηνος ἐνενήκοντα (σταδίων), lib. x. cap. iv.

graphers, neither agrees with Strabo's account as to distance or as to its being a seaport; it is, therefore, erroneous, and the difficulty in question is removed.

In the first edition I prefixed to the voyage "Notices of the Life and Writings of St. Luke," and added a separate dissertation "On the Sources of St. Luke's Writings." In this edition I have rewritten the whole, and combined both articles in "a Dissertation on the Life and Writings of St. Luke." The importance of the matter in a historical view must be my excuse for stating so fully the evidence which St. Luke's own writings, the epistles of St. Paul, and the works of the early fathers furnish. In the former dissertation on the origin of St. Luke's writings, it was necessary to enter at great length into the question of the origin and connection of the first three gospels. Having, however, in a separate work [*], given the whole evidence which a minute comparison of these gospels affords, as well as the conclusions which necessarily flow from it, I limit myself in the present work to so much of the subject as is necessary to elucidate the sources of the writings of St. Luke.

[*] Dissertation of the Origin of the Gospels, &c., 8vo. Edin. 1853.

CONTENTS.

	Page
INTRODUCTION	xvii
Dissertation on the Life and Writings of St. Luke	1

NARRATIVE OF THE VOYAGE.

CHAPTER I. Cæsarea to Myra	59
II. Myra to Fair Havens in Crete	72
III. Crete to Melita — the Gale	94
IV. The Shipwreck	125
V. Melita to Italy	143

DISSERTATIONS.

I. On the Wind Euroclydon	154
II. On the Island Melita	160
III. On the Ships of the Antients	173
IV. On the Geological Changes in St. Paul's Bay	236

APPENDIX.

	Page
I. Letter from David Urquhart, Esq.	243
II. Extracts from Letters from Capt. Spratt, R. N.	244
III. Extract from the Journal of the Yacht St. Ursula, Hugh Tennent, Esq.	246
IV. On Euro-aquilo (from Bentley)	263
V. Note on the Reading "Euro-aquilo" (from Granville Penn)	265
VI. Remarks on the Melita of Acts xxviii.	269
VII. On the Account of the Night March of the Peloponnesians from Thucydides	273

LIST OF ILLUSTRATIONS.

VIEWS.

I. Frontispiece. "The situation of the ship on the fifteenth morning."

Antient ship anchored by the stern in St. Paul's Bay in a gale from E. N. E. Background, Salmonetta Island, on the left, under two seafowl, a place where two seas meet (τόπον διθάλασσον, Acts xxvii. 41.), to which the ship must be driven. This illustration represents the situation of the ship at the moment described in verse 40., when the crew are cutting away the anchors (τὰς ἀγκύρας περιελόντες), loosing the bands of the rudders (ἀνέντες τὰς ζευκτηρίας τῶν πηδαλίων), and hoisting the artemon (ἐπάραντες τὸν ἀρτέμονα).

I am indebted to the talented marine painter, Mr. Smartly of St. Heliers, for having combined artistical effect with the most rigid adherence to the authorities I furnished him with; and as it is my object in every case to put my reader in possession of the evidence upon which my conclusions are founded, I shall here enumerate them.

In the first place, I showed him on the chart the situation in which the ship must have been anchored, and the direction of the wind. He has represented the sea as it must have been running at the time, certainly without exaggeration; the dark clouds indicate the coming rain; whilst a gleam of the morning sun illuminates the sail

(Artemon) which the crew are hoisting, the gilded cheniscus (χρύσεος χηνίσκος), and the

"Carchesium late splendens."

The background is taken from a view taken upon the spot: by enlarging the background in this edition, the place where two seas meet is more fully given. The ship is taken from the following authorities.

    1st. The ship of Theseus from Herculaneum, see figure at page 169.

    2d. The ship on the tomb at Pompeii, figured at page 168.

    3d. The African wheat ship, from a coin of Commodus, figured at page 162.

    4th. The shrouds which support the mast, with the blocks for setting them up, are taken from a coin figured in Montfaucon, iv. pl. 143.

    5th. The undergirding was represented from the directions of the father of the artist, the only naval officer I have met with who had actually seen a ship undergirded.

For the reasons for anchoring the ship by the stern, which this view is meant to illustrate, see page 92.

I have to express my thanks to Mr. Adlard, the engraver, for the pains he took to render the whole scene accurately.

II. "Fair Havens, Crete." From a view taken on the spot, by Signor Antonio Schranz of Valetta. Page 81.

III. "St. Paul's Bay, Malta, from the South." From a view taken on the spot by the author. Page 126.

CHARTS.

1st. General Chart, page 59.

    Constructed on Mercator's projection, in order to give the true bearings. To the west of longitude 24°, it is taken from the English Admiralty chart by Admiral Smyth. To the east of that longitude it is taken from the French Admiralty chart, as being the latest.

2d. "Part of the South Coast of Crete." Page 94.

From the French Admiralty chart of the eastern part of the Mediterranean, from recent surveys. The dotted line, to the east of Fair Havens, marks the traverses which a ship, approaching it from the east, with a north-west wind, would have to make. From that to the point where the compass lines intersect each other, the dotted line represents the course of a ship leaving Fair Havens for the port of Phenice, with a south wind. This point must be near the place where St. Paul's ship encountered the Typhoon. From thence she was driven to Clauda, and beyond it, to about longitude 24° E.; from thence the course must have been in the direction of Malta. See page 121.

3d. "St. Paul's Bay, and west coast of Malta." By Admiral Smyth, R.N., F.R.S., page 125.

WOOD-CUTS.

Page 183. Figure of a Ship taken from an antient bath, in the Borghese Collection, by M. Jal, Arch. Nav. i. 21.

„ 193. An African wheat-ship under sail, from a coin of the Emperor Commodus, in the Museum at Avignon, from a drawing by the author.

„ 194. Coin of the Emperor Commodus (large brass), representing an African wheat-ship under sail, from the Cabinet du Roi.

198. Ship on the tomb of Nævoleia Tyche, at Pompeii, from sketches and measurements made on the spot by the author.

LIST OF ILLUSTRATIONS.

Page 199. The Ship of Theseus from the Pitture Antiche d'Ercolano, t. ii. tav. xiv. p. 91.

„ 202. Antient Anchor, engraved from a sulphur impression of a coin of Adrian in the British Museum.

„ 220. A Bireme, from a coin of Adrian in the British Museum.

„ 221. A Trireme under sail, from the Cabinet du Roi.

The diagrams at pages 222. and 225. represent the supposed position of the Oars in Triremes and Quinqueremes.

The sketch of Port Phenice, now Lutro, at page 88., is taken from one of the French Admiralty charts, of the date of 1738, in the Knights' Library at Malta.

That of Lutro, p. 256., drawn by the Rev. George Brown.

Chart of Fair Havens, p. 257.
     of Lasea, p. 263.

The two last taken from actual survey in Mr. Tennent's yacht by himself and the master.

DIRECTIONS TO THE BINDER.

Situation of the Ship on the Fifteenth Morning	*Frontispiece*
General Chart of St. Paul's Voyage	*to face* p. 59
Fair Havens, Crete	„ 81
Chart of South Coast of Crete	„ 94
Chart of St. Paul's Bay and West Coast of Malta	„ 125
St. Paul's Bay from the South	„ 126

INTRODUCTION.

TRADITION, from time immemorial, has pointed out a bay in the island of Malta as the scene of St. Paul's shipwreck. It has never been known by any other name than "Cala di S. Paolo," or St. Paul's Bay. There is no more effectual mode of perpetuating the memory of events than that of naming places after them; but, although we can scarcely have a stronger case of traditional evidence than the present, in the following inquiry I attach no weight to it whatever. I do not even assume the authenticity of the narrative of the voyage and shipwreck contained in the Acts of the Apostles, but scrutinise St. Luke's account of the voyage precisely as I would those of Baffin or Middleton[*], or of any

---

[*] At the commencement of this century the accounts of those two navigators were held to be apocryphal, and their discoveries expunged from our maps; but in both cases their veracity has been established by the same process to which I am subjecting the account of St. Luke: the localities have been examined by subsequent visitors, and found to agree with the narratives.

antient voyage of doubtful authority, or involving points on which controversies have been raised. A searching comparison of the narrative, with the localities where the events so circumstantially related are said to have taken place, with the aids which recent advances in our knowledge of the geography and the navigation of the eastern part of the Mediterranean supply, accounts for every transaction— clears up every difficulty —and exhibits an agreement so perfect in all its parts as to admit but of one explanation, namely, that it is a narrative of 'real events, written by one personally engaged in them, and that the tradition respecting the locality is true.

Although many volumes have been written upon a question connected with this voyage, namely, whether St. Paul was wrecked at Malta or Meleda in the Adriatic, I am not aware that any such comparison as the one I am about to attempt has yet been made [*]; none, indeed, could have been made with success in the hitherto imperfect

---

[*] Boysen, "De difficili Pauli Itinere," with a promising title, throws no light on the subject. Major Rennel's paper, "On the Voyage and Place of Shipwreck of St. Paul" (*Archæologia*, vol. xxi.), belongs to the series of works on the controversy above alluded to. He had no personal knowledge of the supposed locality, and therefore had to contend with imaginary difficulties. It is written with that caution and candour which distinguishes him. The conclusion he has arrived at is, as might be expected, that Malta was the scene of the shipwreck.

state of our knowledge of the geography of the Levant, and of the ships and seamanship of the antients. For all purposes of minute comparison, our acquaintance with either of these subjects was worse than useless, and only calculated to mislead. Nothing, for instance, could be more erroneous than the charts of the south coast of Crete, where so many events of importance to the right understanding of the occurrences of the voyage took place, or of Malta, where it terminated in shipwreck.*

Had the geographers of former days been contented, without filling up conjecturally the spaces in their maps, about which they were ignorant, or only given us "elephants instead of towns," we should have had but little reason to complain; but they more frequently did the very reverse, and gave us towns instead of elephants. In one of the French Admiralty charts of 1738, the southern promontory of Crete, now called Cape Matala, and the great bight (the Gulf of Messara) to the west of it, are altogether omitted, and the line of the coast represented as nearly straight. On the other

---

* Dr. Bloomfield, in his "Recensio Synoptica," refers to the map of Malta of Cluverius, for the spit of land which forms the place where two seas meet ($\tau o\pi o\nu$ $\delta\iota\theta\alpha\lambda\alpha\sigma\sigma o\nu$). The spit, or "ness," is evidently the present site of Valetta; but the map has scarcely any resemblance to Malta.

hand, Sanson, in his great map of Crete*, "E Conatibus Geographicis," as it is entitled, exhibits projections and indentations where none really exist; and in particular he has represented an extensive promontory in the centre of the Gulf of Messara, upon which he has placed the town of Assos, evidently for the purpose of accommodating his Geography to the narrative of St. Luke; so, that, whether we translate the word "$\alpha\sigma\sigma o\nu$" (Acts, xxvii. 13.) into "Assos," as it is rendered in the Vulgate, or "close by," as in the English translation, we are sure that the account and map will agree with each other.

Recent surveys have, however, corrected these errors, and furnished us with a correct outline of the coasts of Crete.† The soundings are not yet

---

* Appended to "Meursii Creta," *Opera*, iii. 143. In Dapper's map (*Description de l'Archipel.* p. 385.) there is neither cape nor bight. Fair Havens and the city of Lasea are placed at the east end of Crete; and Claudos (the island of Clauda), according to the longitude of Ptolemy, at the opposite extremity.

† The British survey now carrying on has not yet extended to the south coast of Candia. I am, however, assured by officers engaged in it that the coast lines of the late French Admiralty chart are extremely accurate. I have accordingly made use of it in the chart of the south coast of Crete; I have also used it in that part of the general chart of the voyage which lies to the east of long. 24°, the meridian where Admiral Smyth's chart of the "western division of the Mediterranean Sea" terminates. See however the Appendix, Numbers I. II. and III.

INTRODUCTION. xxi

filled in; but this is immaterial in the earlier proceedings of St. Paul and his companions. At Malta, where we require to know not only the outline and peculiar features of the coast, but the soundings and nature of the bottom, we have Admiral Smyth's chart of the island, and, above all, his plan of St. Paul's Bay, to a scale of 8·6 inches to the mile*, which leave nothing to be desired with regard to the hydrography of this part of the voyage.

Next in importance to a correct knowledge of the geography is that of the peculiarities of ancient navigation; but there is no department of classical antiquity about which we are so much in the dark. I have not met with any modern author on the subject who has not left it more obscure than he found it, chiefly from a want of practical knowledge of the science.† Translators and commen-

---

* I question if modern science has ever done more to confirm an antient author than Admiral Smyth's survey of St. Paul's Bay has done in the present case. The soundings alone would have furnished a conclusive test of the truth of the narrative. To the common reader, the mention of twenty fathoms and fifteen fathoms indicates nothing more than the decreasing depth which every ship experiences in approaching the land; but when we come to consider the number of conditions which must be fulfilled in both instances where the depth is mentioned, in order to make the chart and narrative agree, we must admit that a perfect agreement cannot be accidental. I refer the reader for the details of the coincidences to the Narrative of the Voyage.

† M. Jal, author of a late work entitled "Archæologie Navale,"

tators have necessarily had recourse to the writings of authors who have treated *de re navali antiqua* as authorities; and the consequence is, that there is scarcely a single nautical term in the narrative which is correctly rendered, and even when one is, the reader has no certainty that the meaning is the right one, for he will rarely find two commentators agreed in opinion respecting it.

We are not, however, to suppose that men of learning and research offer conjectures at random; all of them have some grounds to go upon, and it is only by testing their conclusions by a careful examination of the data upon which they rest them, and by rejecting such as we can prove to be erroneous, that we can hope to arrive at the true explanation of the terms. This I have attempted; but I found it a work of much greater labour than I anticipated. Even the verification of quotations is anything but an easy task; we often meet with errors in the references, and every antient author has not a verbal index to guide us in searching for passages.

and Captain Beechey, R. N., are to be excepted from this last remark; but M. Jal is rather a mediæval than a classical antiquary; and Captain Beechey's remarks on antient ships, appended to his travels in Africa, are avowedly taken from Potter. His observations on the rate of sailing of antient ships are, however, valuable, and I have availed myself of them.

But it is not enough to discover the passages, or even to assure ourselves, from the context, that we understand the meaning of the author; we must, by comparing him with other authorities, satisfy ourselves that he understood what he was writing about, and is correct in his terminology. Those who trust implicitly to antient authors will not infrequently be led into error, particularly where the object is to arrive at the meaning of technical expressions. The antient scholiasts and lexicographers, and writers *de omnibus rebus* like Julius Pollux and Isidore of Seville, cannot always be right in their explanations, and I should consider inferences drawn from their works of little value, unless supported by independent collateral evidence. But if caution be requisite with regard to the writings of the antients, it is still more so with regard to the engravings of representations of antient ships on coins, marbles, and pictures. To the nautical antiquary the engraved figures, particularly of coins, are of little value, except to guide him to the originals.

It has been my object, in every instance where it was in my power, to get at the best evidence. I cannot accuse myself of want of industry in the research, and I have been placed in circumstances in some respects peculiarly favourable for prosecuting it.

A winter's residence in Malta afforded me ample opportunities for a personal examination of the localities. In the ships of war stationed there, I could consult with skilful and scientific seamen, familiar with the navigation of the Levant, an advantage I did not fail to avail myself of; and as it is my object to put my readers in possession of my authorities, I have never scrupled to name them. In the Knights' Library I had access to an extensive collection of works, printed and manuscript, on the controversy as to the scene of the shipwreck, on the hydrography of the Mediterranean, and on local and classical antiquities. The following summer I spent on the Continent, and devoted my time almost exclusively to the investigation, with the advantages which the museums and libraries of Naples, Florence, Lausanne, and Paris afforded. Since my return, I have continued it with the advantages our own country possesses, particularly in the libraries and medal rooms of the British Museum and records of the Admiralty[*], and with a private library which I may term rich in early sea voyages, formed in a great measure for the purpose of illustrating geographical and nautical antiquities, and with the means of testing

[*] It will be seen that the record of the proceedings of a court-martial on the officers of a frigate wrecked in St. Paul's Bay, furnished very important information, bearing directly on the subject.

experimentally the soundness of my conjectures as to the internal arrangements of antient ships.

It is not enough, however, to be placed in a position favourable for observation, in order to arrive at just conclusions: we must also know "what to observe" and "how to observe;" but the power of doing so with advantage depends in a great measure upon practice; and I think it is due to the reader to state, that none of the channels into which my inquiries on the subject have branched are altogether new to me. I have, in the first place, endeavoured to identify the locality of a shipwreck which took place eighteen centuries ago. An attempt to do this would be of little value, unless the geological changes to which sea coasts are liable, which may or must have occurred in the interval, are taken into account. Now, it so happens that this is a department of geology which I have been engaged many years in investigating.

In like manner, it would be hardly possible to reconstruct the history of a sea voyage out of such scattered and fragmentary notices as we find in the narrative of St. Luke, without some practical knowledge of navigation and seamanship. My knowledge of these subjects is only that of an amateur, yet a yacht sailor of more than thirty years' standing can scarcely fail to have acquired some skill in those principles of nautical science which are common to all times, although he may not always express them in the appropriate language of the quarter-deck. I find, at all events, the knowledge I have thus acquired enables me to consult my nautical friends with advantage. But nautical skill, whether original or borrowed, will not tell us how Greek and Roman vessels, so different from the moderns in rigging and construction, should be managed under given circumstances. Here, also, former pursuits come to my aid. Nautical antiquities have long been a favourite study, and not a little practical experience in planning, building, and altering vessels, has given me definite notions both of external form and internal capabilities, whilst the opportunity of testing my conclusions by experiment, and the success of those I have made, gives me confidence in their accuracy.

I have felt some hesitation in dwelling upon the advantages I possess for conducting such inquiries with success, which are in a certain degree personal, and I turn with satisfaction to those I have derived from recent antiquarian discoveries, from the pictures and marbles exhumed at Herculaneum and Pompeii, and especially from the discovery of the inventories of the Athenian fleet, which were excavated at the Piræus, in 1834. These last are inscribed upon marble tables : they have been published by Professor Böckh, of Berlin, well known for his researches on Attic antiquities, and his great collection of Greek inscriptions. Nothing can be more satisfactory than the manner in which he has edited these important fragments.

He has, in the first place, printed the tables in inscription characters. He has next printed them in the common Greek type, with the lacunæ filled up conjecturally within brackets, as far as that could be done with tolerable certainty, and he has accompanied them with notes and preliminary dissertations.* It will be seen that I frequently dissent from his nautical inferences, but this difference of opinion by no means lessens my sense of the care and fidelity with which he has executed his editorial labours. These tables contain, in the most authentic form, much information on nautical matters, calculated to throw light on difficult and unexplained passages, both in the sacred and profane writers of antiquity.

We are also indebted to M. Jal for having brought forward in his "Archæologie Navale," some important documents respecting the shipping of

* The title of the work is, "Urkunden über das Seewesen des Attischen Staates hergestellt und erläutert von August Böckh," 8vo, Ber. 1840: *i. e.* Archives of the Navy of the Attic States. I have quoted them as "Attic Tables."

the middle ages. They furnish a valuable link connecting the modern and antient nautical language, which I have not failed to avail myself of.

If, therefore, I have succeeded in clearing up unexplained passages in the sacred historians, or other antient writers, my success must be ascribed, in a great measure, to discoveries unknown to the authors who preceded me in the same lines of inquiry.

My original intention was to have confined myself to the illustration of St. Paul's voyage, and that the work should have been, in the strictest sense of the word, a monograph; that my antiquarian researches should have been confined to the wheat ships of Alexandria, and my critical researches to the nautical style of St. Luke. I could not, however, in searching for evidence regarding the merchant ships of the antients, avoid noticing that which regarded the war galleys also, and I could not resist the temptation of attempting a solution of what Dr. Arnold has called "an indiscoverable problem," * namely, the internal arrangement of the rowers.

I have also extended my inquiries respecting the writings of St. Luke much beyond my original intention. In comparing his nautical style with

---

* Roman Hist. iii. 572.

that of other authors, antient and modern, I was led to a minute examination of his account of the miracle of stilling the tempest on the lake of Gennesareth, as compared with those given of the same event in the Gospels of St. Matthew and St. Mark.

With this view I copied them out in the original in parallel columns, placing St. Luke's account, which it was my object to elucidate, in the centre. After repeated transcriptions, I succeeded in adjusting them so as to exhibit at a glance its relation to each of the other two. The results of this comparison were to me unexpected, but in the highest degree interesting and satisfactory. I found I had unintentionally been led to place in juxta-position the passages which were, perhaps, of all others best calculated to show us what were the authorities which St. Luke has made use of in this part of his Gospel. In the parallel passages of St. Matthew and St. Mark, we have all the data, and nothing but the data, which he has employed. There is here no disturbing cause to perplex us, such as the employment of authorities which have perished, or of information procured by personal inquiry. We are thus introduced, as it were, into his study. We see the two rolls from which he composed his narrative open before us. One of these, which is in Greek, is the Gospel according to St. Matthew; the other is in the language of the country (Syro-

Chaldaic, or Aramaic, called by the fathers Hebrew). The original employed by St. Luke, it is true, is no longer extant, but we have what I believe to be a close and literal translation of it in the Gospel of St. Mark.

By thus placing the writings of the first three Evangelists in a new point of view, and employing a new instrument of examination, if I may be allowed the expression, I cannot help thinking that I have succeeded in throwing new light on the origin of their Gospels. I say, a new instrument of examination: for it was the contrast between the *landsmanlike* style in which St. Matthew describes the storm and its effects, and the accurate but provincial style of the fisherman of the lake apparent in St. Mark's account, and the equally accurate but less provincial and more historical style in which St. Luke, in a narrative evidently constructed from the other two, relates the same occurrence, which first arrested my attention. This led me to examine into the nature of the connection of the accounts given of this miracle by St. Luke and St. Mark. The conclusion at which I arrived was, that St. Mark is the translator of a contemporary account by an eye-witness, and that St. Luke has based his account of the miracle, not upon St. Mark's translation, but upon this original narrative, supplying some particulars from St. Matthew's Gospel in Greek.

An important question here presented itself: if St. Mark be a translator, whom did he translate? The answer which I have endeavoured to establish, both by internal and external evidence, I give in the words of Papias and other antient fathers: "Mark is the translator of Peter" (Μαρκος ἑρμηνευτης Πετρου), not, as some of those writers have, as I think erroneously supposed, that he was the translator of what St. Peter remembered and dictated at a distance of years, but that a considerable part of St. Mark's Gospel is a translation of an account of the transactions in which St. Peter was personally engaged, written by St. Peter himself upon the spot, immediately after the events took place which he has recorded.

Since writing the above, I have seen some remarks on this subject by the translator * of Schleiermacher's "Critical Essay on the Gospel of St. Luke," in which he points out the importance of examining it in every point of view, and anticipates the probability that the right clew may thus be discovered. He says:—

"That a problem so complicated may not yet have been viewed from every possible side; and, therefore, that the right clew may still be discovered, is not in itself improbable."†

Now, independently of all the proofs which I have

* Dr. Thirlwall, now Bishop of St. David's.
† Introduction, p. xxii.

brought forward in support of my view of the authorship of the original documents, and the use which has been made of them by St. Luke, I cannot help thinking that I have got possession of the right clew, when I feel the ground so firm under me — when I feel that in every step I have taken, difficulties have disappeared — when I feel assured that I am not wandering amongst the mists of myths, legends, or early traditions, but amidst the clear light of the best of all historical evidence, that of the contemporary accounts of the persons actually engaged in the transactions which they have recorded.

Although it does not come within the plan of this work to discuss the bearing of the conclusions I have arrived at, on the question of the genuineness or authenticity of the writings of St. Luke, there is one remark which, as it depends on the peculiarities of the nautical style of the Acts of the Apostles, I wish here to make. That style, as I shall have occasion more than once to observe, though accurate, is unprofessional. No sailor would have written in a style so little like that of a sailor; no man not a sailor could have written a narrative of a sea voyage so consistent in all its parts, unless from actual observation. This peculiarity of style is to me, in itself, a demonstration that the narrative of the voyage is an account of real events, written

INTRODUCTION. xxxiii

by an eyewitness. A similar remark may be made on the geographical details. They must have been taken from actual observation, for the geographical knowledge of the age was not such as to enable a writer to be so minutely accurate in any other way.

There is one objection to the locality assigned by the Maltese tradition as the scene of the shipwreck, which meets us at the very threshold of our inquiry, and which it is necessary to obviate in a work which aims at exhausting the subject. It is maintained by Giorgi, Bryant, Falconer, and others, that it did not take place at Malta at all, but at Meleda, in the Gulf of Venice, an island which was antiently known by the same name as Malta, namely, Melita.

But for the above-mentioned reason, I should have been much inclined to have noticed this objection very briefly, thinking, with Joseph Scaliger, " that it would not deserve to be confuted, if it had not had supporters."[*] But when I find it adopted by modern commentators [†] and biographers [‡], and read such passages as the sub-

---

[*] " Hæc ridicula opinio, si non sectatores nacta esset, indigna erat quæ vel confutaretur."—*De Emendatione Temporum*, p. 536.

[†] Dr. Valpy, in his edition of the New Testament.

[‡] Chalmers's Biog. Dict. art. " Bryant."

" On sait bien aujourd'hui, à ne plus en douter, que c'est l'île de Meleda dans la Mer Adriatique, sur la côte de la Dalmatie, et qui

joined, I feel called upon to subject the arguments by which it is supported to a minute and sifting examination. This I have attempted to do, following the reasoning of Bryant and Falconer, as

faisait autrefois partie de la république de Raguse, où St. Paul fit naufrage."— *Corresp. de Bar. Zach*, ix. 78.

" The most celebrated treatise with which we are acquainted is that of Mr. Bryant, who has defended his opinion at great length with all his usual learning, and more than his usual judgment, and in the general opinion, I believe, has been supposed to have established his position."— *Townsend's New Testament arranged in Chronological Order*, ii. 445.

" The course of this voyage, related Acts xxvii., in which the Apostle was shipwrecked on the island of Melita, Acts xxviii. 1., has been mistaken by the first geographers and commentators, and their maps of it erroneously constructed, in consequence of the vulgar error that the island in question was the African Melita or Malta, instead of the Adriatic Melita or Meleda. This correction of the received geography we owe to the sagacious Bryant; and it has recently been established with much learning and ability by a layman, in a dissertation on this voyage, Oxford, 1817, the ingenious Dr. Falconer, the physician of Bath, who has furnished a correcter map of the voyage."— *Hales, Chronology*, iv. 406.

" The supposition (that Malta was the scene of the shipwreck) is quite absurd. Not to argue the matter at length, consider those few conclusive facts. The narrative speaks of the barbarous people and barbarians of the island; now our Malta was at the time fully peopled and highly civilised, as we may surely infer from antient and other writings. A viper comes out of the sticks upon the fire being lighted; the men are not surprised at the appearance of the snake, but imagine first a murderer and then a God from the harmless attack. Now in our Malta there are, I may say, no snakes at all." — *Coleridge's Table Talk*, p. 185.

"This (Malta) is not the Malita where St. Paul was shipwrecked." — *Lord Lindsay's Letters from Egypt and the Holy Land*, i. 19.

best known in this country. I have not, however, left any of the arguments of foreign writers on the subject, who have adopted the same side of the question, unnoticed or unanswered.

Jordanhill, 12th March, 1848.

THE
VOYAGE AND SHIPWRECK
OF
SAINT PAUL.

DISSERTATION ON THE LIFE AND WRITINGS OF ST. LUKE.

BEFORE entering upon the following inquiry, there is a preliminary question which must be disposed of—namely, Is the Luke, the physician mentioned by St. Paul in his Epistles as a beloved friend and fellow-labourer, the author of the third Gospel and of the Acts of the Apostles? For most readers it might be sufficient to cite the evidence of Irenæus, who lived too near the time of the Evangelist to render it probable that he could be mistaken on such a matter. By some recent critics, however, the authorship has been assigned to Timothy, and by others to Silas. My first object, therefore, must be to show that neither Timothy nor Silas could have written them, and, next, that they were written by St. Luke.

With regard to Timothy, it is difficult to understand how the authorship could be ascribed to him in direct contradiction to the author's own statements, that when in company with St. Paul he sailed from Philippi, Timothy and others going before "tarried for us." (See Acts, xx— 4—6.) There is another reason against the supposition that Timothy could have been the author, which, as it applies to Silas also, I may be allowed to dwell upon at greater length than might otherwise seem necessary.

In inquiries into the evidence furnished by historical writings, it is of importance to distinguish between the *historical* style, taking the word in the limited sense as that of a narrator relating events on the authority of others, and the *autoptical*, or that in which he describes what fell under his own observation — in other words, in the style of an eye-witness; because by doing so we are enabled to determine whether the author was or was not present at the events which he describes. These characteristics of narration, which appear to be unavoidable when an author writes truthfully and naturally, are peculiarly observable in the writings of St. Luke. Thus, in his account of the second missionary journey of St. Paul, he uses the first person plural, in Acts, xvi. 10., proving that he was then at Troas. Now it is interesting to observe how naturally the change of style from the historical to the autoptical coincides with the change of pronoun. It is in fact one of those undesigned coincidences which afford such conclusive proof of the authenticity of the narration. Let us consider the bearing which this difference of style has on the present case. In this long land journey of Paul and Silas from Antioch to Troas, nothing is mentioned but what is purely historical. At Troas the vision of St. Paul, calling upon him to proceed to Macedonia, is historical, and properly mentioned, as are the events at Philippi. But between Troas and Philippi nothing of historical importance took place; and a historian who did not make the journey would probably have said no more than that St. Paul and his friends, warned by the vision at Troas, proceeded to Philippi, the capital of Macedonia. Let us now see the manner in which this short and uneventful voyage is described. In the first place we are told that they "got under way" (ἀναχθεντες) at Troas, and ran straight (εὐθυδρομησαμεν) to Samothrace, and next day to Neapolis (xvi. 11.). But it was quite immaterial, historically speaking, whether they went by sea or by land, whether they ran straight or circuitously (περιελθοντες), as they did afterwards on the coast of Sicily (xxviii. 13.), whether they passed by Samothrace or landed at Neapolis, for we hear of nothing having occurred at any of these places. We cannot suppose that an author who writes so autoptically when he was present, even in describing a journey of two days, can have described a journey taken by himself, which must have consumed many months, without the notice of a single autoptical incident. I conclude, therefore, that the author was not present on the previous journey from Antioch to Troas; but as both Silas and Timothy were, neither of them could have been the author of the narrative.

I have dwelt longer upon the importance of distinguishing between the *historical* and *autoptical* styles, because it will be seen, in the course of the following inquiry, how much light it throws, not only on the life of St. Luke, but upon the origin of his writings, and their connexion with those of the other Evangelists.

I have now to state other and not less cogent reasons to prove that Silas could not be the author of the Acts. In the first place, how does it happen that his name should so often occur in the narrative of that portion of the life of St. Paul, which begins with his departure from Jerusalem, and ends with his residence at Corinth? In this not very lengthened period, the name of Silas occurs thirteen times. St. Paul also, in writing from Corinth to the Thessalonians, mentions him, along with Timothy and himself, as addressing (i. 1.) that church: in his Second Epistle to the Corinthians (i. 19.), he expressly alludes to his labours along with Silas in that city. We hear no more of him afterwards either in the Acts or St. Paul's epistles. Can we suppose that in the latter and most eventful portion of the history of St. Paul, if he had been in company with him, he should so completely change his style, and that his name should never been have mentioned either in the Acts or the epistles? Lastly, can we suppose that so modest a writer as the author of the Acts unquestionably was, should introduce himself to the reader as one of " the chief men among the brethren" (xv. 22.)?

It may be asked what, then, are the reasons assigned for the supposition that Silas was the author of the writings attributed to St. Luke? A late author* has urged the following:—First, his accurate knowledge of the proceedings of St. Peter, with whom Silas was intimately connected (see 1 Pet. v. 12.): but this proves nothing, for the author of the Acts, whoever he was, was in a position to have ready access to the Apostles, and with the object of writing an account of the first spread

---

* See Kitto's *Journal of Sacred Literature*, Oct. 1850.

of Christianity, he could not fail to have recourse to so unquestionable an authority as that of St. Peter.

Another argument is drawn from the statement in xvi. 10.: "And after he had seen the vision immediately *we* endeavoured to go into Macedonia, assuredly gathering that *the Lord had called us* for to preach the Gospel unto them." This is held to be arrogance if we suppose it was written by St. Luke. But there is no arrogance in the statement of a fact, a fact confirmed, as regards Luke, by St. Paul, who calls him his fellow-labourer (Philem. 24.); and besides it is the universal practice for even the humblest members of collective bodies of men to save circumlocution by speaking of their proceedings in the first person plural. The author does no more in this passage. But if Silas be the author, he may justly be accused of arrogance in the one above quoted, in which he assumes a superiority over others.

The last argument is taken from the meaning of the names " Lucus," grove; " Silva, whence Silvanus or Silas," wood. This admits that Luke is the author; but if we can identify Silas with Luke, we also prove that Silas is the author. To this I reply, that we have the names Wood and Grove still, but who would dream of trying to identify them?

I am not aware that the authorship has been ascribed to any other companion of St. Paul, except St. Luke and the two above mentioned. It has, indeed, been supposed that the latter portion of the Acts is not written by the author of the Gospel; but the difference of style is simply that of the historian and eye-witness, in every other respect the same hand is perceptible in both works.

Having, as I believe, cleared away the claims that have

been advanced for others, I come now to the positive evidence, which proves that Luke, who is mentioned by St. Paul in his epistles, was the author of the Gospel and the Acts. In the epistles Luke is mentioned as a "fellow-labourer," as one who was with him on his first visit to Rome, and as a physician. Here then are three conditions, which if shown to be fulfilled in Luke, and in him alone of all the companions of St. Paul, we cannot avoid the conclusion that he is the author of the works in question. I shall, therefore, endeavour to show that they are all fulfilled in the writer of the Acts and the third Gospel.

1st. He was a fellow-labourer (Philem. 24.). This is proved by the text already quoted (Acts, xvi. 10.), wherein he states himself as one of those called to preach the Gospel in Macedonia.

2nd. He was with St. Paul on his first arrival at Rome, proved by Col. iv. 14., written immediately after, and by Acts, xxviii. 16., where the writer states his arrival there in the following terms: "And when *we* were come to Rome," &c.

3rd. He was a physician (Col. iv. 14.).

It is not easy for a professional man in treating of professional matters to avoid betraying his profession. From the simplicity of St. Luke's style and entire absence of anything like professional pedantry, his professionalisms are never obtrusive; when, however, we subject his accounts of the cures of diseases to a searching examination, we find that he is always careful to state their precise nature and extent, and that he does so in the technical language of the Greek physicians. It would be easy to multiply instances; I content myself with one from the Gospel and one from the Acts. In the account of the cure of Peter's wife's mother, she is said to be "*labouring under* a *great* fever" (Luke iv. 38.) (ἦν συνεχομενη πυρετῳ μεγαλῳ). Now we are expressly told by Galen, in his treatise on the difference of fevers, that physicians were accustomed to distinguish fevers as the *great* and small fevers.* In an excellent paper on the medical style of St. Luke, signed J. K. Walker (*Gent. Mag.* June, 1841, p. 585.), the author remarks: —

"Nor does he (St. Luke) fail, as often as he has occasion to mention diseases or their cure, to select such appropriate language as none but a professional man could have used. . . . . In speaking of Simon's wife's mother, who was taken with a great fever (Luke. iv. 38.), he uses the term συνεχομενη in the same sense as the Greek writers do."

Compare the above quoted text with that describing the disease of the father of Publius in Melita (Acts, xxviii. 8.), wherein we are told that he was "*labouring under fevers* and dysentery," πυρετοις και δυσεντεριῳ συνεχομενον. Here also we have the testimony of Hippocrates, who uses πυρετοι, fevers, in the plural (*Epid.* iii.). In both these cases we have the best evidence as to the technical character of St. Luke's medical terminology; but we know also from St. Jerome that ecclesiastical authors who wrote before him, whose works have perished, bore the strongest testimony to the medical skill of St. Luke.

"Evangelistam Lucam tradunt veteres ecclesiæ tractatores medicinæ artis fuisse scientissimum." (Com. in Isaiam, 43. cap. 6.)

I may add, that modern medical authors familiar with

---

* Και συνηθες ἤδη τοις ιατροις ὀνομαζειν ἐν τουτῳ τῳ γενει τας διαφορας του μεγαν τε και μικρον πυρετον. De Feb. diff. l. i. c. 1.

the writings of the Greek physicians* have observed, that when he mentions diseases, he uses the appropriate language with accuracy. He also speaks with the natural feelings of a professional man, of which we have an interesting instance in his account of the cure of the woman with the issue of blood, taken, as I have shown elsewhere, from the original account of Peter, in the second Gospel, evidently derived from personal knowledge. The downright Mark (Peter) speaks with indignation, no doubt justly, of the treatment she had received from the physicians, probably quacks, such as might be found in a fishing village. He tells us that this woman "had suffered many things from many physicians, had wasted (δαπανησασα) all that she had upon them, and was nothing bettered by them, but rather grew worse" (Mark, v. 26.).

This is, as Dr. Bloomfield expresses it, " strong language," and although no doubt in this particular case true, yet from the unqualified manner in which it is expressed, it leads to an imputation on the profession in general. St. Luke states it so as to remove the harsh inference implied in Mark's account, but in doing so adheres rigidly to the facts of the case. He tells us that the woman "had expended her whole living upon physicians, neither could be healed by any" (viii. 43.). We may conclude, therefore, with confidence, that the fact of his having been a physician is established, and that the

---

* I am indebted to Dr. Stroud, author of the " Physical Death of Christ," not only for a statement of his own conviction on the subject, entirely agreeing with that mentioned in the text, but for pointing out a similar opinion on the part of Dr. Mead, in his " Medica Sacra."—See Works, Lond. 1762, p. 625. See also Freind, " Historia Medicinæ," p. 433.

conditions which identify Luke the friend of St. Paul with the author of the Acts are fulfilled.*

The only unquestionable sources of information respecting St. Luke's life are his own writings, and the epistles of St. Paul. There are indeed scattered notices in the works of the Fathers, which, whether we consider them authentic or not, are useful in guiding us in our inquiries, and which in many cases are confirmed by the incidental notices which occur so frequently in those writings. Thus, St. Luke does not tell us that he was a physician, and St. Paul does not tell us that he was the author of the works which pass under his name, but we have seen that a minute examination establishes both points.

Eusebius and Jerome state that he was a physician of Antioch. The latter refers to his writings in proof of the statement: "Lucas medicus Antiochiensis ut ejus scripta indicant" (*De Vir. Illust.* c. vi.). It is not quite clear whether he refers to his country or profession in this passage. If to the former, Jerome had means of noticing national peculiarities in a language still spoken when he wrote, which would escape the researches of modern critics, for he who could detect Cilicisms in the language of St. Paul could as easily detect Antiochianisms in the language of St. Luke.

There are, however, other indications in his writings, not depending on idiomatic expression, which tend to prove that he was an Antiochean at least by residence, if not by birth.

* A full statement of this evidence will be found in the 14th chapter of Briscoe's "Hist. of the Acts," vol. ii. p. 474.

We learn from St. Paul's Epistle to the Colossians that he was not " one of the circumcision" (iv. 11. 14.). If, therefore, he was an Antiochean, he was in all probability one of the Grecian proselytes of that city, converted either by the first Christian missionaries (see Acts, xi. 21.), or by St. Paul himself (Ib. v. 26.).

The first indication of his country occurs in his enumeration of the seven deacons, in Acts, vi. 5. He stops in relating their names to tell us that Nicolas was "a proselyte of Antioch," but he does not say a word of the country of any of the others. Now, if St. Luke himself was an Antiochean, nothing could be more natural than his notice of a circumstance which could not fail to interest him, and of which he must have been personally cognisant. How otherwise can we account for his particularising this individual alone of all the seven?

The earliest notice of Antioch connected with the history of Christianity occurs in Acts, xi. 19., where we are informed that " they who were scattered abroad, upon the persecutions that arose about Stephen, travelled as far as Antioch" (Acts, xi. 19.). St. Luke's account of this part of the history of the church is so minute and circumstantial as to indicate the pen of one who was then residing at Antioch. Thus he mentions the different places from whence the disciples came, and distinguishes those who addressed the Jews from those who addressed the Grecians. He also mentions the names of certain Antiocheans, men of consequence no doubt in their own city, but never heard of elsewhere. The manner too in which he relates the events which took place at Antioch at this time indicates no less clearly that his is the narrative of an eye-witness. Thus, in speaking of the men of Cyprus and Cyrene, he tells us that "when they were *come* to Antioch, they spake unto the Grecians (xi. 20.), that Barnabas *departed* (from Antioch) (v. 25.), and *brought* him (Paul) *to* Antioch; prophets *come from* Jerusalem (v. 27.); relief *is sent to* Jerusalem" (v. 29.). And at the end of the following chapter, after narrating the persecutions of Herod and his death, he tells us without prefatory explanation that St. Paul and Barnabas *returned from* Jerusalem (xii. 25.). This is the language of a person who was at Antioch at the time; any other would have said, they returned to Antioch.

The evidence drawn from the autopticity of the narration of St. Luke's presence at Antioch at this time receives a strong confirmation from a reading in the Codex D. (Cantabrigiensis), in which he expressly declares that he was present when Agabus foretold the famine in the days of Claudius Cæsar (Acts, xi. 27, 28.). The passage is as follows: "And in these days came prophets from Jerusalem to Antioch, and *there was great joy; and when we were assembled**, one of them stood up," &c. This passage, although not included in the received text nor in any of the late critical editions, is supported by evidence quite as strong as some which are. In the first place, it cannot be an interpolation, for it is expressly quoted by Augustine at least a century before the date of the MS., but must be taken from preceding MSS. The passage is in the following terms: "In the Acts of the Apostles *it is written,* that what was necessary for sustenance was provided

---

* Ἦν δε πολλη αγαλλιασις, συνεστραμμενων δε ἡμων.

against future famine—for *we thus read,* 'In these days prophets came down to Antioch, *and there was great joy; and when we were assembled,* there stood up one of them named Agabus,'* &c. The same passage also occurs in the pre-Hieronymian Latin version which accompanies the Greek text in Codex D.† It occurred, therefore, in manuscripts and versions of a much earlier date. It is one of those passages to which none of the causes to which interpolations are ascribed can apply, such as the subjective views of transcribers, the insertion of marginal explanations or of parallel passages, neither could it be accidental. On the other hand, its absence from other MSS. might be accidental, for nothing is more common than the omission of a line in copying, and in the present case the sense of the passage is complete without it, so that the omission might pass unobserved. I can only attribute the want of attention bestowed by commentators on this passage to the depreciatory remarks of Tillemont and Lardner, which we find stated in the following note appended by the latter to his account of St. Luke (vol. vi. p. 104., 8vo. ed.): —

"From some words in the Cambridge manuscript, Bishop Pearson has argued that Luke was in Paul's company from the year 43 : 'Dein peragrat (Paulus) Phrygiam et Galatiam et per Mysiam venit Troadem ubi se illi comitem adjunxisse indicat Lucas (xvi. 10.). Qui antea etiam Antiochiæ cum Paulo fuit, et jam eum Troade assecutus

---

* "Item in Actibus Apostolorum scriptum est, ea quæ ad victum sunt necessaria procurata esse in futurum famem. Sic enim legimus. 'In illis autem diebus descenderunt ab Ierosolymis prophetæ Antiochiam, *eratque magna exultatio. Congregatis autem nobis,* surgens unus ex illis nomine Agabus.'" De Serm. Domini, lib. ii. c. 57.

† "Revertentibus autem nobis."

est; ut colligere licet ex Act. xi. 28., ubi Codex Cantabr. habet συνεστραμμενων δε ἡμων, ab anno igitur 43 per octennium discipulus fuerat Antiochiæ ' (*Annal. Paulin.* p. 10.). But it is not safe to rely upon one manuscript only, different from all others, and of no great authority. As Mr. Tillemont took notice of this observation of Pearson, I transcribe his thoughts about it: 'Selon le manuscrit de Cambridge, S. Luc dit qu'il estoit avec S. Paul à Antioch dès l'an 43, ce que Pearson a reçu. Mais il ne seroit pas sur de fier à un manuscrit différent de tous les autres. Et quand cela se pourrait en quelques occasions, ce ne seroit pas à l'égard du MS. de Camb., qui est plein d'additions et alterations contraires au véritable texte de S. Luc' (Mém. Eccl. t. 2. S. Luc, note 3.). Some may argue from these words that Luke was a Gentile converted by Paul at Antioch. And others might argue that he is the same as Lucius, mentioned Acts, xiii. 1., but I should think it best for neither side to form an argument from this reading. Mr. Wetstein has referred us to a place from St. Augustine, where the text is quoted very agreeably to the Cambridge manuscript: 'In illis autem diebus descenderunt ab Ierosolymis Prophetæ Antiochiam, eratque magna exultatio; congregatis autem nobis, surgens unus ex illis nomine Agabus,' &c. (*De Serm. Dom.* ii. 17.) But it is observable that Irenæus (iii. 14.), a more ancient writer, enumerating St. Luke's journeys in St. Paul's company, begins at Troas (Acts, xvi. 8. 10.). I presume it must be best to rely upon him, and the general consent of all MSS. except one in the common reading."

Having shown that the passage in question is not an interpolation in the Cambridge MS., the objections of Tillemont do not apply to the case, neither is it the only manuscript which contains it; according to Lachmann it also occurs in the cursive MS. d. It is mere assumption to say that the so called interpolations are contrary to the true text. Whatever may be the character of codex D. as to correctness, its remarkable agreement with antient versions proves the great antiquity of the text. Irenæus does not contradict the passage; he quotes from memory.

and confuses the arrival at Troas — "Nos venimus in Troadem" (Acts, xx. 6.) — the only one where the first person plural is used with that of Paul (Acts, xvi. 8.). The testimony of St. Augustine to the reading in Codex D. remains, therefore, unshaken by that of Irenæus.

The autopticity of the account of St. Paul's first missionary journey to Cyprus and Asia Minor, in company with Barnabas, narrated in Acts, xiii. and xiv., affords strong presumptive proof that Luke accompanied them. He tells us, in the first place, that they "departed into Seleucia, and from thence sailed to Cyprus" (xiii. 4.); but nothing is recorded as having happened at Seleucia, and it was quite immaterial whether they embarked there, or descended to the sea by the river Orontes. At Salamis, where they landed, nothing happens except that they preached to the Jews, but nothing occurred in consequence; and as this was their usual practice, it would scarcely have been mentioned had the author not been present. They afterwards proceed to Paphos, which is at the opposite end of Cyprus from Salamis; hence the propriety of the world "διελθόντες," passing *through* it (xiii. 6.), naturally used by one who had made the journey. At Paphos the notices of the particular species of blindness, "ἀχλὺς καὶ σκότος,"† and groping for assistance, mark at once the physician and the eye-witness.

---

* Irenæus evidently supposes that Luke was with Paul and Silas on their arrival at Troas (Acts, xvi. 8.). He says, " Lucas inseparabilis fuit a Paulo, et cooperarius ejus in Evangelio, ipse facit manifestum, non glorians sed ab ipsa productus veritate. Separatis enim inquit a Paulo et Barnaba et Joanne, qui vocabatur Marcus, et cum navigassent Cyprum nos venimus Troadem."

† Galen, who wrote after the time of St. Luke, states that a certain

Mr. Alford, in his notes on this journey, has noticed several traits of autopticity, and conjectures from the change of his style that St. Luke remained at Antioch in Pisidia from the time St. Paul left it till his return, a conjecture which is fortified by a text (xiii. 52.), in which the state of the church there is noticed after St. Paul's departure.*

I am satisfied, therefore, from the concurring evidence just stated, that St. Luke was a resident inhabitant of Antioch when St. Paul first visited it, and from that time was a fellow-labourer with him in the spread of the Gospel, and joined with him in many of his missionary journeys. After the return of Paul and Barnabas to Antioch (xiv. 26.), he appears to have remained there till the Apostle and Silas finally left it (xv. 40). There is nothing in the account of the journey which Paul and Barnabas made to Jerusalem to indicate that he accompanied them. He tells us indeed that they passed through Phenice and Samaria, where we do not hear of anything being done; but it is probable that he accompanied them so far, for he informs us that they were "brought on their way by the Church" (xv. 3.).

When St. Paul left Antioch, St. Luke must have proceeded to Troas, where the Apostle meets him; and here it falls from him that he was engaged with St. Paul in preaching the Gospel, for he infers from St. Paul's vision that the Lord called *us* to preach, &c. From Troas he accompanies the Apostle to Philippi—the circum-

---

disorder of the eye is called ἀχλυς. See Mr. Walker's paper on the medical style of St. Luke. *Gent. Mag.* June, 1841., p. 585.

* See Notes on Acts, xiii. 13., and xiv. 22.

stantiality with which he relates this short voyage, when he was actually present, as we know from the use of the first person plural, forms, as formerly observed, a strong contrast with the manner in which he describes the previous journey of Paul and Silas from Antioch to Troas.

At this and the other cities of Macedonia St. Luke appears to have remained when St. Paul, Timothy, and Silas left it, till the Apostle rejoined him at the end of several years. It is evident, not only from the change of pronoun from the first to the third person, but also from the change of style from the autoptical to the historical, that St. Luke did not accompany them; and as the next time we hear of him he was at Philippi, we are warranted in supposing that he remained in charge of the church there. The peculiar nature of the connexion which subsisted between this church and the Apostle bears every mark of personal attachment, of such a knowledge of his wants, and such exertions to supply them* as we might expect to find in a faithful and devoted friend.

It is during this period that a circumstance in the life of St. Luke mentioned by Jerome—namely, that he was "the brother whose praise was in the Gospel throughout all the Churches," who was sent by St. Paul to Corinth to receive the contributions of the church there (2 Cor. viii. 18.) —took place.

As this is an important event, and one which throws much light upon a portion of his life, about which he is entirely silent, it becomes desirable to ascertain how far the statement of Jerome is confirmed by other and

* See Paley's admirable illustrations on this character of the Philippian church, in "Horæ Paulinæ."

independent authorities. Origen, in noticing St. Paul's praise of Luke's Gospel, evidently understands that he was " the brother," &c., and it is expressly so stated in the (longer) epistle of Ignatius to the Ephesians.

But these are not the only authorities which have come down to us which prove that St. Luke was one of the companions of Titus in the mission in question. In the subscription to the Second Epistle to the Corinthians, it is expressly stated that he was: this is not indeed canonical authority, but it is one of great antiquity, and quite independent of that of Jerome. He has not introduced it into the Vulgate, and he cannot have taken his statement from it, for it says nothing about Luke being " the brother whose praise is in the churches; " whilst, on the other hand, Jerome says nothing about Luke being the companion of Titus.

It is true that several of the subscriptions to the epistles have been shown by Paley to have been erroneous; but this is not one of them, and is unquestionably of the very highest antiquity, for it occurs both in ancient MSS. and ancient versions. The subscriptions which are shown to be erroneous are evidently the conclusions which transcribers have drawn from the matter of the epistles; but as the name of Luke is not mentioned in the body of the epistle, its insertion in the subscription must either be the record of a fact or an arbitrary interpolation—a supposition in which there is not a shadow of probability.

The manner in which St. Paul's second visit to Macedonia is related in the Acts is precisely what might have been expected from St. Luke, on the supposition that he was sent to Corinth upon St. Paul's arrival in Macedonia,

He was too intimately connected with the apostle, and too anxious to record his proceedings, to have noticed them in so cursory a manner had he not been absent at this time. It has been well observed, that the importance of the Philippian church would of course cause St. Paul to "halt there for some time."* Now, we know that St. Luke was at Philippi at the time of this visit, for he left it with St. Paul on his departure from Macedonia. We must infer, from his usual style of writing when with St. Paul, that he neither was with him during his stay at Philippi, nor accompanied him in his progress through Macedonia, the whole of which is related in these words— "He departed (from Ephesus) for to go into Macedonia; and when he had gone over those parts, and had given them much exhortation, he came into Greece" (Acts, xx. 1, 2.). St. Luke therefore, although in Macedonia, was not with St. Paul either during his stay at Philippi or on his journey through Macedonia. I account for his absence by the supposition that St. Paul's first business, on his arrival, was to despatch him with Titus to Corinth, and that he returned to Philippi before St. Paul (xx. 2.). We can thus explain the manner in which he describes St. Paul's proceedings on this occasion, which is so different from that which he uses when he was in his company.†

---

* Note to "Conybeare and Howson's St. Paul," vol. ii. p. 89.

† Mr. Stanley, in his edition of the Epistles to the Corinthians, in proceeding by the method of exhaustion to ascertain who was the brother whose praise was in the churches, excludes St. Luke, "If the view be correct which supposes the author of the Acts to have joined him from Philippi" (Acts, xvi. 10—40.). There can be no doubt, I apprehend, that the author of the Acts was with Paul during that portion of the narrative xvi. 10—40. This carries him to Philippi. And it is from

The next peculiarity I would advert to is, the remarkable contrast between the writings of St. Paul and St. Luke respecting the contributions. It is quite obvious, from both of his epistles to the Corinthians and that to the Romans, that St. Paul attached the highest importance to them: the very circumstance of his declining to take charge of them is a proof that they were of great importance; and yet, were it not that it incidentally drops from St. Paul, in his address to Felix (Acts, xxiv. 17.), that he came to Jerusalem to bring alms and offerings, nothing whatever respecting this matter would have been known from the Acts. I attribute this silence on the part of St. Luke to the entire abnegation of self, which characterises his writings. I believe that the history of the contributions belongs in a great measure to the history of St. Luke, and that he was not merely the selected trustee, but a principal mover in the contributions of the earliest European churches, both to St. Paul personally, and to the church at Jerusalem. Assuming then, as I do, that the fact mentioned in the subscription to the 2 Cor. with respect to Luke is established, it follows that he is " the brother whose praise is in the Gospel in all the churches" of Macedonia. I do not, with Jerome and many commentators, suppose that St. Paul, in mentioning the Gospel, alludes to the Gospel written by St. Luke, but to his

Philippi he is sent according to the subscription, from Macedonia according to the context; and as he left Philippi with St. Paul, he must have been in Macedonia during the visit when the mission in question took place: there is therefore no antecedent improbability in the supposition, and the style of narration shows that he was not with St. Paul at the time when it took place.

success in preaching the Gospel, and adopt the translation of Mr. Conybeare: —

"The brother whose praise, in publishing the glad tidings, is spread throughout all the churches;"

to which he appends the following note:

"Τῷ εὐαγγελίῳ here cannot refer, as some have imagined, to *a written* Gospel; the word is of constant occurrence in the New Testament (occurring sixty times in St. Paul's writings, and sixteen times in other books), but never once in the supposed sense." *Life of St. Paul*, ii. 109.

Agreeing with this view, let us revert to the circumstances under which St. Luke first visited Philippi. We learn from Acts, xvi. 10., that the members of St. Paul's mission, of whom St. Luke was one, proceeded to Philippi, where St. Paul founded the first European church; Paul, Silas, and Timothy then left Philippi, or rather were driven from it (Acts, xvi. 40., and xvii. 14.); but St. Luke certainly did not, as I have already shown, accompany them. This church, notwithstanding the absence of St. Paul, and all the other members of the mission except St. Luke, continued to flourish. Immediately after leaving it, St. Paul proceeded to Thessalonica; and here we learn that he repeatedly received relief to his necessities from the Philippian church. I cannot doubt but that this assistance was mainly due to the personal friend who remained with that church,— who knew his wants, and who exerted himself to supply them. St. Luke felt he was called upon to teach the Gospel to the Macedonians, and we must suppose that he obeyed the call, and laboured assiduously and successfully, as every indication connected with the Macedonian churches proves.

Years roll on, and St. Paul again visits Macedonia. St.

Luke, after fulfilling the mission to Corinth, returns to Philippi with the contributions, and is there joined by St. Paul, whom he accompanies to Jerusalem; his journey thither is circumstantially related in the Acts, xx. 6. to xxi. 17., and need not be repeated here.

St. Luke, as usual, is entirely silent respecting his own proceedings. There are, however, the strongest reasons for believing that, during the two years of St. Paul's imprisonment at Cæsarea, he composed his Gospel.

There are several indications in that work which tend to prove that it was written in Judea. In the first place, he tells us in his preface that his object was to give an account of " the things which had been accomplished *amongst us* " (πεπληροφορημενων εν ημιν πραγματων), showing that he was then writing in the scene of the events. In the next place, his descriptions are those of a person familiar with the localities, and who was upon the spot at the time of writing: thus, in relating the triumphant entry of our Lord into Jerusalem, he informs us of the exact place where the attendant multitudes burst out into Hosannas — it was on " the descent of the Mount of Olives " (Luke xix. 37.), a circumstance only noticed by him. The last proof of the Judean origin of the Gospel is the manner in which he makes use of the national denomination, " the Jews," as compared with the use he makes of it in the Acts. A person writing in the country does not think of giving the national denomination to its inhabitants, except in cases where it is unavoidable; but writing out of it he very naturally does. Now in the Gospel St. Luke only uses the word " Jew " five times, and that in cases where he could not help it — namely, " the King of the Jews," " the elders of the Jews," " a city of the Jews;" but he never uses it when speaking of the people in general. In the Acts, on the other hand, it is used no less than eighty-two times.

I infer from these indications that St. Luke's Gospel was written in Judea; but if so, it must have been written before he quitted it with St. Paul on his voyage to Rome, for there is no later period to which its composition can be referred. It was therefore written between A.D. 58 and A.D. 60, under circumstances of all others the most favourable for historical investigation, on the spot where the transactions took place, and with constant opportunities of intercourse with those chiefly engaged in them. To this beloved friend of the Great Apostle of the Gentiles, himself, as I have shown, a leading member of the mission which first bore the light of the Gospel into Europe, every means of information at that time in the possession of living witnesses must have been accessible.

In the narrative of the voyage we have a minute account of the events of the life of St. Luke till the arrival of St. Paul at Rome, and we learn from the Epistles to the Colossians and Philemon that he was still there when they were written. The only subsequent notice in Scripture respecting him is that in 2 Tim. iv. 11., where we are told that he alone was with the apostle in the very crisis of his fate, " when the time of his departure was at hand," and when all but Luke had forsaken him. From his not being included in the greetings to the Philippians, it has been inferred, with great probability, that he had previously left Rome. This is confirmed by his silence as to the events alluded to in Philip. i. 12., as "having fallen out unto the furtherance of the Gospel." St. Luke mentions the results of these events when he states that St. Paul taught the "things which concern the Lord Jesus Christ with all confidence, no man forbidding him" (Acts, xxviii. 31.). We can only account for this silence by supposing that he was not present when they took place. The change of style also, from that of an eye-witness, when he relates what took place on their arrival at Rome, to that of a historian, when he gives an account of the two succeeding years, points to the same conclusion.

When St. Paul ascertained that his case could not come before the Emperor for a considerable length of time, and that till it was decided he was in no personal danger, we find that his first care was to despatch Tychicus to the churches in Asia Minor. We may suppose that Luke would be sent on a similar mission; but if so, the church at Philippi is clearly the one to which conjecture would lead us. Now, there is, I think, very strong reason for believing that he actually was there when the epistle to that church was written, and that the " true yoke-fellow " (iv. 3.), addressed in it, was no other than St. Luke. Had it been a Philippian presbyter that was meant, we must suppose that he would have named him; whereas, if he sent Luke to the Philippians, as he did Tychicus to the Asiatic churches, it would be unnecessary. The terms in which the message is expressed show clearly that it was addressed to one of the class of St. Paul's friends to which St. Luke belonged; and from the evident allusions to what took place on his former visit to Philippi (compare Philip. iv. 3., with Acts, xvi. 13.), it must have been one of those who were with him at the time. Now, we know very accurately those who were the members of the mission. It consisted at first of Paul and Silas. Timothy joined them at Lystra (Acts, xvi. 1.), and the author of the Acts at Troas (Ib. v. 10.). There is no mention of any other of the apostle's companions; nor does St. Luke's style of narration afford any warrant for supposing that there were any except those mentioned. The true yoke-fellow must, therefore, have been either Timothy, Silas, or Luke. Timothy it could not be, for he was at Rome when St. Paul wrote the epistle (2 Cor. i. 1.). Neither, I apprehend, could it be Silas; he disappears from the page of sacred history at least ten years before the date of the epistle, a circumstance which could not have happened had he continued a fellow-labourer of St. Paul. The last time we hear of him is with St. Paul at Corinth, where he wrote the Second Epistle to the Thessalonians, about A.D. 56., in which city he preached along with St. Paul (see 2 Cor. i. 19.), and where he appears to have remained. After St. Paul's departure, he probably returned to Jerusalem, and joined St. Peter, for next time we hear of him is in connection with that apostle (1 Peter, v. 12.). We are thus led to fix upon St. Luke. The very terms of the message point to one who was a beloved friend as well as a fellow-labourer.

Assuming that the true yoke-fellow and the author of the Acts are identical, we are furnished with the date of the Acts, both with respect to time and place. It was written, or at any rate finished, at Philippi, and sent from thence to Theophilus, in the summer of A.D. 63. It ends in one respect abruptly, as every history written by a contemporary inevitably must; but in so far as respects the history of the progress of the Gospel, which it was the author's object to record, the work is brought down to a period at that time certainly the brightest which had yet occurred in its annals. In order to estimate its importance, we must lay aside our knowledge of subsequent events, and view it from the same point as the author did, and, as far as we can, enter into it with the same feelings. His object in the Acts was to record the progress of Christianity, as it had been his object in his "former treatise" to record its rise. He begins the Acts when the number of Christians together was about an hundred and twenty, and traces the progress of the Gospel throughout Syria, Asia Minor, into Europe. At the first planting of a Christian church in this quarter of the globe Luke himself assisted; and we have every reason for believing that he continued to labour with success in the same field; that the church at Philippi, with which he was more immediately connected, had received the unqualified approbation of St. Paul; that other churches had sprung up in Macedonia and the more distant regions of Greece; and that the Great Apostle of the Gentiles, he whose career it was his special object to narrate, was then in the capital of the civilised world, "preaching the kingdom of God, and teaching those things which concern the Lord Jesus Christ with all confidence, no man forbidding him." If we can divest ourselves of our knowledge of the persecutions which were so soon to follow, it is difficult to imagine a conjuncture which afforded brighter prospects of the success of the cause in which he laboured.

As a history, therefore, "the Acts" concludes at a well-marked epoch, and bears the most perfect evidence of having been finished two years after St. Paul's arrival at Rome, which was in spring A.D. 61, and thereby furnishes a date of the utmost importance, for it establishes the earlier date of his Gospel; and that, in its turn, as I shall endeavour to show, establishes the still earlier date of the Gospels of Matthew and Mark. The works of the three first evangelists were therefore written within thirty years after the death of Christ, and the events recorded were within the memory of the then existing generation.

I have stated that Luke concludes the history of the Acts of the Apostles, as all contemporary historians must. Let us compare it with one in modern times. Elliot's "Life of Wellington" contains no mention of the Battle of Waterloo. What modern critic, applying the usual rules of critical research, but would at once explain this omission, by assuming that the book must have been written before the battle was fought, although there is nothing in the date (1815) to prove that it was? But biblical critics, misled by their own preconceived views, have exhausted their ingenuity to explain away so obvious an inference. What would be said of a modern critic who would account for this author's silence as to the Battle of Waterloo by saying it was an event so well known as to render any notice of it superfluous? yet the same is actually said of St. Luke's silence as to the release of St. Paul. It is interesting to compare the last notices of the career of Wellington given by this author with that of St. Paul as given by St. Luke. After informing us that he went as ambassador to Paris, the author adds, "since which period he has resided in that capital, fulfilling the important duties of his station with a degree of judgment and skill which prove that he is no less qualified to support the honour of his country by his diplomatic talents than by his military ones," p. 572.

Having thus traced St. Luke with a considerable amount of proof to what I believe to have been the great scene of his labours, we hear no more of him till near the conclusion of St. Paul's course, when, as he (St. Paul) says, "he had fought the good fight, and finished his course; when Demas and others had forsaken him, and only Luke was with him." Such was the termination of the public life of one who but for his modesty must have ranked as high as a man of action as he ever must as one of the most able and faithful of historians. We have no other well authenticated notice of him, but tradition says that he died at an advanced age a natural death. St. Jerome, in his life of St. Luke, says that he died, unmarried, at the age of eighty-four, and that his bones were transported from Achaia to Constantinople, in the 28th year of the reign of Constantius.*

Although at the distance of time at which Jerome wrote much dependence cannot be placed upon the particular details we may at least infer from the silence of antiquity that he did not suffer martyrdom. Irenæus states that he was one of the seventy disciples, but I see no evidence of this; neither is there any proof of the conjecture that he was a freed man, nor of the tradition that he was a painter.

The style of St. Luke as a historian is clear, animated, and picturesque. This last attribute is of course most obvious when he describes scenes which fell under his

* Hieronomi Vita D. Lucæ.

own observation; but it is not confined to them. It distinguishes his descriptions in the Gospels: witness his account of the disciples plucking and eating ears of corn on the Sabbath—"rubbing them in their hands" (vi. 1.); and in that of the Denial of Peter, where we are told that, when "the cock crew," "the Lord turned and looked upon Peter" (xxii. 6.).

Combined with these excellences, we find the total want of any thing like display or attempt at fine writing, his sole object being to convey the truth to his readers, not to enhance his literary reputation.

When he describes events on the authority of others his style is purely historical; when he describes those which fell under his own observation it is eminently autoptical, and has all the minuteness and circumstantiality which almost unavoidably characterise the descriptions of eye-witnesses.

We are indebted to the autopticity of his style for the numerous facts which, combined with the inferences we draw from them, enable us to reconstruct the narrative of the Voyage and Shipwreck. It enables us also to judge with tolerable certainty as to the presence or absence of the author in the transactions which he has recorded. I may here observe that nothing but the most perfect truthfulness could have enabled us to draw conclusions in every instance consistent with themselves and in numerous cases with facts, the knowledge of which we arrive at by recent discoveries, and which could only have been known to the author from personal observation.

As a voyage writer St. Luke is possessed of another most essential qualification,—he is thoroughly versant in nautical matters, and describes them in the appropriate language of seamanship.

No man could by any possibility attain so complete a command of nautical language who had not spent a considerable portion of his life at sea, not, however, as a seaman, for his language, although accurate, is not professional. The difference in the manner of describing nautical events by seamen and landsmen is too obvious to require remark; but there is a third class of authors who are, properly speaking, neither seamen nor landsmen. I mean those who from some cause or other have been much at sea, who from living with the officers of the ship, and hearing nautical matters constantly discussed, necessarily acquire the use of the technical language of seamen. An attentive examination of St. Luke's writings shows us that it is to this class of authors that he belongs. How he acquired this knowledge we have no means of knowing; but I cannot help thinking that he must, at some period of his life, have exercised his profession at sea. From the great number of persons which we often hear of in ancient ships*, we must suppose that they carried surgeons. Whether St. Luke ever served in that capacity or not is, of course, mere matter of conjecture: one thing is certain, no one unaccustomed to a sea life could have described the events connected with it with such accuracy as he has done.

But although his descriptions are accurate, they are, as I have already observed, *unprofessional*. The seaman in charge of the ship has his attention perpetually on the stretch, watching every change or indication of change

---

* The ship in which Josephus went to Rome carried 600.—*Life.*

of wind or weather. He is obliged to decide on the instant what measures must be taken to avail himself of favourable changes or to obviate the consequences of unfavourable ones. Hence in describing them he naturally dwells upon cause and effect. He tells us not only what was done, but why it was done. The impression produced by incidents at sea upon the mind of the passive observer is altogether different, and of course his mode of describing them equally so. He tells us what has happened, but rarely tells us how or why the measures connected with it were taken. In doing so he often mentions circumstances which a seaman would not think of noticing from their familiarity, or from being matters of course; and is frequently silent as to those which are of the greatest importance, and which no seaman would pass over.

Now these are exactly the peculiarities which characterise the style of St. Luke as a voyage writer; for instance, when the ship was run ashore, he tells us that they loosed the bands of the rudders. A seaman would rather have told us, in the previous stage of the narrative, how they were secured,—a matter of necessity in an ancient ship when anchored by the stern; and when we remember that it was in the face of a lee shore, in a gale of wind, it must have been one of difficulty, whereas loosing them when they made sail was a mere matter of course. Thus, also, when the shipmen became aware of the proximity of land, no seaman would have neglected to mention what were the indications which led them to "deem that they drew near to some country" (xxvii. 27.).

It would be easy to multiply instances from the narrative, or to cite analogous ones from the published works of medical men who have written narratives of their voyages; for those who are led by the love of science or adventure to make long voyages frequently become their historians. I prefer, however, making the comparison with a fragment of a journal of an officer in Captain Cook's ship, from the "United Service Magazine" (May, 1842, p. 46.). There can be no doubt but that in this case the author was a medical man.* The correspondent who communicates it infers that he is so, from the circumstance of a medical case being in the same book. The professional manner in which he describes Captain Cook's remains would have been proof sufficient to me that he was one. I prefer this as a case in point, because we have it as it was written on the spot, without being pruned or worked up for effect, and because we can compare it with the published accounts of the same events written by professional seamen. It exhibits the same peculiarities which I have alluded to as characterising the style of St. Luke.† The author re-

* I have no doubt but that the author of this interesting fragment is Mr. Anderson, surgeon of the Resolution, Captain Cook's ship, for the following reasons:—He calls the other ship the Discovery, but does not name his own. I find his description of Captain Cook's remains in Captain King's narrative of the voyage. Now it was natural that he should apply to the surgeon of the ship for it; and he accompanies the two captains when they land on a newly-discovered island—circumstances which clearly point to the principal surgeon of the expedition.

† In this respect the fragment presents a curious contrast with Captain King's eloquent account of the recovery and solemn committal to the deep of Captain Cook's remains. By the surgeon's account, some of the bones could not be those of Captain Cook, but he adds, "we said nothing about it; and some of the bones were brought to the ship the day after the funeral, and dropt into the sea as near as possible to the spot where the other bones were dropt the day before," a circumstance Captain King says nothing about.

lates the events as they fell under his observation in correct nautical language, but offers no explanation of the reasons which induced the officers to take the measures which he narrates. Take the following examples: —

"24th Feb. (1779).—In the evening hauled our wind, and stood out clear of the islands." *Journal*, p. 46.

Compare this with Captain King's account —

"At sunset, observing a shoal which appeared to stretch a considerable distance to the west of Mowee, towards the middle of the passage, and the weather being unsettled, we tacked and stood to the south." *King's Voyage*, p. 84.

Or the following: —

"28th.—Hauled our wind, and are to stand off and on for the night." *Journal*, p. 46.
"It being too late to run for the road on the south-west side of the island, where we had been last year, we passed the night in standing on and off." *King's Voyage*, p. 88.

Here it will be observed that the nautical language is quite as correct in the one case as in the other, the only difference being, that the seaman relates the causes of their proceedings, whilst the medical author of the journal omits them.

When St. Luke mentions the incident of hoisting the boat on board, he informs us that it was a work of difficulty (μολις, xxvii. 16.), but he does not tell us wherein the difficulty consisted. In like manner, when the author of the journal notices the incident of getting the Resolution's foremast into its place, he merely says: —

"The mast after much trouble and risks was got in."

Compare this with the accounts given by seamen of the same circumstance : —

"We had the satisfaction of getting the foremast shipped. It was an operation attended with great difficulty and some danger, our ropes being so exceedingly rotten that the purchase gave way several times." *King's Voyage*, p. 79.

In a journal by an officer of the Discovery (8vo. London, 1785), it is thus narrated : —

"We had the satisfaction of getting the foremast of the Resolution shipped, a work of great labour and some difficulty, as the ropes were now become rotten and unable to sustain the purchase." P. 314.

This mode of writing accounts for the omission in the narrative of St. Luke of circumstances which, nautically speaking, were of much importance, and the insertion of others which were of none. But, notwithstanding these omissions, it is the style of all others best calculated to give us a clear idea of the events of the voyage. We can, generally speaking, infer the causes of the events from the effects, provided they are stated truthfully and accurately; while the familiarity which a professional man acquires, leads him to pass over circumstances which he knows others with professional knowledge will conclude must have taken place. Walter Scott in one of his letters notices the description of one of the battles in Spain by a volunteer officer who was present, thus : —

"The narrative was very simply told, and conveyed better than any I have seen the impressions which such scenes are likely to make when they have the effect (I had almost said the charm) of novelty. I don't know why it is, I never found a soldier could give me an idea of a battle." *Life*, vol. ii. p. 324.

D

Had St. Luke's object been to describe a sea-voyage, this style of narrating the events would no doubt have been liable to objections; but it was no part of his intention to do so, except in so far as the events of the voyage illustrated passages in the life of St. Paul; and but for his circumstantiality when relating events at which he was present, we should probably have known no more than that the apostle was shipwrecked at Melita on his voyage from Syria to Italy. His notices of events are altogether accidental and fragmentary. He records them simply because he observes them, not because they are intrinsically important. They drop unintentionally from his pen, and are never thrown in for the purpose of heightening the effect, although no doubt they very often do so, as in the account of the visit to Philippi, for it is impossible to write autoptically without at the same time writing graphically. Still less are the circumstances thrown in for the purpose of lending probability to his narrative. On the contrary, they often detract from it — "*Le vrai n'est pas toujours le vraisemblable.*" The most important circumstances probably did not fall under his notice, and he never stops to offer explanations. St. Luke, however, possesses two qualifications as a writer, which in a great degree compensate for his omissions, and which enable us to supply many of them with the greatest certainty. The first of these is his perfect acquaintance with his subject, and the second his accuracy. No man who was not in an eminent degree gifted with this quality could have given a narrative capable of being tested as his has been in the following examination. He must not only have been an accurate observer, but his memory must have been accurate, and his habits of thought and reasoning not less so. Hence his facts afford the firmest grounds for resting inferences upon, and these, in their turn, furnish data for mathematical reasoning. The reader may give an incredulous smile at working the dead reckoning of a ship from such disjointed and apparently vague notices: yet I have done so, and the result is nearer than I could have expected beforehand, had it been the journal of a modern ship, and had her log book been lying before me. I admit that a coincidence so extraordinary is, to a certain extent, accidental; but it is an accident which could not have happened had there been any inaccuracy on the part of the narrator. Had he made an error of a single day, it would have been difficult to have reconciled his statements; and had it been any other island upon which the ship was wrecked, it would have been impossible. I refer the reader to the account of the voyage for the calculations and the authorities upon which they are founded.*

* Extraordinary as the coincidence above alluded to is, it has received a confirmation not less extraordinary. My friend Mr. Howson found amongst the papers of the late Admiral Sir Charles Penrose a calculation of the course and distance. "With respect to the distance," Admiral Penrose observes, "allowing the strength of the gale to vary a little occasionally, I consider a ship would drift at the rate of about one and a half mile an hour, which at the end of fourteen complete days would amount to 504 miles. But it does not appear that the calculation is to be made for fourteen entire days. It was on the fourteenth night the anchors were cast off the shores of Melita. The distance from the south of Clauda to the north of Melita, measured on the best chart I have, is 490 miles; and is it possible for coincident calculations of such a nature to be more exact? In fact, on one chart, after I had calculated the supposed drift as a seaman to be 504 miles, I measured the distance to be 503."—"Conybeare and Howson's St. Paul," vol. ii. p. 346, note.

Before comparing Admiral Penrose's calculation with mine, it will be

The care which St. Luke takes, on all occasions, to select the most appropriate expressions, and the precision which results from it, are very remarkable; thus, to express the progression of a ship, we have not only the substantive πλοος (xxvii. 9.), but not less than fourteen verbs expressing the same thing, but with a distinction, indicating the particular circumstances of the ship at the time. I may add that, with the exception of the last three, they are all nautical expressions. They are also peculiar to the writings of St. Luke, occurring both in the Gospel and the Acts, but are not used by any of the other New Testament writers. The following is the list:—

1. Πλεω. Luke, viii. 23.; Acts, xxi. 3, &c. &c.
2. Αποπλεω. Acts, xiii. 4., xiv. 26., xx. 15., xxvii. 1.
3. Βραδυπλοεω. Acts, xxvii. 7.
4. Διαπλεω. Acts, xxvii. 5.
5. Εκπλεω. Acts, xv. 39., xviii. 18., xx. 6.

---

right to estimate, as nearly as the narrative will allow, the time elapsed rom the departure of the ship from Fair Havens till her departure from Clauda, and from thence till "the shipmen deemed they drew near to some country" (Acts, xxvii. 27.). The departure from Clauda must have been on the first day after mid-day; and before midnight; taking the mean, the time is about thirteen days and six hours. Now the distance of the point at the entrance of St. Paul's Bay from Clauda is, according to the accurate determinations of longitude and latitude of Admiral Smyth, 476·6 miles, which, at the rate of drift assumed by Admiral Penrose, would take 13 days, 5 hours, 47 min. According to my calculation it would take 13 days, 1 hour, 21 min.; or, reckoning the distance, that given by the rate assumed by Admiral Penrose is 477 miles, by mine 483½, the actual distance from Clauda to St. Paul's Bay being 476½ miles. I may well say with Admiral Penrose, "Is it possible for coincident observations of such a nature to be more exact?" Certainly none could have been more independent of each other, as my calculations, which were first published, were made in entire ignorance of the previous calculations of Admiral Penrose.

6. Καταπλεω. Luke, viii. 26.
7. Ὑποπλεω. Acts, xxvii. 4. 7.
8. Παραπλεω. Acts, xx. 16.
9. Ευθυδρομεω. Acts, xvi 11., xxi.
10. Ὑποτρεχω. Acts, xxvii. 16.
11. Παραλεγομαι. Acts, xxvii. 8. 13.
12. Φερομαι. Acts, xxvii. 15.
13. Διαφερομαι. Acts, xxvii. 27.
14. Διαπεραω. Acts, xxi. 2.

The reader cannot fail, in perusing his writings, to remark how much precision is thus given to his descriptions, and in how few words they are expressed.

It may be asked, how can we be certain that the nautical language of St. Luke is so correct?

The reply is, in the first place, that it must be a real language, and correctly used, which admits of being deciphered as it has been. In the account of the voyage I have cited the case of a German physician, who made a voyage in the same seas, and in some part of it under very similar circumstances; but although he obviously intended to give an account of his voyage, his statements are not only confused, but impossible, and we have no difficulty in seeing that he does not understand what he is writing about.

Independently, however, of this consideration, it so happens, that although ancient literature is scanty in the department of voyages, it is not so in the terminology of seamanship. Julius Pollux, in his "Onomasticon," has given many pages of Greek nautical terms and phrases. His arrangement is confused, and he sometimes mistakes the meaning of words; but for our present purpose explanation is not required, it is sufficient to know that such were the terms used by the ancients. It will be seen by the notes that a large proportion of those employed by St. Luke are to be found in this author.

I now proceed to inquire into the nature of the materials from which St. Luke drew up his historical works; but before I do so, it will be convenient to state shortly what I believe were the historical records of Christianity when St. Luke visited Judea, circa A.D. 58, and when, as I have already stated, there is good reason to believe that he wrote his Gospel.

In my "Dissertation on the Origin and Connection of the Gospels," I have stated the evidence from which I conclude — first, that several of the apostles, including Matthew, Peter, and John, drew up memoirs of our Lord's transactions immediately after they took place, some of which, certainly Peter's, were in the language of the country, *i. e.* Syro-Chaldaic, or Aramaic, known in the New Testament and works of the Fathers as Hebrew, or as the *native* language (πατριῳ): second, that Peter's memoirs were the original, which, being afterwards translated by St. Mark, now forms the Gospel of Mark: third, that when the apostles were driven by persecution from Judea, Matthew drew up from these memoirs a history of our Lord's life in Hebrew and Greek; the Greek version being the same as our first Gospel.

That several such narratives had been written when St. Luke composed his Gospel, may be gathered from his preface, in which he informs us: first, that "many had undertaken to draw up a digest of the things which had been accomplished" (v. 1.); and, next, that "those who from the beginning were eye-witnesses and ministers of the word had delivered such accounts unto us" (παρεδοσαν ἡμιν); or, in other words, that he was in possession of such accounts, for the word "us" must include St. Luke. Eusebius clearly understands that Luke means himself in particular, for he quotes the passage in the third person, παρεδοσαν αυτῳ, "delivered to him,"—and rightly concludes that he meant to assure Theophilus that such were the authorities which he had made use of. He tells us—

"One of these (St. Luke's writings) is his Gospel, in which he testifies that he has recorded as those who were from the beginning eye-witnesses and ministers of the word delivered *to him*, whom also, he says, he in all things followed." (H. E. iii. 4. *Cruze's Translation*.)

The word "many" is a relative term, and has reference probably to the literary habits of Judea, and the time which had elapsed since the events which he has recorded occurred; just as Alison, in his preface to the history of the French Revolution, speaks of his authorities: "Although so short a time has elapsed since the termination of these events, the materials which have been collected for their elucidation have already become, beyond all precedent, interesting and ample" (vol. i. p. 29.). Neither Luke nor Alison say that they made use of such materials. Why should they? Is it possible that Luke should write to Theophilus that he was anxious that he should know the certainty of the things in which he had been instructed,—that he had carefully investigated every thing from the beginning—and that he was in possession of the accounts of those personally engaged in the transactions, and yet that we should be in doubt as to whether or not he made use of such authorities? I conclude, therefore, that St. Luke's preface was meant to assure his readers that his authorities were eye-witnesses and ministers of the word. St. Matthew was an eye-witness and minister of the word; and it becomes a question, whether St. Luke made any use of his Gospel in drawing up his own.

This can only be ascertained by comparing the two accounts. Now we have not to go far before we have evidence to prove that he did make use of Matthew's Gospel. The parallelism between the Gospels begins with the public life of our Lord (Matt. iii. 1., Luke, iii. 1.); and at the seventh verse of the third chapter of St. Luke we find a passage, extending to three verses, agreeing verbally with four verses of the same account in the Gospel of St. Matthew (vv. 7, 8, 9, 10.). Here, at least, St. Luke must have taken from a *written* account in the same language; and when I find such a passage in the works of an eye-witness and minister of the word, I am satisfied that I have traced it to its source. We have not to go far for another example of the same kind, for the 16th and 17th verses of the same chapter correspond verbally with the 11th and 12th verses of Matthew's account. There are many others of the same nature. If examples can be adduced where similar agreements arise from any other cause than transcription from a work in the same language, I am quite ready to abandon my hypothesis; but as I am confident that no such case can be adduced, I feel entitled to call the attention of the reader to the consequences which flow from the establishment of a point of such importance in the evidences of the origin of the Christian religion. Had St. Luke's writings never been heard of till now, had they been discovered for the first time amongst the papyri of Herculaneum, would any doubt have been entertained, with such evidence before us, that the author had made use of the Gospel of St. Matthew as one of his authorities? It would have been held as the most valuable of all the ancient external evidences of the authenticity of that Gospel, as indeed it is, because it is at once the fullest and the most ancient, and because the author had the most ample means of knowing that it was indeed the work of an eye-witness. It proves that the Gospel of Matthew as we now have it was known to an author who wrote less than thirty years after the transactions, and when they must have been within the memory of a large portion of the then existing generation.

My present object, however, is not to look at the consequences of my researches, but to consider the evidences upon which my conclusions rest. I must, therefore, if I can, obviate the objections which have been made to the supposition that Luke made use of the Gospel of Matthew. They all resolve themselves into the negative one, that if Luke had known of the previous Gospel he would have written differently from what he has done. Arguments which rest upon the opinion of critics never can overthrow positive proofs. Amongst those who have called my conclusions respecting the connection between Luke and Matthew in question, I may mention Mr. Alford and Professor Thiersch of Marburg. Both of these critics admit the identity of the above cited passages. Mr. Alford in his note observes that the agreement "indicates a common origin;" and Professor Thiersch, who agrees with me entirely as to the originality of the second Gospel, and the use made of it by St. Luke, observes in a letter to me that "There were more written accounts than St. Mark's

Gospel which they could make use of; and it is in this way that I should like to explain those coincidences in Matthew and Luke for which there are no parallels in Mark. In Germany we are in a continual struggle with Strauss and other sceptical antagonists of sacred history; and therefore we feel more of that difficulty, with which you are less urged in England—viz. If Luke had before his eyes the two first chapters of Matthew, how could he neglect them entirely?—if he did so he must have ascribed very little value to them." The explanation of the connection between Luke and Matthew which I have to offer is, that the former meant to make his Gospel at once supplementary for those who possessed Matthew's Gospel, and intelligible to those who did not. But it would not have been intelligible had he resolutely omitted everything in Matthew; whilst, on the other hand, had he included everything in Matthew, his Gospel would have exceeded the length consistent with a wide circulation, when the only means of multiplying copies depended on transcription. Admitting this conjecture, which at least is a probable one, it furnishes us with a reason for the omissions in Luke's Gospel of important matter which we find in Matthew's Gospel. St. Luke leaves it out because St. Matthew had already recorded it.

Both Professor Thiersch and Mr. Alford adduce the difference in the two first chapters of Matthew's and Luke's Gospels as proofs that Luke could not have seen that of Matthew. But there is nothing contradictory in the two accounts. Mr. Alford observes, truly enough, that "The *only* inference from the account in these two chapters, *which is inevitable,* is that they are wholly independent of one another." It is quite true that they are independent of one another; but independence is no proof that the later writer was ignorant of the work of his predecessor. Selection is the rule of all the evangelists. John repeatedly tells us that there were many things which Jesus did that are not written in his Gospel. It has been supposed, and, I think, with much probability, that St. Luke's authority for the first two chapters in his Gospel was the mother of our Lord. The events related are such as his mother must have known and was likely to narrate; they relate to private and domestic matters, whilst those in Matthew relate to public and historical events—events about which Luke was silent because they were already related by Matthew. It is, however, foreign to my present purpose to enter at large into a consideration of all the negative arguments which have been adduced to prove that St. Luke was not acquainted with, or did not make use of, the first Gospels, as I have done so elsewhere.

The conclusion to which a minute comparison between the two Gospels has led me is, that St. Luke was in possession of the present Greek Gospel of Matthew; that he did make occasional use of it, chiefly for the purpose of rendering his own account of the transactions and sayings of our Lord more complete, thereby proving that it (the Greek Gospel) was the work of "an eye-witness and minister of the word."

This is no contradiction to the patristic evidence that St. Matthew wrote in Hebrew; nor do I hold the supposition that he wrote in two languages to be a compromise between competing evidence. The state of Judea with respect to language at the time, required that any work meant for all classes of its inhabitants should be bilingual. Josephus, the contemporary of Matthew, and who wrote, as he did, for the use of the Jews, informs us, in his preface to his Greek history of the Jews' Wars, that he had also written it in his native language ($\pi\alpha\tau\rho\iota\wp$, the word used by Eusebius for the original language of Matthew), for the use of those who did not understand Greek (οἱ βαρβαροι).

The conditions of the agreements which subsist between Luke and Mark are altogether different from those which subsist between Luke and Matthew. In Luke and Matthew we have two historians writing in the same language; but in Luke and Mark we have a historian (Luke) who uses an original autoptical memoir in another language (Peter), which is translated by Mark, and which had also been made use of by the preceding historian (Matthew). These are the agreements of contemporary historians, and are so simple in themselves, and of such every day occurrence, that I question if we can examine any series of contemporary writers, who narrate the same transactions in a language different from that of the persons engaged in them, without meeting with them all. I have elsewhere illustrated this view of the connection of the three first Gospels by examples from the historians Alison, Napier, and Suchet, who hold the same relation to the events of the peninsular campaigns in respect to time, which Luke, Matthew, and Mark hold to the events in the life of our Saviour; Alison being a historian who takes as his authorities the accounts of those who witnessed the transactions, and when it suits his purpose to give extracts from the originals, he transcribes from Napier and translates from Suchet; just as Luke, when he extracts from the originals, transcribes where the language is the same, translates where it is different. Now I find, when I compare the passages peculiar to Luke and Matthew, the phenomena are those of transcription, when I compare the passages peculiar to Luke and Mark, the phenomena are those of translation. Hence, I arrive at the conclusion that Mark is a translator. But it may be asked, if the Gospel of Mark be a translation of memoirs written by Peter, why is it not called the Gospel of Peter? To this I answer, that the title it bears is only that affixed to it by tradition, for the work itself is anonymous; and I cannot admit that traditional evidence can supersede that which is the result of inductive reasoning.

In holding that Mark is the translator of Peter's memoirs, I do not rest altogether on the evidence drawn from the study of the phenomena, for the earliest quotation from the second Gospel is that by Justin Martyr, who gives it expressly *as it is written* in his (Peter's) memoirs — γεγραφθαι εν τοις απομνημονευμασιν αυτου (Πετρου).* So also Jerome, in speaking of Mark's Gospel, says it is called his (Peter's).† The question therefore ought to be, Why has the less important name of Mark prevailed over the more important name of Peter?—Answer, perhaps to distinguish it from the apocryphal Gospel of Peter.

---

* *Apol.* II. p. 333.
† *Cat. Sacr. eccl.* c. 1.: "Evangelium juxta Marcum... hujus (*sc.* Petri) dicitur."

Bishop Pearson says on this point, "Marci evangelium credebant veteres nihil aliud fuisse quam Petri απομνημονευματα" (*Vindiciæ Ignatianæ*). And Bishop Gleig: "I am inclined to think likewise, that the Gospel by St. Mark contains little more than similar notes and memorandums which had been made by St. Peter, which will sufficiently account for many of the antients calling it St. Peter's Gospel." (*Directions for the Study of Divinity*, p. 409.)

Assuming that we have in the three first Gospels a case of contemporary historians, the same as the very common one of Alison, Napier, and Suchet, the nature of the agreement between them ought to be the same as that which we find between the modern historians. I have already adduced one between Luke and Matthew. As an example of that between Luke and Mark, I take that which I have alluded to in the introduction, as having first called my attention to the subject. It is perhaps the most instructive I could select, because it is entirely free from the complication which arises from being mixed up with matter drawn from other authorities. It is also one of the few cases in which Matthew makes no use of the original of Mark, *i. e.* the memoir of Peter. We have here then the very simple case of an historian drawing up an account of an event from two preceding works, one of which is in a different language.

CHRIST STILLS THE TEMPEST.

MATT. VIII.	LUKE VIII.	MARK IV.
	22 Εγενετο δε εν μια των ημερων,	35 Και λεγει αυτοις εν εκεινῃ τῃ ημερᾳ, οψιας γενομενης.
23 Και εμβαντι αυτῳ εις το πλοιον ηκολουθησαν αυτῳ οἱ μαθηται αυτου	και αυτος ανεβη εις πλοιον και οἱ μαθηται αυτου· και ειπεν προς αυτους, Διελθωμεν	
See v. 18.		*See* 1st. line.
	εις το περαν της λιμνης·	Διελθωμεν εις το περαν.
		36. Και αφεντες τον οχλον παραλαμβανουσιν αυτον ὡς ην εν τῳ πλοιῳ και αλλα δε πλοια ην μετ' αυτου.

AND WRITINGS OF ST. LUKE.

MATT. VIII.	LUKE VIII.	MARK IV.
	Και ανηχθησαν. 23 Πλεοντων δε αυτων αφυπνωσεν,	
24 Και ιδου σεισμος μεγας εγενετο εν τη θαλασση, ωστε το πλοιον καλυπτεσθαι υπο των κυματων.	και κατεβη λαιλαψ ανεμου εις την λιμνην·	37 και γινεται λαιλαψ μεγαλη ανεμου, και τα κυματα επεβαλλεν εις το πλοιον ωστε ηδη γεμιζεσθαι το πλοιον.
	και συνεπληρουντο, και εκινδυνευον.	
αυτος δε εκαθευδε.		38 Και ην αυτος εν τη πρυμνη επι το προσκεφαλαιον, καθευδων,
25 Και προσελθοντες ηγειραν αυτον, λεγοντες, Κυριε, σωσον, απολλιμεθα.	24 Προσελθοντες δε διηγειραν αυτον, λεγοντες, Επιστατα, επιστατα, απολλυμεθα.	και εγειρουσιν αυτον, και λεγουσιν αυτω, Διδασκαλε, ου μελει σοι οτι απολλυμεθα;
26 Και λεγει αυτοις, Τι δειλοι εστε, ολιγοπιστοι; τοτε εγερθεις επετιμησε τοις ανεμοις και τη θαλασση,	Ο δε εγερθεις επετιμησε τω ανεμω και τω κλυδωνι του υδατος,	39 Και διεγερθεις επετιμησε τω ανεμω, και ειπε τη θαλασση, Σιωπα, πεφιμωσο. Και εκοπασεν ο ανεμος,
και εγενετο γαληνη μεγαλη.	και επαυσαντο και εγενετο γαληνη. 25 Ειπε δε αυτοις, Που η πιστις υμων;	και εγενετο γαληνη μεγαλη. 40 Και ειπεν αυτοις, Τι δειλοι εστε ουτως; πως ουκ εχετε πιστιν;
27 Οι δε ανθρωποι εθαυμασαν,	Φοβηθεντες δε εθαυμασαν,	41 Και εφοβηθησαν φοβον μεγαν,

MATT. VIII.	LUKE VIII.	MARK IV.
λεγοντες, Ποταπος εστιν οὑτος, ὁτι οἱ ανεμοι και ἡ θαλασσα αυτῳ ὑπακουουσιν;	λεγοντες προς αλληλους, Τις αρα οὑτος εστιν ὁτι και τοις ανεμοις επιτασσει και τῳ ὑδατι, και ὑπακουουσιν αυτῳ;	και ελεγον προς αλληλους, Τις αρα οὑτος εστιν, ὁτι και ὁ ανεμος και ἡ θαλασσα αυτῳ ὑπακουει;

TRANSLATION.

MATT. VIII.	LUKE VIII.	MARK IV.
	22 And it came to pass on one of the days,	35 And on that same day, when even was come,
23 And when he was entered into the boat, his disciples followed him.	that he entered into a boat with his disciples; and he said to them, Let us go over to the other side of the lake.	he said unto them, Let us go over to the other side. 36 And having sent away the people, they take him just as he was into the boat; and there were also other boats with him.
	And they put off. 23 And as they sailed he fell asleep.	
24 And, behold, there arose a great disturbance in the sea, so that the boat was covered with the waves;	And there came down a squall of wind in the lake,	And there arises a great squall of wind;
	and they were filled and in jeopardy.	but the waves beat into the boat so that it was now full.

MATT. VIII.	LUKE VIII.	MARK IV.
but he slept.		And he was sleeping at the stern, on the seat cover:
25 And going to him they awoke him, saying, Lord, save us, we perish.	24 And going to him they awoke him, saying, Master, Master, we perish.	And they awake him, and say to him, Teacher, carest thou not that we perish?
26 And he saith to them, Why do you fear, Oh ye of little faith? Then he arose, and rebuked the winds and the sea;	But he arose, and rebuked the winds and the raging of the water;	And he arose up, and rebuked the wind, and said unto the sea, Peace, be still.
and there was a great calm.	and they ceased, and there was a calm. But he said to them, Where is your faith?	And the wind fell, and there was a great calm. And he said to them, Why are you afraid? How is it that ye have no faith?
27 But the men wondered, saying, What man is this, that the winds and the sea obey him?	But they being afraid wondered, saying one to another, Who then is this, that even the winds he commandeth and the water, and they obey him?	41 And they feared with great fear, and said one to another Who then is this that even the wind and the sea obey him?

Here the accounts of Luke and Mark are obviously too closely connected to admit the supposition that they are separate and independent accounts of the same event, one of them must therefore be taken from the other, or both from a common source. This last supposition is so far true, for the accounts bear internal proofs of being derived from an original in another language. But St. Mark's account bears the strongest internal evidence of having been written by an eye-witness. It must, therefore, be a translation of an autoptical memoir; and a literal translation of an autoptical memoir may be held as an original authority where the original itself is lost.

It is right, however, to observe that the second Gospel is held by Griesbach and others to be a compilation from the Gospels of Matthew and Luke. According to this view, what I hold to be omissions on the part of Luke are additions on the part of Mark, and what I hold to be additions on the part of Luke are omissions on the part of Mark.

I come first to the matter which is peculiar to Mark. He states —

1st. The particular day on which the miracle took place.

2nd. The time of day.

3rd. The dismissal of the multitude.

4th. That the disciples took our Lord into the boat "even as he was."

5th. That there were other boats in company.

6th. That our Lord was in the stern of the boat.

7th. That he was reposing on the seat cover.

8th. The words with which he rebuked the storm.

Here are no less than eight facts mentioned in this short account, not one of which could possibly be taken from either of the other evangelists; for they are neither expressly noticed, nor can they be inferred from their accounts. With the exception of the date, they are all purely autoptical, such as an eye-witness would very naturally relate, but such as a historian would omit, because they do not affect the main event, neither do they render the other accounts clearer.

Let us subject the matter which is peculiar to Luke's account to a similar examination —

1st. He leaves the date undetermined.

2nd. He adds that it was "the lake" to which the expression "the other side" refers.

3rd. The nautical expression "They shoved off, and when under way."

4th. That the squall "came down on the lake."

5th. That they were in danger.

6th. That the disciples were astonished at the events as well as terrified.

1st. With regard to the date, when we examine the context carefully, it will be found that there is a slight difference between Matthew and Mark with respect to the time when the event took place. I have already shown that Luke made use of Matthew's Gospel. I am now showing that he also made use of Mark's. Had he in this case adopted the arrangement of Matthew, he must have differed from that of Mark; with both before him, by using the expression "on one of the days," he differs from neither. We have, therefore, an obvious reason why he left the exact day undetermined.

2nd. The expression το περαν, "the other side," applied to the eastern side of the lake, is a provincialism, or rather Capernaumism, which Luke corrects by explaining that it is "the other side of the lake" which is meant. Here also the reason for the addition is obvious.

3rd. The nautical expressions are characteristic of Luke's

style of describing nautical events; they give great clearness to the narrative, and they can be inferred with certainty from the other accounts.

4th. The expression "there came down," in Luke's account, is in apparent contradiction to that of Mark, according to our authorised version, "there arose;" but there is none in the original. Luke by a single word ($\kappa\alpha\tau\epsilon\beta\eta$) gives the effect of the particular kind of squall with perfect precision, and at the same time corrects the Hebraism of Matthew, who speaks of a great disturbance in the *sea*.

5th. "They were in danger" ($\kappa\alpha\iota\ \epsilon\kappa\iota\nu\delta\upsilon\nu\epsilon\upsilon\sigma\nu$). Luke here supplies a qualification, the want of which in the other Gospels is remarked by Dr. Bloomfield in his notes on the passage.

6th. The effects of the miracle upon the disciples are described by Matthew as those of "wonder," by Mark, of "fear." Luke combines them both, "They, being afraid, wondered."

There are none of these additions but what are either inevitable inferences from the statements in Mark's account, or are taken from Matthew's, and in each of them we can see a reason for its insertion.

I hold, therefore, that in the preceding Gospels we have the materials from which Luke drew up his account of this miracle — that it is based upon that in the second Gospel, but completed from that in the first. I hold, also, that the original of the second Gospel existed in a different language from Greek when Luke wrote his.

In order to ascertain this point, we must lay out of sight all the changes made by Luke as a historian, and also the matter which he has taken from Matthew, and confine the comparison to passages in which he has adhered to the account in Mark. Where he has done so, I find twenty-one lines in which there is no change except that which arises from translation. Of these, eight lines are expressed in identical terms and thirteen in synonymous terms. This is about the usual proportion which we find in independent translations. Thus, in the example of independent translations from the French given in my former work, consisting of nineteen lines, I find that there are eight lines identical and eleven synonymous or translational. St. Mark then is a translator; but if a translator he must be the translator of Peter, and by that designation he is known by the earliest Christian writers "Mark the translator of Peter,"—Μαρκος ἑρμηνευτης Πετρου, being the designation given to him by Papias, the first writer by whom he is mentioned.

I have already glanced at the external evidence which would lead us to conclude that Peter was the original author of the second Gospel. The internal evidence furnished by a minute examination is not less conclusive. The author of the account of stilling the tempest, whoever he was, was a Galilean residing on the western shore of the lake; he must have been in the boat when the event happened, and he must have been familiar with the navigation of the lake, all of which characteristics agree with those of Peter. But we can come still nearer to him, for he relates, as an eye-witness would, things which could only be known to three of the disciples,—Peter, James, and John; such as what took place in the house of Jairus, at the transfiguration, and in the house of Peter. In this last case we can strike off James and John. They are mentioned as being present, but only as spectators; and no mention is made of Peter, who must also have been present. But a man does not think it necessary to say he was in his own house. Lastly, he speaks of Peter's house exactly as the owner would. Who but Peter would think it necessary to tell us that Andrew was a joint tenant. I have elsewhere entered into the evidence at greater length: for my present purpose it is sufficient to show that St. Luke, in making use of such an authority as we find in Mark, was making use of the best historical evidence, that of "an eye-witness and minister of the word."

St. John also was an eye-witness and minister of the word; and although his Gospel was given to the world long after that of Luke, yet his details of events are occasionally so minute and circumstantial as to indicate not only the presence of the author, but that they were written when the impression was yet fresh upon him; such as his account of his own visit to the sepulchre in company with Peter. But if he wrote such accounts at the time, a man of research like Luke would naturally endeavour to avail himself of them. Now, if we compare his account of Peter's visit to the sepulchre with that in the Gospel of John, agreements will be found which can scarcely be accidental.

LUKE XXIV. 12.	JOHN XX. 3.
Ὁ δε Πετρος αναστας	Εξηλθεν ουν ὁ Πετρος, και ὁ αλλος μαθητης, και ηρχοντο εις το μνημειον, ετρεχον δε οἱ δυο ὁμου και ὁ αλλος μαθητης
εδραμεν	προεδραμεν ταχιον του Πετρου, και ηλθεν πρωτος

επι το μνημειον· και παρακυψας βλεπει τα οθονια κειμενα.	εις το μνημειον. Και παρακυψας βλεπει κειμενα τα οθονια.
Then arose Peter,	Peter therefore went forth and that other disciple, and came to the sepulchre. So they ran both together; and the other disciple
and ran into the sepulchre, and stooping, down he beheld the linen clothes lying.	did outrun Peter and came first to the sepulchre, and stooping down he beheld the linen clothes lying, &c.

Mr. Alford observes that the similarity of diction indicates a common origin, and one distinct from the rest of the chapter. I agree with him; and add that the original is in John's own account; for who but an eyewitness would enter into such minute detail? Luke's silence as to John's presence proves nothing, for we are informed afterwards that there were more than one present. In the 24th verse of the same chapter, he says, " Certain of them went to the sepulchre, and found," &c.

So, also, in the account of the disbelief of Thomas we meet with two passages agreeing verbally.

LUKE XXIV. 36.	JOHN XX. 19.
Εστη εν μεσω αυτων, και λεγει αυτοις· Ειρηνη υμιν.	Εστη εις το μεσον, και λεγει αυτοις· Ειρηνη υμιν.
* * *	
40 Και τουτο ειπων, επεδειξεν αυτοις τας χειρας.	και τουτο ειπων, επεδειξεν αυτοις τας χειρας.
Stood in the midst of them, and said to them, Peace be with you.	Stood in the midst and said to them, Peace be with you.
* * *	

40 And when he had so said, he showed them his hands.	And when he had so said, he showed them his hands.

This agreement can scarcely be accidental. Perhaps the reason why there is not a greater amount of it between Luke and John may be that, having given his writings to Luke, and they having been incorporated by Luke in his Gospel, John refrained from repeating them in his own, in accordance with its supplementary character. We can thus account for St. John passing over certain remarkable events in the life of our Lord, such as the transfiguration. As John was one of the three disciples present on that occasion, he could supply Luke with matter not mentioned by the other evangelists. Accordingly, we find in Luke's account circumstances not mentioned by them, which St. Luke must have received from one of those present, as in the following passage: — "Who (Moses and Elias) appeared in glory, and spake of his decease which he should accomplish at Jerusalem. But Peter and they that were with him were heavy with sleep; and when they were awake, they saw his glory and the two men that were with him" (Luke ix. 31, 32.). This is evidently the account of an eye-witness; but as it is not in Mark's (Peter's) account, it must be either from John or James. I am inclined, therefore, to place John amongst the authorities made use of by Luke in the composition of his Gospel.

St. Luke's connection with St. Paul gave rise to an early tradition that he was indebted to that Apostle for the matter of his Gospel. Tertullian mentions it, but only as a tradition, which he accounts for by saying that "it was natural to ascribe to the master what the disciple promulgated."* Origen states that the Gospel was praised by Paul.† Irenæus, indeed, goes farther, and says that "Luke wrote what Paul preached;" but he says elsewhere that "Luke delivered to us what he had learned from the Apostles, as he himself testifies in his preface,"‡ we can lay no weight, therefore, upon this assertion, farther than that when he wrote, the tradition alluded to was prevalent and in his mind at the time.

We must, however, suppose that Paul communicated to Luke accounts of his own transactions and spoken addresses; but we cannot suppose that St. Paul preached in the historical style in which St. Luke wrote. There is indeed one great historical event in the life of our Lord narrated by St. Paul, which he stated that he had received by revelation—namely, the institution of the Lord's Supper —which, if my views of the time and place of writing the Gospel be correct, we should expect to find made use of by Luke as an authority. Now it has been long observed that Luke's account agrees more nearly with Paul's than any of the others. There are indeed, or rather there were, difficulties which a minute comparison suggested, difficulties which have not escaped modern criticism; for example, the passage in the received text—"και ειπε, λαβετε, φαγετε," "and said, take eat"—occurs in Matthew's account,

---

* Lucæ digestum Paulo ascribere solent. Capit magistrorum videri quæ discipuli promulgarint. *Adv.* Marcion. iv. 5.

† Και το τριτον το κατα Λουκαν, το υπο Παυλου επαινουμενον ευαγγελιον. *Ap.* Euseb. H. E. vi. 25. Origen evidently alludes to 2 Cor. viii. 18., and supposes Paul meant the gospel of Luke by the expression τον αδελφον ου ὁ επαινος εν τῳ ευαγγελιῳ.

‡ Lucas . . . ea quæ ab eis (Apostolis) didicerat tradidit nobis sicut ipse testificatur, dicens, &c.

but not in Luke's. Upon this, De Wette observes, "It is not probable that Matthew was acquainted with Paul's account;" and it would contradict Paul's account, that he had received it from the Lord, were we to suppose he got it from Matthew. In the early uncial MSS., however, no such difficulty exists, for the passage does not occur in the account in the Epistle to the Corinthians. The agreement is then too close to admit of any supposition, except that one of the accounts must be taken from the other; and as Paul informs us that he had received his "of the Lord," Luke must have taken his from it.

The result of this enquiry into the sources of the writings of St. Luke goes to prove that, on every occasion in which it is possible to trace them, we find that those sources are written accounts of Apostles; and we are warranted in supposing from his preface, that those portions of his writings which we cannot trace to any existing authority were drawn from similar sources; and from the perfect fidelity with which he adheres to his authorities, where we can put it to the test, we cannot entertain a doubt that he is a true and faithful historian of events which either fell under his own observation, or which he derived immediately from those who were engaged in them.

CHART OF S

NARRATIVE OF THE VOYAGE.

CHAPTER I.

CÆSAREA TO MYRA.

(Acts, xxvii. 1—6.)

AFTER two years' imprisonment at Cæsarea, and after repeated examinations before Felix and Festus, successive Roman governors of Judæa, and before King Agrippa, the last of the Herod family, St. Paul appealed unto Cæsar.

In consequence of this appeal it was determined that

1 Ὡς δε εκριθη του αποπλειν* ἡμας εις την Ιταλιαν, παρεδιδουν τον τε Παυλον και τινας ἑτερους δεσμωτας ἑκατονταρχῃ, ονοματι Ιουλιῳ, σπειρης Σεβαστης.	1 And when it was determined that we should sail into Italy, they delivered Paul and certain other prisoners unto one named Julius, a centurion of Augustus' band.

* αποπλειν. Literally "to sail from." St. Luke, by his accurate use of nautical terms, gives great precision to his language, and expresses by a single word what would otherwise require several. Mitford observes, that "we are often at a loss to render the verb Πλεω otherwise than by our word *to sail*, though they are far from being of the same precise import. The use of oars, so prevalent in Grecian navigation, is so little known in our seas, that to sail is our only general term for going by sea."—*Hist. of Greece*, ii. 362. St. Luke alone of the sacred writers uses this nautical term, either simply, or, as in the present instance, in composition.

he should be sent, along with other prisoners, by sea to Italy. He was accordingly committed to the charge of a centurion named Julius, of the Imperial band, a person who, upon all occasions, treated the apostle with humanity and consideration.

Cæsarea was at that time the principal seaport of Syria.* It would appear, however, that there were no ships bound for Italy in the harbour capable of accommodating the party of Julius, including the prisoners and their guard. He therefore embarked them in a ship of Adramyttium †, a seaport of Mysia, on the eastern shore of the Ægean Sea, opposite Lesbos. This ship was evidently bound for her own port, and her course from Cæsarea thither necessarily led her close past the principal seaports of Asia.‡

---

* See account of Cæsarea in Josephus, Antiq. xv. 13. Bryant, absurdly enough, supposes that Ptolemais (Acre) was the port of embarkation; and adds, as if it were a mere conjecture, "Grotius is of opinion that they went from Cæsarea:" it would have been quite contrary to St. Luke's usual method to have omitted the land journey from Cæsarea to Ptolemais, had it actually taken place. See Acts, xxi. 7, 8.

† See a very full account of the notices in ancient authors of this place, in Wetstein ad loc.

‡ By Asia St. Luke means pro-consular Asia, of which Ephesus was the capital, i. e., the western part of Asia Minor, which, according to Cicero, comprehended Caria and Lycia; and according to St. Luke, did not include Pamphylia. Acts, ii. 9, 10. By attending to this, we are left in no doubt as to "the places" (τους τοπους) meant in the text, which they would arrive at by the route they pursued. The places "κατα την Ασιαν," which may be translated "along the coast of Asia," were then flourishing sea-ports, three of which are mentioned by St. Luke; namely, Myra (Acts, xxvii. 5.), Patara (xxi. 1.), and Cnidus (xxvii. 7.). For an account of the present state of Myra, see Spratt and Forbes, Travels in Lycia, i. 125. It has been observed that the magnitude of ancient cities may be inferred from that of their theatres; the diameter of that of Myra is 360 feet and

Now this is also the course which a ship would take in making a voyage from Syria to Italy; they would, therefore, be so far on their voyage when they reached the coast of Asia, and in the great commercial marts on that coast, they could not fail to find opportunities of being carried on to their ulterior destination. On St. Paul's former voyage from Philippi to Syria (Acts, xx. 6. to xxi. 7.) the same plan was adopted: they sailed to the places on the coast of Asia (κατα την Ασιαν), and changed ship at one of them, Patara, just as we find was done in the present instance at Myra. We have, therefore, an obvious reason why they took their passage in this ship. The apostle was on this occasion accompanied by Aristarchus, the Macedonian of Thessalonica, and St. Luke, the historian of the voyage. The former appears to have been a prisoner, for St. Paul, in his epistle to the Colossians, designates him as his fellow-prisoner.† iv. 10.

---

2 Επιβαντες δε πλοιω Αδραμυττηνω μελλοντι πλειν εις τους* κατα την Ασιαν τοπους, ανηχθημεν, οντος συν ἡμιν Αρισταρχου Μακεδονος Θεσσαλονικεως.

2 And entering into a ship of Adramyttium, we launched, meaning to sail by the coasts of Asia; *one* Aristarchus, a Macedonian of Thessalonica, being with us.

---

the "arena is now a corn-field." Ib. 132. The theatre of Patara is also a magnificent structure; see a view of it in the Ionian Antiquities, published by the Dilletante Society (vol. ii. pl. 56, 57.), and an account of it in Beaufort's Caramania, p. 5.; for an account of Cnidus, see Clarke's Travels, vol. ii. p. 216.

* μελλοντι πλειν εις τους, &c., is the reading both of the Vatican and Alexandrian MSS., the two earliest, and, in a case like the present, best authorities, and is that adopted by Lachmann; the common reading is μελλοντες πλειν τους, &c.; the preposition εις renders the meaning obvious, by showing that the ship was to touch at "the places," &c.

† This companion of St. Paul is very unceremoniously mentioned by

On the day after they left Cæsarea they touched at Sidon. From the distance accomplished, sixty-seven geographical miles, we must infer that they had a fair, or at least a leading wind, probably westerly, which is the wind which prevails in this part of the Mediterranean.* We are not informed of the cause of their stopping at Sidon; probably, however, it was for the purposes of trade.† Whatever was the cause of the delay, it afforded the centurion an opportunity of showing kindness to St. Paul, for we are told in the narrative that he "gave him liberty to go unto his friends to refresh himself."

---

3 Τῃ δε ετερᾳ κατηχθημεν εις Σιδωνα.

3 Φιλανθρωπως τε ὁ Ιουλιος τῳ Παυλῳ χρησαμενος, επετρεψεν προς τους φιλους πορευθεντα, επιμελειας τυχειν.

3 And the next *day* we touched at Sidon.

3 And Julius courteously entreated Paul, and gave *him* liberty to go unto his friends to refresh himself.

---

our English translators, by the gratuitous insertion of the word "*one*." He is twice previously noticed in the Acts, once as a Macedonian (xix. 29.), and once as a Thessalonican (xx. 4.); here he is mentioned as both.

* "The wind continues to the westward. I am sorry to find it almost as prevailing as the trade winds." (4th July, 1798, near Alexandria.)— *Life of Lord de Saumarez*, i. 210. "We have just gained sight of Cyprus, nearly the track we followed six weeks ago, so invariably do the westerly winds prevail at this season." (19th Aug. 1798.)—Ib. i. 243. A westerly wind would be fair between Cæsarea and Sidon, as the bearing of the coast line between the two places is about N.N.E. See sailing Directions for the Coast of Syria, by Capt. E. Smith, R. N.

† According to Strabo, Sidon was situated on the finest harbour of the continent, and contested with Tyre the supremacy of the Phœnician cities (lib. xvi. c. 2.). Achilles Tatius calls it the metropolis of the Phœnicians, μητηρ Φοινικων ἡ πολις; he describes it as having two harbours, one of

Loosing* from thence they were forced, by contrary winds, to run under the lee of Cyprus.† A question here

---

4 Κἀκειθεν αναχθεντες ὑπεπλευ- | 4 And when we had launched
σαμεν την Κυπρον δια το τους | from thence, we sailed under
ανεμους ειναι εναντιους. | Cyprus, because the winds were contrary.

---

which is large with a narrow entrance, where merchant ships can winter in safety (lib. i.). To judge from its present state, the shelter was afforded by a ridge of rocks, parallel to the coast, forming a natural breakwater. The harbour was filled up during the wars of the middle ages. For an account of its present state, see Robinson's Biblical Researches, and Wilson's Lands of the Bible. The latter author gives a plan of the harbour. See a view of it in Carne's Syria and the Holy Land illustrated, vol. iii. p. 6.

* αναχθεντες is one of those nautical terms about which there is no doubt as to the meaning — which is, to depart from a place; it is used by St. Luke both in the Gospel and Acts, and is rendered in the authorised version, "to launch," "to loose," "to sail," "to set forth," "to depart." Αναγεσθαι is amongst the nautical terms of Julius Pollux. There is no precisely corresponding term in English. Mitford observes, that in rendering it "we must risk the sea phrase *to get under way*, or content ourselves with the inaccurate expression *to set sail.*"—*Hist. of Greece,* vol. ii., p. 232, note.

St. Luke uses the words αποπλεω, εκπλεω, and αιρω, to express the same thing. The last is an elliptical expression: it occurs in verse 13 of this chapter, and is translated "loosing." It would have been more accurately rendered "weighed," τας αγκυρας, the anchors, being understood. Thus, in Plutarch, Pompey, p. 1208., αραμενοι τας αγκυρας. It is, however, generally used absolutely, as in the present case, and as its English equivalent to weigh. See Wetstein ad loc. The corresponding word for coming to land, καταγεσθαι, Jul. Pollux, Onom. i. 102., occurs in the preceding verse.

† ὑπεπλευσαμεν, "we sailed under the lee" Dr. Falconer, in his Dissertation on St. Paul's Voyage, supposed it meant to sail to the south of a place, because the maps of the ancients, like those of the moderns,

arises, which was the lee side of Cyprus? In passing it, did they leave it upon their right or upon their left? Commentators are divided on the subject, but it is generally supposed that they left it on their right, that is, that they passed to the south of that island. This opinion is evidently founded upon the erroneous suppositions that the coast of Syria is comprehended by St. Luke in the term *Asia*, and that the ancients only made coasting voyages. The question is not one of importance, farther than that it is desirable to leave nothing uncertain where certainty can be attained, and because, in the next place, if we are sure of the meaning of the author, in this case we can compare the proceedings of the ancient navigators with those of modern ones, who have been placed under similar circumstances in the same locality, and can thus form a more correct estimate of their seamanship.

As I dissent from the generally received opinion that they sailed by the south of Cyprus, I shall, in the first place, state the arguments upon which that opinion is founded. Dr. Falconer, in his Dissertation on St. Paul's Voyage, says,—

"On their loosing from Sidon, they found that their intention of continuing their voyage along the coasts of Asia Minor would be frustrated by contrary winds, which obliged them to pursue their

---

were constructed with the north point uppermost. The explanation of Wetstein is, however, unquestionably the true one: "ubi navis vento contrario cogitur a recto cursu decedere, ita ut tunc insula sit interposita inter ventum et navem, dicitur ferri *infra* insulam." We meet with the same word again in the 7th verse, where ample proof will be given that this is the meaning of the term. Kuinöel erroneously supposes that it means to sail close to the shore: "sublegere, oram *cominus* legere."

voyage under or on the southern side of the island of Cyprus, instead of the northern, as according to their plan of sailing along the coast they had at first proposed."

Dr. Bennet, a late commentator on the Acts, expresses himself thus:—

"Sailed under or to the south of Cyprus, on account of the winds being contrary, when they would otherwise have taken them to the north, along the Asiatic coasts."—*Lectures*, p. 399.

Dr. Bloomfield, whilst he correctly renders ὑποπλειν, "*to sail under the lee of any high land*," and admits that, had the weather been fair, it is probable they would have taken a course to the south of Cyprus, but at a distance from it, adds,—

"Since, however, we are told that the winds were contrary (though varying, yet all more or less adverse), they changed that course, and ὑπεπλευσαμεν την Κ. Now, for the winds to have been contrary, they must have been N., or N. E., or N. N. E., or such like, and then the best way to evade their force would be to sail close under the coast of Cyprus, after having cut across to the promontory of Pedalium, so as to reach the Bay of Catium. That they coasted along Palestine, and then made for the *eastern* promontory of Cyprus (as the best commentators think), is improbable, because they would thus be brought more into the wind's eye (as the sailors say), and into tempestuous seas."—Note ad loc.

When we hear of contrary winds, and wish to ascertain their direction, the chief points to be determined are the ship's actual position and intended course. Now, when St. Luke talks of contrary winds, we know that the ship had left Sidon, and must have been in sight of Cyprus, for he tells us the winds forced them to leeward of that island. Their ultimate object was Italy and their proximate one was one or other of the "places in Asia," which

F

I have already shown lay in the same direction. As St. Luke does not include Pamphylia in Asia, the nearest part of that region to Syria is Lycia, and a ship's course from Sidon thither is W. N. W., leaving Cyprus on the right. St. Luke was perfectly aware of this, for upon the former voyage, in which he accompanied St. Paul, he tells us that on their passage from Patara, one of the "places in Asia," to Phenicia, "they left Cyprus on the left hand," *i.e.* on the north. (Acts, xxi. 3.) The winds, therefore, which prevented them from taking the straight course to the places in Asia must have been from the westward. Now these are the very winds which might have been expected in this part of the Mediterranean at this season (summer). Admiral de Saumarez writes, 19th August, 1798,—

"We have just gained sight of Cyprus, so invariably do the westerly winds prevail at this season."—*Life*, i. 243.

Under these circumstances, sailing under Cyprus is equivalent to saying that they left Cyprus on their left hand; but this point is put out of doubt by St. Luke himself, for he tells us in the 5th verse that they *sailed through* the sea of Cilicia (διαπλευσαντες), not *over*, as in the authorised version; but as this sea lies altogether to the north of Cyprus, they could not have sailed through it without leaving the island on their left.

---

5 Το, τε πελαγος το κατα την Κιλικιαν και Παμφυλιαν διαπλευσαντες, κατηλθομεν εις Μυρα της Λυκιας.

5 And when we had sailed over the sea of Cilicia and Pamphylia, we came to Myra, a city of Lycia.

In pursuing this route they acted precisely as the most accomplished seaman in the present day would have done under similar circumstances; by standing to the north till they reached the coast of Cilicia, they might expect when they did so to be favoured by the land wind, which prevails there during the summer months, as well as by the current, which constantly runs to the westward, along the south coast of Asia Minor.*

In April, 1844, the Belvidera frigate, commanded by the Honourable George Grey, sailed from Beyrout for Athens; her course, therefore, till she reached the Archipelago, was nearly the same as that of the ship of Adramyttium; but instead of taking the direct course, they "sailed under (*i.e.* to the east of) Cyprus, because the winds were contrary." Captain Grey informed me that he did so because he expected, by standing to the north, "to get the wind off the land:" in this he was disappointed, probably because it was too early in the season. But M. de Pagés, a French navigator, who made a voyage from Syria to Marseilles, took the same course, and has given the reasons why he did so. He informs us, that after making Cyprus,

"The winds from the west, and consequently contrary, which prevail in these places during the summer, forced us to run to the

---

* "From Syria to the Archipelago, there is a constant current to the westward." *Beaufort's Description of the South Coast of Asia Minor*, p. 39. Dr. Pococke found this current running so strong between Rhodes and the continent, that it broke into the cabin windows even in calm weather.—*Description of the East*, ii. p. 236.

north. We made for the coast of Caramania (Cilicia) in order to meet the northerly winds, and which we found accordingly."*

Fynes Moryson, in his Itinerary, narrates a sea voyage from Syria to Crete, in which the circumstances of wind and weather bear a still more marked resemblance to those experienced by the ancient 'mariners than any of the above. He sailed from Scanderoon, the port of Aleppo, with the intention of disembarking at the city of Candia, on the north side of Crete, and therefore his course so far was the same as that of St. Paul and his companions. At first he tells us,—

"We sayled prosperously, but after the winds grew so contrary as we were driven to the south of Candia."—p. 251.

Here, in the seas where I infer from the silence of St. Luke that the circumstances of St. Paul's voyage were favourable, they " sayled prosperously ; " and in the seas where St. Paul's ship met with contrary winds, μη προσεωντος ἡμας του ανεμου, "the winds grew contrary," and had precisely the same effect upon the ship, which it drove to the south of Crete; and, what is still more remarkable, Moryson is carried to Fair Havens. It is not, perhaps, easy to recognise in "the wild rocks called Calis Miniones" the Fair Bays which give the harbour its name, and which it still retains in Calos Limeones. There is no doubt, however, of the identity of the places, for Moryson marks the position of Calis Miniones by saying it is

---

* "Nous fîmes route sur l'isle de Chypre. Après l'avoir cotoyée, les vents de l'ouest, par conséquent contraires, qui règnent pendant l'été dans ces parties, nous firent élever au nord, nous cherchions la côte de la Caramanie, pour rencontrer les vents du nord, que nous y trouvâmes en effet." *Voyages autour du Monde*, tom. i. p. 406.

"Some three miles distant from a monastery called Santa Maria Aggidietra,"
just as St. Luke marks it, "as nigh unto the city Lasea." The monastery still remains: in Pashley's map it is spelt Hodhetria, and is exactly three miles above the "rocky promontory" which separates the two bays upon which Moryson was landed. (See view of Fair Havens.)

Favoured, as they probably were, by the land wind and currents, they arrive without any recorded incident at Myra of Lycia, then a flourishing seaport, now a desolate waste. The stupendous magnitude of its theatre attests the extent of its former population; the splendour of its tombs*, its wealth. But it is not my intention to describe the ancient or modern state of the places visited, farther than as they illustrate the events of the voyage.

This city is situated, according to Capt. Beaufort, about three miles from the sea; according to Strabo, the distance is twenty stadia, or about two geographical miles, the difference being probably caused by the silting up of the river Andriaki, which flows past it into a spacious bay. This river, which Appian calls the port of the Myrians (Μυρεων επινειω), Bell. Civ. lib. iv. cap. 82., was navigable to Myra, for he informs us that Lentulus, having broken the chain of the harbour, ascended to that city.

The voyage has hitherto been prosperous, and the object which the party had in view in proceeding to "the places in Asia" is attained. At the first of them which lay in

---

* "Sepulchres, which for the elegance of their design, costliness of execution, and size, seem to have been suited rather for the keeping of the ashes of rulers and kings, than of common citizens." — *Spratt and Forbes*, i. p. 132.

their way, the centurion found a ship of Alexandria, loaded, as we afterwards learn, with wheat, bound for Italy, in which he embarked his charge. Egypt was at this time one of the granaries of Rome, and the corn which was sent from thence to Italy was conveyed in ships of very great size.* From the dimensions given of one of them by Lucian †, they appear to have been quite as large as the largest class of merchant ships of modern times. We need not be surprised, therefore, at the number of souls which we afterwards find were embarked in this one ‡, or that another ship of the same class could after the shipwreck convey them to Italy, in addition to her own crew.

Some commentators have supposed that Myra lay so much out of the track from Alexandria to Italy that the term Alexandrian must mean the particular "build" of the ship, just as we say Liburnian galleys, and not as marking the port to which she belonged. Now it is quite true that Myra is out of the direct course from Alexandria to Italy, which is by the south of Crete. But with the westerly winds which prevail in those seas,

---

6 Κἀκει εὑρων ὁ ἑκατονταρχης πλοιον Αλεξανδρινον πλεον εις την Ιταλιαν, ενεβιβασεν ἡμας εις αυτο.

6 And there the centurion found a ship of Alexandria sailing into Italy; and he put us therein.

---

* After the capture of Jerusalem the Emperor Titus returned to Italy in one of these ships, touching at Rhegium, and landing at Puteoli. Sueton. Vit. ch. 5.; see also Vit. Augusti, 98.; and Seneca, Epist. 77.

† In the Dialogue Πλοιον η Ευχη, see the Dissertation on ancient ships, post.

‡ Granville Penn, on the authority of the Vatican MS., reads "seventy-six," instead of "two hundred and seventy-six." See his note on the subject; the Alexandrian and other uncial MSS., however, have two hundred and seventy-six.

ships, particularly those of the ancients, unprovided with a compass, and ill calculated to work to windward, would naturally stand to the north till they made the land of Asia Minor, which is peculiarly favourable for navigation by such vessels, because the coast is bold and safe, and the elevation of the mountains makes it visible at a great distance; it abounds in harbours, and the sinuosities of its shores and the westerly current would enable them, if the wind was at all off the land, to work to windward, at least as far as Cnidus, where these advantages ceased.*
Myra lies due nòrth from Alexandria †, and its bay is well calculated to shelter a wind-bound ship. The Alexandrian ship was not, therefore, out of her course at Myra, even if she had no call to touch there for the purposes of commerce.

We may suppose that the same westerly winds which forced the Adramyttian ship to the east of Cyprus, drove the Alexandrian ship to Myra. The land wind on the Cilician coast appears to be quite local, and, therefore, might enable St. Paul's ship to reach Myra, although the prevalent wind did not admit of the ships in that harbour proceeding on their voyage.

* We learn from Thucydides (viii. 35.), that Cnidus was frequented by merchant ships from Egypt, απ' Αιγυπτου ὁλκαδες.

† According to Ptolemy it lies just east of the meridian of Alexandria, which is precisely its position. I have never had occasion to consult this great geographer without being astonished at the extent and accuracy of his information. It is easy for modern writers to find fault with him; the very precision he introduced into the science enables them to detect errors unavoidable in the state of knowledge which the ancients had of distant regions, or caused by errors in transcription. The edition of Tauchnitz, which I have used, though unpretending in form, is, I believe, the most correct.

CHAP. II.

VOYAGE FROM MYRA TO FAIR HAVENS IN CRETE.

(Acts, xxvii. 7, 8.)

In this ship of Alexandria, in which the centurion and his party embarked, they proceeded on their voyage. Their progress, after leaving Myra, was extremely slow; for we are told that it was "many" days before they were "come over against Cnidus," that is, before they reached the entrance of the Ægean Sea. As the distance between the two places is not more than 130 geographical miles, which they could easily have accomplished with a fair wind in one day, they must either have met with calms or contrary winds. I infer that the delay was caused by contrary winds, from the expression μολις, which is translated in our authorised version "scarce," producing the impression that the ship had scarcely reached Cnidus when the winds became contrary; but which ought to be rendered "with difficulty," expressing the difficulty which ships experience in con-

---

7 Εν ικαναις δε ἡμεραις βραδυπλοοῦντες, και μολις γενομενοι κατα την Κνιδον, μη προσεωντος ἡμας του ανεμου, ὑπεπλευσαμεν την Κρητην κατα Σαλμωνην.

7 And when we had sailed slowly many days, and scarce were come over against Cnidus, the wind not suffering, us we sailed under Crete, over against Salmone.

tending with adverse winds. The same word occurs in the following verse, where it is translated "hardly," where there can be no doubt as to its meaning, for the general trending of the south coast of Crete, which they were navigating (παραλεγομενοι, v. 8.), was the same as that of Asia, east and west; and we are now told that the winds were contrary. (v. 7.) Cicero, in one of his epistles, uses very similar terms to express the effects of contrary winds: —

"Adversis ventis usi essemus, *tardeque et incommode* navigâsse-mus."*
"We met with contrary winds, and *sailed slowly and with difficulty*."

I am satisfied, therefore, that the words in the original, βραδυπλοουντες, και μολις γενομενοι, " sailing slowly and with difficulty were come," &c., express the delays which a ship experiences in working to windward.

The question now occurs, what was the direction of the wind which produced the effects recorded in the narrative. We are told, that when they "were come over against Cnidus, the wind not suffering us, we sailed under Crete, over against Salmone." (v. 7.) The direct course of a ship on her voyage from Myra to Italy, after she has reached Cnidus, is by the north side of Crete, through the Archipelago, W. by S. Hence a ship which can make good a course of about seven points from the wind, which I have shown elsewhere † cannot be far from the truth, would not have been prevented from proceeding on her course, unless the wind had been to the west of N.N.W.

---

* Epist. ad Familiares, Lib. xiv. Epist. v.
† Dissertation on ancient ships, *post*.

We are next told that she ran " under Crete, over against Salmone," which implies that she was able to fetch that cape, which bears about S.W. by S. from Cnidus; but unless the wind had been to the north of W.N.W., she could not have done so. The wind was, therefore, between N.N.W. and W.N.W. The middle point between these points is North-West, which cannot be more than two points, and is probably not more than one, from the true direction. The wind, therefore, would in common language have been termed North-west. Now, this is precisely the wind which might have been expected in those seas towards the end of summer. We learn from the sailing directions for the Mediterranean, that

"Throughout the whole of the Mediterranean, but mostly in the eastern half, including the Adriatic and Archipelago, the northwest winds prevail in the summer months." *

which agrees with Aristotle's account of these winds.† According to Pliny, they begin in August, and blow for forty days.‡

With north-west winds the ship could work up from Myra to Cnidus; because, until she reached that point she had the advantage of a weather shore, under the lee of which she would have smooth water, and, as formerly mentioned, a westerly current; but it would be "slowly and with difficulty." At Cnidus these advantages ceased; and unless she had put into that harbour, and waited for

* Purdy's sailing directions for the Mediterranean, p. 197.
† Οἱ Ετησιαι λεγομενοι μιξιν εχοντες των τε απο της αρκτου φερομενων και ζεφυρου.—*Arist. de Mundo*, cap. iv.
‡ Perflant diebus quadraginta quos Etesias vocant.—*Plin.* lib. ii. cap. 4.

a fair wind, her only course was to run under the lee of Crete, in the direction of Salmone* (κατα Σαλμωνην), which is the eastern extremity of that island. After passing this point, the difficulty they experienced in navigating to the westward along the coasts of Asia would recur; but as the south side of Crete is also a weather shore, with northwest winds, they would be able to work up as far as Cape Matala. Here the land trends suddenly to the north and the advantages of a weather shore cease, and their only recourse was to make for a harbour. Now, Fair Havens is the last harbour before arriving at Cape Matala, the farthest point to which an ancient ship could have attained with north-westerly winds.

The delays experienced by navigators proceeding westward in this part of the Mediterranean during the summer months, are of such constant occurrence that I have scarcely found an instance in which they have not been encountered.

Rauwolf, a German physician, who travelled in the Holy Land in the 16th century †, passed and repassed by the same track which St. Paul did. On his voyage eastward, the winds were favourable, *i. e.* westerly. The ship touched at and watered at a port which he calls Calismene (p. 16.), which is evidently Fair Havens. After passing Cape Salmone, they met with a ship coming from the eastward, which had been seven weeks on her passage from Tripoli, which they were obliged to supply with

---

* This promontory still retains its ancient name.—See *Strabo*, lib. ii. cap. 14. *Apol. Rhod.* lib. iv. ver. 1693. *Ptol.* lib. iii. cap. 17.

† Leonharti Rauwolfen Raiss in die Morgenlander, Augsburg, 1582. It is translated by Rav and included in his Collection of Travels, vol. ii.

biscuit. On their return, they met with the same contrary winds which that ship, as well as St. Paul's, had encountered when off the coasts of Lycia and Pamphylia. At length, when they had reached the small mountainous island of Scarpanto, he tells us that a *north* wind sprung up, which, he says, drove them *on their right course* towards Salmone.*

It is interesting to compare the confused and blundering account of the physician of Augsburg with the few but accurate notices of the physician of Antioch. In the first place, had the wind been northerly, no ship bound for the westward would have run down from Scarpanto to the south side of Crete; and in the next place, this was not "the right course," which was W. by S. across the Ægean Sea, to the north of Crete, for which a northerly wind would have been favourable. Rauwolf's ship could, as we learn, lie within about six points of the wind †; hence a northerly wind would have been quite fair. St. Luke, in a ship in the same position between Carpathus (Scarpanto) and Cnidus, and meeting with the same winds, says, shortly but correctly, that the winds did not permit of their proceeding on their course ‡, and that they ran to leeward of Crete. (v. 7.)

---

* P. 465.

† He tells us that, as they were proceeding eastwards, there were only three out of eight winds that were contrary, Sirocco, Levante, and Gregale (p. 18.); hence the ship could lie within six points of the wind.

‡ Commentators very generally suppose that μη προσεωντος ημας του ανεμου, meant that the winds defeated the purpose of taking shelter in the harbour of Cnidus. Dr. Hacket in his commentary on the Acts observes, "That προσεαω does not occur in the classics. Προς cannot well mean *farther*, as some allege, since they would have no motive to continue the

It appears to me, that in the ancient ship they had, not only a more accurate historian, but more skilful seamen. St. Luke tells us that they succeeded in reaching Fair Havens, although it was with difficulty. Rauwolf says, that, although they got into smooth water, under the lee of Crete, in their apprehensions of being driven towards Africa, they kept so close to the high land that they had much difficulty in avoiding being shipwrecked on Candia*; a proceeding which argues any thing but good seamanship.† They saved their ship, but failed in their attempt

---

voyage in that direction, even if the weather had not opposed it."ᵃ Admiral Penrose, however, a better authority in such a matter, takes the same view as I have done. He explains the passage thus: "*The wind not suffering them to get on in the direct course.*" See "Conybeare and Howson," II. p. 326. *note.* We are not told wherein the difficulty of entering Cnidus, if they wished it, lay. Mr. Alford takes what I have no doubt is the correct view: see his note on the passage.

* "Also wurden wir des Getöses und Rauschen der Winden und Wellen wol loss: dargegen cam unser Schiff den Gestadten Candiæ so nahe, das wir alle Augenblicke müsten eines Schiffbruchs gewartig sein."—P. 465.

† Should this meet the eyes of my gallant friends Captains the Hon. G. Grey and J. Lunn, R.N., it may recall to them the result of a similar blunder, on the part of a foreign sloop of war, in the Bay of Gibraltar. I was standing beside the former when our attention was attracted by this vessel passing close by the New Mole, with her top-gallant sails set, staggering under a stiff Levanter. Captain Grey immediately exclaimed, "That gentleman will find himself in a scrape; I must run down and make Lunn get up his steam." The event very soon justified Captain Grey's precaution; before she reached the Ragged Staff, an eddy squall took her aback; in a moment sheets and halyards were gone, and the anchor dropt; the next squall struck her in the opposite direction; the anchor did not hold, she was nearly ashore on Gibraltar, and but for the assistance of Captain Lunn in the Locust steamer, she would probably have drifted on the rocks of Algesiras.

to reach a harbour, which could be no other than Fair Havens, and were obliged to put back to the Calderon Islands.

Sir James afterwards Lord de Saumarez, returning from Aboukir, after the battle of the Nile, with a detachment of Lord Nelson's fleet, stood to the north till he discovered the island of Cyprus, from whence he intended to pass by the north side of Candia (Crete); but the winds proved contrary, and he was forced, like the ancient voyagers and Rauwolf*, to run to the south of that island. His delightful journal, addressed to Lady Saumarez, and written from day to day, throws much light upon the circumstances which affect the navigation of this part of the Mediterranean, and shows how perfectly they agree with those experienced by St. Paul and his companions.

On the 28th of August, 1798, he writes: —

"We are still off the island of Rhodes, which appears fertile and well cultivated. We have also sight of Candia, at the distance of above thirty leagues; our present route is different from any of the former, as we go to the northward of Candia, amidst the innumerable islands that form the Archipelago." †

This was precisely the course which St. Paul's ship was pursuing. The contrary winds, however, forced Sir James Saumarez, as they had forced the ancient navigators, to run to the south of Crete. On the first of September, 1798, he thus writes to Lord Nelson: —

"After contending three days against the adverse winds which are almost invariably encountered here, and getting sufficiently to the northward to have weathered the small islands that lie more immediately between the Archipelago and Candia, the wind set in so

---

* P. 465.   † Life, p. 248.

strong from the westward that I was compelled to desist from that passage, and was compelled to bear up between Scarpanto and Guxo (Carpathus and Casus)."*

It is to be observed, that the fleet could not "fetch" Salmone with the wind at west; which shows that in the apostle's case the wind must have been to the north of west.

I have already adduced the case of Fynes Moryson, whose ship was also forced to deviate from the original intention of going to the north of Crete, and take the same course as St. Paul's.

After these instances, it will scarcely be thought necessary to have recourse to an ancient scholiast for the reasons which induced the navigators of St. Paul's ship to pass by the south of Cape Salmone; yet recent commentators assure us that "this question is resolved by the account of Eustathius, who on another occasion mentions that there were no good ports on the northern side of that island (Crete) — Δυσλιμενος ἡ Κρητη προς την βορῥαν." †
In fact, it so happens that there are excellent harbours on the north side of Crete, namely, Souda and Spina Longa.

After working up along the southern coast of Crete, they reached Fair Havens, which we have seen is the farthest point which an ancient ship, navigating under

---

8 Μολις τε παραλεγομενοι αυτην, ηλθομεν εις τοπον τινα καλουμενον Καλους Λιμενας, ᾧ εγγυς ην πολις Λασαια.

8 And hardly passing it, came unto a place which is called the Fair Havens; nigh whereunto was the city of Lasea.

---

* Life p. 253.

† Valpy's edit. of N. Test. *ad loc.* quoted from Dr. Falconer. Even Barthelemy, in his Anacharsis, is misled by Eustathius, and assures us there are no harbours on the north side of Crete.

the lee of Crete, could reach with north-west winds. As this is an important point in the voyage, it becomes necessary to ascertain precisely its situation, as well as that of the port of Phenice and the island of Clauda. St. Luke marks the position of Fair Havens by its vicinity to the city of Lasæa; but neither Fair Havens nor Lasæa are noticed by any other ancient authority, nor have the ruins of the city been discovered in modern times.* Commentators have generally supposed that Καλους Λιμενας, or Fair Havens, of St. Luke, is the same as Καλη Ακτη, or Fair Strand †, of Stephanus Byzantinus.‡ This, however, is said to be a city of Crete; but St. Luke, by mentioning Fair Havens as in the vicinity of a city, seems to show that there was no city there. Mr. Pashley found a district in Crete bearing the name of Akté, and supposes, with probability, that the city mentioned by Stephanus was situated there. This district is, however, at the west end of Crete, and cannot be the same as Fair Havens, which from the context must be on the south coast.

Mr. Pashley afterwards visited the place, which still bears the ancient name, and which I am prepared to show

---

* Since the above was written, the ruins of this city have been independently discovered by my friends Capt. Spratt, R.N. and the Rev. George Brown. Appendix Nos. 2 & 3. It lies just east of Fair Havens, and still retains its name.

† Ακτη ὁ αιγιαλος, και ὁ παραθαλασσιος τοπος, " the beach, and place along the sea."—Hesych. Notwithstanding the authority of Hesychius, which, however, is not great in such matters, I suspect that ακτη and αιγιαλος are not synonymous; that the latter means a sandy beach (see note on v. 39.); the former, a more general term, equivalent to the English strand. Julius Pollux distinguishes the χωρια επιθαλαττιδια into ακτη, ῥων, αιγιαλος, χηλη, ὑφορμος, ὁρμος, λιμην.—Lib. i. 99.

‡ Καλη Ακτη πολις Κρητων, &c.

FAIR HAVENS, CRETE. (To face p. 81.)

is identical with the Fair Havens of St. Luke; but, unfortunately, the work terminates without any account of his observations. I am, however, indebted to Signor Antonio Schranz*, the able artist who accompanied him, for the view of this interesting locality taken upon the spot.

Dr. Pococke appears to have been the first who ascertained its exact situation; he says—

"In searching after Lebena farther to the west, I found out a place which I thought to be of greater consequence, because mentioned in Holy Scripture, and also honoured by the presence of St. Paul, that is, the Fair Havens, near unto the city of Lasea; for there is another small bay, about two leagues to the east of Matala, which is now called by the Greeks Good or Fair Havens (Λιμεονες Καλους)."†

Dr. Pococke found no ruins here, nor is there reason to suppose that it ever was more than it is at present—an open roadstead, or rather two roadsteads contiguous to each other.

Its retention of its name is owing, no doubt, to its appropriateness. In the old sailing directions, Licht der Seevaert (Amst. 1621), and Miroir de la Mer, it is thus described:—

"Right to the east of Cabra (an islet) lies a fair bay (een schoone bay, Dutch; une belle baie, Fr.), where there is good anchorage; there is, also, one immediately to the west of it where there is also good anchorage." ‡

---

* It will be seen that this view enabled my friends Messrs. Tennent and Brown to identify the locality. Appendix No. 3.

† Travels in the East, vol. ii. p. 250.

‡ " Recht beeosten Cabra leygt een schoone bay daer seer goedt rede is

The most conclusive evidence, however, that this is the Fair Havens of Scripture is, that its position is precisely that where a ship, circumstanced as St. Paul's was, must have put in. I have already shown that the wind must have been about N. W., but with such a wind she could not pass Cape Matala ; we must, therefore, look near, but to the eastward of this promontory, for an anchorage well-calculated to shelter a vessel in north-west winds, but not from all winds, otherwise it would not have been in the opinion of seamen an unsafe winter harbour. Now, here we have a harbour which not only fulfils every one of the conditions, but still retains the name given to it by St. Luke.*

Here, we learn, they were detained till "navigation had become dangerous,"† in consequence of the advanced

---

desheliger ook een der recht bewesten daer't saer goedte legghen is."—*Licht der Seevaert,* p. 217.

"Il y a, droit à l'est de Cabra, une belle baie, où il y a une fort bonne rade, comme aussi encore une autre droit a l'ouest de la, où il fait aussi bon d'ancrer."—*Miroir de la Mer,* p. 80.

* "We have now examined the journeys and voyages of St. Paul and his companions ; and of the numerous places named therein, we find but seven which are omitted by Strabo, the chief of the ancient geographers that are come down to us. The rest are described by him in exact agreement with the history of the Acts. Of the seven omitted by him, five are fully and clearly spoken of by other ancient authors. There remain only two, therefore, of which a doubt can be admitted," Biscoe, p. 383. He adds in a note, "The two are *The Fair Havens* and *Lasea,* of which the former is probably the Καλη Ακτη of *Stephanus,* the latter the *Lasos* of *Pliny.*" The position of *Lasea* agrees with the Lisia of the Peutingerian tables, *i. e.* about the centre of the south coast of Crete. See note, p. 80.

† V. 9. επισφαλους του πλοος, the appropriate nautical term, πλους ασφαλης, Jul. Pollux, i. 105.

state of the season. The fast, supposed of the expiation, which took place about the period of the autumnal equinox, was now past. It would appear that by this time all hope of completing the voyage during the present season * was abandoned; and it became a question whether they should winter at Fair Havens, or move the ship to Port Phenice, a harbour on the same side of Crete, about forty miles farther to the westward.

St. Paul assisted at the consultation, and strongly urged them to remain, addressing them in the following terms:—

"Sirs, I perceive that this voyage will be with hurt and much damage, not only of the lading and ship, but also of our lives."

---

9 Ἰκανου δε χρονου διαγενομενου, και οντος ηδη επισφαλους του πλοος, δια το και την νηστειαν ηδη παρεληλυθεναι, παρῃνει ὁ Παυλος,

10 Λεγων αυτοις· Ανδρες, θεωρω ὁτι μετα ὑβρεως και πολλης ζημιας ου μονον του φορτιου και του πλοιου, αλλα και των ψυχων ἡμων, μελλειν εσεσθαι τον πλουν.

11 Ὁ δε ἑκατονταρχης τῳ κυβερνητῃ και τῳ ναυκληρῳ επειθετο

9 Now when much time was spent, and when sailing was now dangerous, because the fast was now already past, Paul admonished *them*,

10 And said unto them, Sirs, I perceive that this voyage will be with hurt and much damage, not only of the lading and ship, but also of our lives.

11 Nevertheless the centurion believed the master and the owner of the ship, more than those

---

* According to Vegetius, the sailing season did not close so early; he states that "ex die igitur tertio iduum Novembris, usque in diem sextum iduum Martiarum, maria clauduntur. Nam lux minima noxque prolixa, nubium densitas, aeris obscuritas, ventorum, imbrium, vel nivium geminata sævitia." These dates correspond better with their stay in the island of Melita: Chap. xxviii. v. 11. Μετα δε τρεις μηνας ανηχθημεν, &c.

The officers of the ship were, however, of a different opinion, and the centurion naturally deferred to it. The event justified St. Paul's advice. At the same time it may be observed, that a bay, open to nearly one half of the compass, could not have been a good winter harbour.*

It was determined at this consultation to attempt to reach Phenice, a harbour of Crete, which looked, according to St. Luke, κατα Λιβα και κατα Χωρον, which is rendered in our version, " lieth toward the south west and north west." The intermediate point between these two winds is west; and it is generally understood that the

μαλλον η τοις υπο του Παυλου λεγομενοις.	things which were spoken by Paul.
12 Ανευθετου δε του λιμενος υπαρχοντος προς παραχειμασιαν οί πλειους εθεντο βουλην αναχθηναι κἀκειθεν, ει πως δυναιντο καταντησαντες εις Φοινικα παραχειμασαι, λιμενα της Κρητης βλεποντα κατα Λιβα και κατα Χωρον.	12 And because the haven was not commodious to winter in, the more part advised to depart thence also, if by any means they might attain to Phenice, *and there* to winter; *which is* an haven of Crete, and lieth toward the south west and north west.

* I have allowed this passage to remain as it stood in the first edition; for it is interesting to observe how each addition to our knowledge of the scene of the narrative confirms its authenticity and accuracy. It now appears from Mr. Brown's observations and survey, that Fair Havens is so well protected by islands and reefs, that though not equal to Lutro, it must be a very fair winter harbour; and that considering the suddenness, the frequency, and the violence with which gales of northerly wind spring up, and the certainty that, if such a gale sprung up in the passage from Fair Havens to Lutro, the ship must be driven off to sea, the prudence of the advice given by the master and owner was extremely questionable, and that the advice given by St. Paul may probably be supported even on nautical grounds.

harbour looked to, or was open to, the west. Father Giorgi, aware that if it could be proved Phenice was on the south side of Crete, a ship could not be driven off the island towards the Adriatic Gulf, infers from this that it was at the west end of the island *, and that the situation of Clauda is uncertain. Dr. Falconer, a man of undoubted learning, admits that it is not easy to determine the exact import of this passage; but supposes it to be "open to both quarters of the heavens from whence these winds proceed, and of course unsheltered from these winds:" he then observes that " this would, according to Vitruvius, leave 105° open to the west.† Such a harbour would certainly not be 'commodious to winter in,' and would not have warranted the attempt which was made to move to it."

Although they never reached this harbour, it becomes of importance to ascertain its position; because, unless we do so, we can draw no safe inferences respecting the ship's place when she encountered the gale, a point which it is of importance to determine. Phenice no longer retains its name ‡; there is, indeed, a place named Phœnikias in Pashley's map, not far from the position assigned to it by Strabo and Ptolemy; but this cannot be the port of Phenice, for it is not on the coast; although it may possibly be the

---

* "Quo modo Phenice Australis si ad eam ex Bonis Portibus Paulus secundo Austro tendebat . . . . . incertus est Claudæ situs."—P. 195.

† Grotius takes the same view of the meaning of this passage; he remarks, "Βλεποντα κατα Λιβα, respicientem *ad* Africum . . . . και κατα Χωρον, et *ad* Caurum."

‡ So in the first edition. But this is a mistake, Lutro is still known by the name of Phenice: see Mr. Brown's letter, App. 3.

city of that name, for Ptolemy mentions both a city and port of Phenice, or rather Phœnix.

Lutro, Sphakia, and Franco Castello, places on the south coast of Crete, have each been supposed to be Port Phenice. For our present purpose of ascertaining the ship's course it is not very material which of them is meant: I am, however, satisfied that it is the harbour of Lutro.

This harbour, however, looks to the east. I have already shown that the words of St. Luke in the original are generally supposed to indicate a harbour open in the opposite direction; unless, therefore, we get over this difficulty, we must give up the idea that Lutro is meant. The question as to the import of the passage must depend on the meaning we affix to the preposition "κατα," in connection with the winds. I apprehend it means "*in the same direction as*" (in Latin, secundum); if I am right, βλεποντα κατα λιβα does not mean, as is generally supposed, that it is open to the point *from* which that wind (Libs) blows, but to the point *towards* which it blows — that is, it is not open to the south-west but to the north-east.

Herodotus speaks of a ship being driven κατα κυμα και ανεμον *; now it is quite clear that, in this sense, a ship driven κατα Λιβα must be driven to the north-east. There is a passage in Arrian still more opposite to this point. In his Periplus of the Euxine he tells us, that when navigating the south coast of that sea, towards the east, he observed during a calm a cloud suddenly arise, " driven before the east wind " † — εξερραγη κατ' ευρον.

---

* Lib. iv. c. 110.; in the Latin translation, "secundum fluctus et ventum."

† αφνω νεφελη επαναστασα εξερραγη κατ' ευρον.—Periplus Euxini, p. 3.

Here there can be no mistake; the cloud must have been driven to the west. When St. Luke, therefore, describes the harbour of Phenice as looking κατα Λιβα και κατα Χωρον, I understand that it looks *to* the north-east, which is the point towards which Libs blows; and to the south-east, that *to* which Caurus blows.* Now this is exactly the

* Professor Hacket, in his commentary on the Acts, p. 358., contests the above view of the meaning attached to κατα in the following note : —" This mode of explaining κατα Λιβα involves, I think, two incongruities: first, it assigns opposite senses to the same term, viz. *south-west* as the name of a wind, and north-east as a quarter of the heavens ; and, secondly, it destroys the force of βλεποντα, which implies certainly that the wind and the harbour confronted each other, and not that they were turned from each other. Mr. Smith adduces κατα κυμα και κατα ανεμον, from Herod. 4. 110. ; but the expression is not parallel as regards either the preposition or the noun : κατα there denotes conformity of motion, and not of situation, where the objects are at rest; and ανεμος does not belong to the class of proper names like Libs and Corus, which the Greeks employed in such geographical designations." Professor Hacket then quotes the passage in which I refer to Arrian, and observes that, " to quote the passage in that manner assumes the point in dispute," and adduces the authority of Professor Felton of Cambridge, U. S., in support of the view he takes respecting the meaning of the passage in Arrian. To these remarks I would reply, that ευρος means either a point of the compass, or the wind which blows from that point. If Arrian meant the bearing of the phenomenon which he has recorded, then no doubt the meaning attached to the passage by Professors Hacket and Felton is the correct one; but it was of no consequence in what quarter of the heavens it was observed, and a seaman who draws his inference from the observed effects of the action of the winds upon clouds, would be more apt to notice the direction in which the clouds were flying, than the direction in which he first observed them.

Professor Lushington of the University of Glasgow, also a high authority in such questions, observes to a friend who applied to him on the subject, " I think the κατα question is very fairly dealt with by Mr. Smith; to pronounce positively, one should have hunted the maritime usages of wind language, of which blasts probably constitute a great portion with all nations. The phrase κατ' ευρον is favourable, and also a passage in description of Lutro, which looks or is open to the east; but, having an island in front which shelters it, it has two entrances, one looking to the north-east, which is κατα Λιβα, and the other to the south-east, κατα Χωρον. The island is not laid down in Pashley's map; I find it, however, in Lapie's map, and in the French admiralty chart of 1738. There is an anchor laid down inside, showing 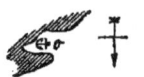 that it is a harbour. I cannot discover in sailing directions, ancient or modern, any hydrographical description of it.* I have found it to be the general impression amongst naval officers, acquainted with the navigation of these seas, that there are no ship harbours on the south side of Candia; but this is one of those harbours which, from the configu-

---

Thucyd. vi. 104., where a wind from the north is called κατα βορεαν ἑστηκως."

Mr. Howson, in his "Life of St. Paul," considers "my criticism quite tenable though unnecessary," and cites a passage from Josephus, who, in speaking of the places between Joppa and Dora, says they were all δυσορμα δια τας κατα λιβα προσβολας. Mr. Howson's explanation is, that "sailors speak of everything from their own point of view, and that such a harbour does 'look,' *from the water towards the land which encloses it*,—in the direction of south-west and north-west."—Vol. ii. p. 333.

The fact that the harbour is open to the east, admits now of no doubt; and as κατα is admitted to employ "conformity of motion," I am still of opinion that, looking in conformity with the motion of the winds mentioned is what is meant. The island shelters the harbour, but it does not lie exactly in front of it, and the water between it and the land is too shallow to have formed an entrance. Mr. Brown observes, "that there is only from three to six feet between it and the land." See Appendix No. 3. It may indeed have been used as an entrance by small craft; and as Luke did not visit it, it might have been so described by native coasting seamen, from whom we must suppose St. Luke derived his information.

* See chart of south coast of Crete.

ration of the land, must inevitably fill up in time. A mountain stream flows into it; and it is only necessary to look at the view given in Pashley's Travels* to see, in the ravine which, in the course of ages, it has hollowed out for itself, a proof that if the harbour could shelter the smallest craft in 1738, it must have been capable of sheltering the largest ships seventeen centuries before.†

---

* Frontispiece to vol. ii.

† When the above was written, the harbour may be said to have been unknown except to the native navigators. Upon reading the passage, Mr. Urquhart, M. P., well known for his writings on the East, kindly wrote to me that he had, when cruising with Lord Cochrane, now Lord Dundonald, during the Greek war, visited it, and thus expresses himself: "Loutro is an excellent harbour. It opens like a box: unexpectedly the rocks stand apart, and the town opens within * * * Excepting Loutro, all the roadsteads looking to the southward are perfectly exposed to the south or east." See Appendix No. 1. Captain Spratt, R.N., also writes me, that "Having in 1853 examined generally the south coast of Crete, I was fully convinced that Lutro was the Phenice of St. Paul, for it is the only bay to the westward of Fair Havens in which a vessel of any size could find any shelter during the winter months. * * * By hauling inside of the island (see chart of the south of Crete), and securing to the south shore of the bay, a vessel is nearly land-locked. South-east and east only could endanger her; but with the former, where the fetch is greatest, the wind would not blow home against such a mountain as the White Mountains, so immediately over the bay, and rising to an elevation of 9000 feet." See Appendix No. 2. It will be seen from Mr. Brown's letter (Appendix No. 3.) how completely Captain Spratt's conclusions respecting the goodness of this harbour are verified by the information he received upon the spot. The health officer informed him "that though the harbour is open to the east, yet the easterly gales never blow home, being *lifted* by the high land behind, and that even in storms the sea rolls in gently (piano, piano); he says *it is the only secure harbour in all winds on the south coast of Crete.*" When we add to all this evidence that the name of Phenice is still preserved by the natives, the evidence confirmatory of the conclusions respecting this locality is complete.

The next question is, does Lutro agree with the notices of Phenice, which we find in the narrative of the voyage, and in ancient writers? In order to agree with the narrative, the south wind must be a fair wind for a ship going from Fair Havens towards it. The first part of the course must lead a ship ασσον την Κρητην, "close past the land of Crete;" and the last part must be at a certain distance from the land, for the expression in the fourteenth verse, ου πολυ, "not long," shows that they had passed the point where they were close to the land. On consulting the chart of the south coast of Crete, it will be seen that the position of Lutro agrees perfectly with every one of these notices.

Phenice, or rather Phœnix, is mentioned by Strabo, Ptolemy, Stephanus Byzantinus *, and in the Synecdemus of Hierocles. The last two authors merely mention it as a city of Crete. Hierocles, however, mentions it along with the island of Clauda †; now, that island is exactly opposite to Lutro. According to Strabo, Phœnix is situated on the south side of the narrow part of Crete, which he calls an isthmus, on the north side of which is Amphimalla ‡, which also agrees with the situation of Lutro.

---

* Φοινικους πολις Κρητης.—Steph. Byz.

† Φοινικη ητοι Αραδενα, νησος Κλαυδος.—Hierocles.

‡ το δε ενθεν ισθμος εστιν ὡς ἑκατον σταδιων, εχων κατοικιαν προς μεν τῃ βορειῳ θαλαττῃ Αμφιμαλλον, προς δε τῃ νοτιῳ Φοινικην των Λαμπιων.—Lib. x. c. 4.

"From thence is an isthmus of about a hundred stadia, having Amphimallus on the North Sea, and Phœnix of the Lampeans on the south." The isthmus is, as nearly as possible, ten geographical miles, or one hundred stadia across.

Ptolemy mentions both a city and port of Phenice. His longitudes, although they cannot be depended upon for the absolute position of places on the surface of the earth, are extremely useful in giving the relative positions of places with respect to places situated to the east or west. Now the difference of longitude between the eastern and western extremities of Crete, Κριου μετωπον ακρον (Cape St. John), and Σαμμωνιον ακρον (Cape Salmone), is, according to him, 3° 5′: the actual distance is about 140 geographical miles. Hence the mean length of a degree of longitude in Crete is, according to Ptolemy, 45½ miles. Port Phenice is placed by him three-quarters of a degree to the east of Κριου μετωπον, which is equal to thirty-four geographical miles; the actual distance of Lutro from the same point is thirty-two. He places it 2° 20′ to the west of Salmone, which is equal to 106 miles; the actual distance on the French chart is 108 miles.*

The only traveller who has collected evidence upon the spot, bearing upon this point, is Mr. Pashley. It is not so complete as could have been wished, because that part of his work has been left unfinished; he has, however, stated enough to confirm the foregoing evidence. He found, a short distance above Lutro, two villages, bearing the names of Anopolis and Aradhena, and observes that,—

"The mention of an ancient city called Aradena, along with Anopolis and Port Phœnix in the Synecdemus of Hierocles, seems to point plainly to Lutro as the site of the last named city."—Vol. ii. p. 257.

* Ptol. lib. iii. c. 17.

Mr. Pashley subsequently visited Lutro, and has marked on his map ruins near it, to which he gives the name of Port Phœnix.

If we compare his map with the notices in Hierocles and Stephanus, it will be found that they throw light on each other. According to Hierocles, Phenice was also named Aradena.* According to Stephanus,

"Aradena, a city of Crete, also called Anopolis, or Upper Town, because it is upper." †

Now, upon the map these three places are little more than a mile from each other, and Anopolis is *above* Lutro. I think that we may conclude, therefore, with certainty, that the port of Phenice is the present port of Lutro.

With regard to the position of the island of Clauda there is no difficulty; it is unquestionably the same as the Claudos of Ptolemy, which he places to the south-west of Crete, and the Gozzo of the modern charts. Ptolemy, it is true, places it a degree too far to the west, which is, perhaps, a clerical error; but there is no island nearer his position, or for which it can be mistaken. The mention of it in the Synecdemus of Hierocles along with Port Phenice points very clearly to its true position. In many manuscripts it is spelt Cauda, which agrees with the spelling of Pliny and Suidas. Pomponius Mela spells it Gaudos, which is its present Greek name, Gaudonesi, or Island of Gaudos, which has been Italianised

---

* Hierocles merely says, Φοινικη ητοι Αραδενα, which implies that Phenice was also called Aradena.

† Αραδην πολις Κρητης ἡ δε Ανωπολις λεγεται, δια το ειναι ανω.

into Gozzo.* We have, therefore, the relative positions of the three places mentioned in the proceedings of the day on which the Apostle and his companions left Crete, the events of which I shall now take into consideration.

* Mr. Brown was informed upon the spot that the island still retained its ancient name Chlauda or Chlauda nesi, Χλαυδα or Κλαυδα Νησος. See Appendix No. 3.

CHAP. III.

CRETE TO MELITA.—THE GALE.

(Acts, xxvii. 13.)

THE ship, as we have seen, remained wind-bound at Fair Havens till the advanced state of the season rendered navigation dangerous. They had, however, resolved, at the consultation mentioned in the 10th and 11th verses, to move to Port Phenice, as a more secure winter harbour; and a moderate breeze from the south having sprung up, it was considered favourable for their purpose. They accordingly weighed anchor.* After clearing the harbour, their course, till they had passed Cape Matala,

---

13 Ὑποπνευσαντος δε Νοτου, δοξαντες της προθεσεως κεκρατηκεναι, αραντες ασσον παρελεγοντο την Κρητην.	13 And when the south wind blew softly, supposing that they had obtained *their* purpose, loosing *thence* they sailed close by Crete.

---

* αραντες may be translated either "weighed" or "set sail;" for ancient authors sometimes supply τας αγκυρας, "anchors," and sometimes τα ιστια, "sails." See note on v. 4., and by Dindorf on Xenophon, Hellen. vi. 2. Julius Pollux, however, like St. Luke, supplies neither, which is certainly the most nautical way of expressing it; he says, αιροντες απο της γης.—Lib. i. 103. In the Romaic (modern Greek version) it is rendered καμνοντες αρμενα, "set sail."

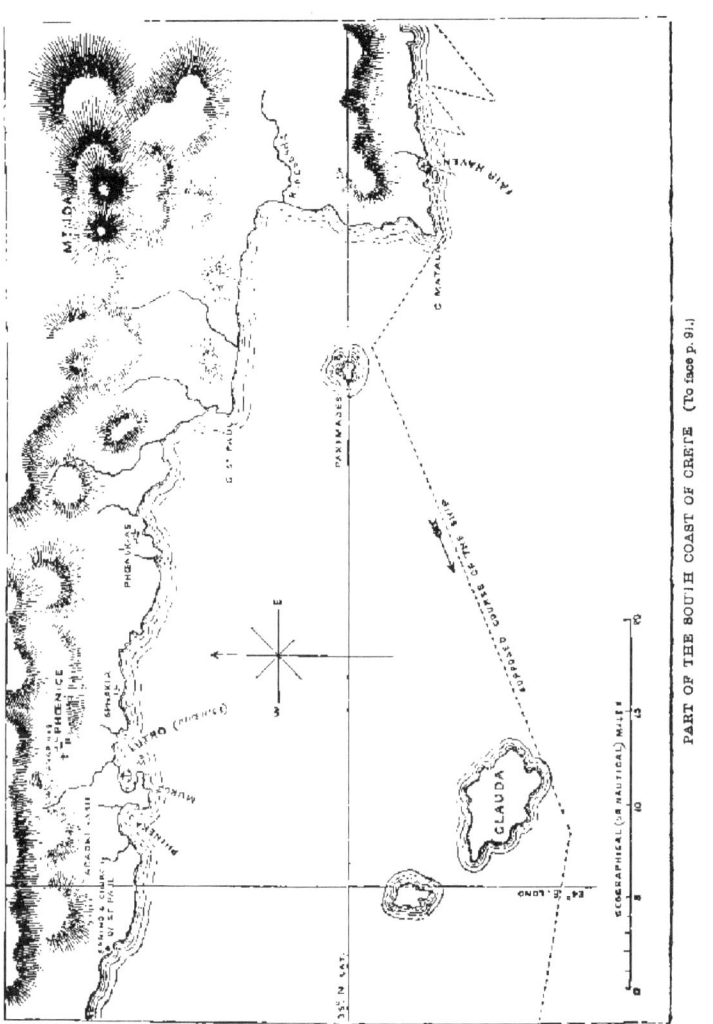

PART OF THE SOUTH COAST OF CRETE (To face p. 91.)

CRETE TO MELITA. 95

was close to the land. A ship which could not lie nearer to the wind than seven points would just weather that point which bears W. by S. from the entrance of Fair Havens. We see, therefore, the force and propriety of the expression, "they sailed *close* by Crete" ("ασσον* παρελεγοντο την Κρητην"), which the author uses to describe the first part of their passage. From the anchorage at Fair Havens to Cape Matala the distance is four or five miles, and from thence to Port Phenice the distance is thirty-four miles; and, as the bearing of the course is W. N. W., the south wind was as favourable as could be desired, being two points abaft the beam. They had every prospect, therefore, of reaching their destination in a few hours. Their course lay across the great southern bight to the west of Cape Matala. They had not proceeded far (ου πολυ), however, when a sudden change in the weather took place.

> "The flattering wind that late with promis'd aid
> From Candia's bay th' unwilling ship betray'd,
> No longer fawns beneath the fair disguise,
> But like a ruffian on his quarry flies."
>
> FALCONER's *Shipwreck*, canto ii.

The ship was "caught" (συναρπασθεντος) in a typhoon (ανεμος τυφωνικος), which blew with such violence that they could not face it†, but were forced, in the first in-

---

* Ασσον, πλησιον, εγγυς· ασσον ιτε, εγγυς ερχεσθαι.—Hesych.

† αντοφθαλμειν, "to face it;" literally, "to look at it." The meaning of the expression is sufficiently obvious; the origin of it is probably drawn from the practice of the ancients of painting an eye on each side of the bow of their ships, a practice which still prevails in the coasting craft in the Mediterranean.

stance, to scud before it*, for such is the evident meaning of the expression—επιδοντες εφερομεθα—"yielding to it we were borne along by it." It follows from this that it must have blown off the land, for had it not they must have been stranded upon the Cretan coast, if they had been unable to gain their harbour. The expression therefore, εβαλε κατ' αυτης, "there arose against it," cannot mean that it "arose against Crete," as some writers contend. The most obvious meaning is, that the typhoon struck the ship. It is quite true that, according to strict grammatical rule, the pronoun should stand for the last-mentioned noun; yet in practice it frequently refers to what is uppermost in the mind of the person who uses it at the time. St. Luke, who was in the ship, could not avoid thinking of its effects on the ship, but would certainly never dream of its effects upon an island.† We

---

14 Μετ' ου πολυ δε εβαλε κατ' αυτης ανεμος τυφωνικος ὁ καλουμενος Ευρακυλων.

15 Συναρπασθεντος δε του πλοιου, και μη δυναμενου αντοφθαλμειν τῳ ανεμῳ, επιδοντες εφερομεθα.

14 But not long after there arose against it a tempestuous wind called Euro-aquilo.

15 And when the ship was caught, and could not bear up unto the wind, we let her drive.

---

* The appropriate nautical term, equivalent to the English one, to scud, is, ανακωχευειν, "dicitur cum exorta tempestate in mari demptis velis navigium ventis sine repugnatione permittitur."—*Suidas*. The translation of Giorgi expresses the same meaning, "non potente aspicere contra ventum, concedentes ferebamur."

† It is objected to this interpretation of κατ' αυτης that πλοιον, a neuter noun, has hitherto been used to designate the ship, and therefore, had the ship been in the mind of the writer, it would have been κατ' αυτου. Now, without pretending to know the reason, I think it not improbable that there

know that it blew them out of their course towards the island of Clauda; if, therefore, we know whereabouts the ship was when the gale overtook her, we can form a tolerable estimate of the direction of the wind which drove

may be occasions in which ναυς would be a more appropriate term than πλοιον, and that this may be one of them, just as in modern language there are cases in which the less general term "ship" would be used in preference to the more general one "vessel." In verse 41., St. Luke says "they ran the ship ashore," επωκειλαν την ναυν, although in verse 39., where this measure was only contemplated, he speaks of "thrusting the vessel, το πλοιον, into a creek." Assuming this to be the case, I do not consider that we must of necessity refer the pronoun to the last preceding noun.

Dr. Johnson remarks on the omission of the nominative " *My father*," at the commencement of *As you Like it* :—" What is there in this difficult or obscure? The nominative, ' *My father*,' is certainly left out; but so left out that the auditor inserts it in spite of himself."— *Note on passage*.

I, however, defer to the opinion of better scholars than myself, and admit the interpretation of Mr. Alford, Mr. Howson, and I may add the Rev. Mr. Drake of Coventry, and the Rev. Dr. Miller of Glasgow, who did me the honour to write to me on the subject; the former of whom, alluding to my explanation of κατα λιβα, &c., observes, " exactly according with your views, κατ' αυτης means *down from it*, down from the mountain gorges of the island." So also Mr. Alford understands it as " *down the high lands forming the coast.*" Mr. Alford supposes that when they had doubled, or were perhaps now doubling Cape Matala, the wind suddenly changed, and the typhoon " *came down upon them from the high lands.*"

When I compare what Mr. Alford supposes must have happened to St. Paul and his companions, with what did happen to my friend Captain Spratt, R.N., and in the same circumstances, I am more persuaded that his view of the passages is the right one. Captain Spratt thus writes me: " In respect to the gale of wind I met with after starting from Fair Havens for Messara Bay, we left *with a light southerly wind* and clear sky — every indication of a fine day, until we rounded the cape (Matala), to haul up for the head of the bay. Then we saw Mount Ida covered in a dense cloud, and met a strong northerly breeze— one of the summer gales so frequent in the Levant, but which in general are accompanied by terrific gusts from those high mountains, the wind blowing direct from Mount Ida."

H

them thither. According to the narrative, it was not long "ου πολυ," after the ship was close to Crete, which can only mean that she had not passed over much of the space interposed between that point and the intended termination of her voyage, Port Phenice. The term employed by the evangelist is a relative one, and must mean less than the half. Hence the ship must have been somewhere between Cape Matala, and a point bearing W. N. W., distant seventeen miles. But the former point bears E. 7° N. from Clauda, to which they were driven, and the latter E. 43° N. The wind, therefore, which drove them thither, must have been to the north of E. 7° N., but to the east of E. 43° N. The intermediate point, which cannot be so much as a point and a half from the true direction, is E. 25° N., or E. N. E.$\frac{1}{4}$° N. Another circumstance mentioned in the narrative indicates the direction of the wind within still narrower limits. When under Clauda they were apprehensive of being driven towards the Syrtis (v. 17.); but the winds, which blow from Clauda towards the Syrtis, range between E. 18° N. and E. 37° N., the mean of which is E. 27° 30′ N., and the mean of both deductions is E. 26° 15′ N., or about E. N. E.$\frac{1}{2}$° N., which cannot deviate so much as one point from the true direction of the wind, and does not differ a quarter of a point from the former determination.

Writers, such as Bentley and Penn[*], who have drawn their conclusions from etymological reasons, infer that the wind was from the point between Eurus and Aquilo,

---

[*] See Appendix for the remarks of these writers.

or E. N. E. We have, therefore, three separate modes of estimating the direction of the gale perfectly independent of each other, and none of them differing from the other so much as half a point. Now there is not one circumstance mentioned in the subsequent part of the narrative which is not perfectly accounted for upon the supposition that this was the true direction of the wind; I differ, therefore, from the commentators who think that it was not a " point wind," that is, a wind blowing steadily from one point, for I consider that no change took place in its direction during the remainder of the voyage.

The sudden change from a south wind to a violent northerly wind is a common occurrence in these seas.* The term "*typhonic*," by which it is described, indicates that it was accompanied by some of the phenomena which might be expected in such a case, namely, the agitation and whirling motion of the clouds caused by the meeting of the opposite currents of air when the change took place, and probably also of the sea, raising it in columns of spray. Pliny, in describing the effects of sudden blasts, says that they cause a vortex, which is called "ty-

---

* Capt. J. Stewart, R.N., in his remarks on the Archipelago, observes, " It is always safe to anchor under the lee of an island with a northerly wind, as it dies away gradually; but it would be extremely dangerous *with southerly winds, as they almost invariably shift to a violent northerly wind.*"

See also the note at p. 97. So also Messrs. Tennent and Brown, when they landed to examine Port Phenice, their vessel being becalmed with light airs from the south and south-east, before they could reach the bay, saw a heavy squall from the north blowing out of it; this blew the yacht, a large powerful vessel of about 200 tons, out to sea, and left the visitors on shore for the night. See Appendix No. 3.

phoon;"* and Gellius, in his account of a storm at sea, notices "frequent whirlwinds," " . . . . and the dreadful appearances in the clouds which they call typhoons."†

St. Luke, therefore, by the single word "typhonic," expresses the nature and violence of the gale, and, by another, its direction. In the dissertation on the wind Euroclydon I have stated my reasons for preferring the reading of the most ancient manuscripts and versions, Euro-aquilo, which must be between Eurus and Aquilo, or E. N. E.

I now proceed to inquire into the effects it produced upon the ship. Nothing more is said in the narrative than that it defeated their object of reaching Port Phenice, and forced them to run under the lee (ὑποδραμοντες ‡) of Clauda. It will, however, be found that the ship must have strained and suffered severely in her hull,

---

16 Νησιον δε τι ὑποδραμοντες, καλουμενον Κλαυδην, μολις ισχυσαμεν περικρατεις γενεσθαι της σκαφης.

16 And running under a certain island, which is called Clauda, we had much work to come by the boat.

---

* Lib. ii. c. 48. De repentinis Flatibus: "Vorticem faciunt qui Typhon vocatur."

† Lib. xix. c. i.: "Turbines etiam crebriores . . . et figuræ quædam nubium metuendæ quas τυφωνας vocabant." Hesychius merely calls it the "great wind," τυφων ὁ μέγας ανεμος.

‡ ὑποδραμοντες, "*running* under the lee of." St. Luke exhibits here, as on every other occasion, the most perfect command of nautical terms, and gives the utmost precision to his language by selecting the most appropriate; they ran before the wind to leeward of Clauda, hence it is ὑποδραμοντες: they sailed with a side wind to leeward of Cyprus and Crete; hence it is ὑπεπλευσαμεν.

and that the leaks she then sprang were gradually gaining upon the crew, and that if they had not providentially made the land, and been thereby enabled to save their lives by running the ship on shore, she must have foundered at sea, and all on board perished.

As the knowledge of this fact can only be gained by circumstantial evidence, and as it throws a clear light upon the subsequent proceedings, it is necessary to state the proofs at some length; but before I do so, I would observe that such a result of a typhoon, not unfrequent in modern times, seems to have been almost inevitable in ancient times. Pliny calls the typhoon —

"The chief pest of seamen, destructive not only to the spars but to the hull itself."*

In the accounts of shipwrecks which have come down to us from ancient times, the loss of the ship must, in a great number of instances, be ascribed to this cause. Josephus tells us that on his voyage to Italy the ship sank in the midst of the Adriatic Sea.† He and some of his companions saved themselves by swimming; the ship therefore, did not go down during the gale, but in consequence of the damage she sustained during its continuance. One of St. Paul's shipwrecks must have taken place under the same circumstances; for he tells us, " a day and a night I have been in the deep," supported no doubt on spars or fragments of the wreck. In Virgil's

* "Præcipua navigantium pestis non antennas modo verum ipsa navigia contorta frangens."—Lib. ii. cap. 48.
† βαπτισθεντος γαρ ἡμων του πλοιου κατα μεσον την Αδριαν.—Vita, c. iii.

description of the casualties of the ships of Æneas, some are driven on rocks, others on quicksands; but,

> "Laxis laterum compagibus *omnes*
> Accipiunt inimicum imbrem, rimisque fatiscunt."

The fact, that the ships of the ancients were provided with hypozomata, or cables ready fitted for undergirding, as a necessary part of their stores, proves how liable they were to such casualties, and I may add, as another proof, the frequent notice of lightening ships we meet with in ancient authors. In the present narrative they occur not less than three times. In the ship of Jonah it is stated that "they cast forth the wares that were in the ship into the sea to lighten it" (c. i. v. 5.); and Juvenal, in describing the dangers encountered by Catullus, not only uses similar language, but assigns the reason —

> "Cum plenus fluctu medius foret alveus, . .
> . . . . . .
> . . . decidere jactu." *Sat.* xii. v. 30.

It is easy to account for the comparative immunity of modern ships from such casualties. The most obvious cause is the improvement in naval architecture; but another, and, I suspect, more efficient one, is the manner in which they were rigged. In modern times the strain is spread over three masts, with small sails, which can be quickly taken in; but the ancient ships had to sustain the leverage of a single mast, with a ponderous yard at the upper end. We can scarcely suppose that St. Paul's ship escaped uninjured. The circumstances mentioned, of her being undergirded, lightened, and finally run ashore, afford conclusive evidence that she did not.

Keeping this in view, we may form some idea of the hardships the ship's company endured. St. Luke shared them all; but he never mentions them, except on one occasion, and that was to illustrate a passage in the life of St. Paul.

At the time the ship was caught in the gale, she must have been near a small group of islands, called the Paximades, in the Gulf of Messara. The island of Clauda lay about twenty-three miles to leeward, and thither they were driven, as the expression επιδοντες εφερομεθα (v. 15.) implies, before the gale. Upon reaching it they availed themselves of the smooth water under its lee, to prepare the ship to resist the fury of the storm. Their first care was to secure the boat, by hoisting it on board. This had not been done at first, because the weather was moderate, and the distance they had to go short. Under such circumstances, it is not usual to hoist the boats on board, but it had now become necessary. In running down upon Clauda it could not be done, on account of the ship's way through the water. To enable them to do it, the ship must have been rounded to, with her head to the wind, and her sails, if she had any set at the time, trimmed, so that she had no head way, or progressive movement.

> "The boats then hoisted in are fix'd on board
> And on the deck with fastening gripes secured."
>
> *Shipwreck*, canto ii.

In this position the ship would drift, broadside to leeward. I conclude that they passed round the east end of the island; not only because it was nearest, but because there are dangers at the opposite end.* In this case the ship would be brought to on the starboard tack,—that is, with the right side to windward.† This must be kept in mind, because it throws light upon a subsequent passage. St. Luke tells us that they had much difficulty in securing the boat (v. 16.). He does not say why; but independently of the gale which was raging at the time, the boat had been towed between twenty and thirty miles after the gale sprung up, and could scarcely fail to be filled with water. Having accomplished this necessary task, their next care was to undergird the ship, which the state in which she was had rendered imperative. This expedient is so rarely had recourse to in modern times, that I have only met with one naval officer who had seen it put in practice, although almost all of my nautical friends whom I have consulted, could furnish me with instances in

---

| 17 Ἡν αραντες, βοηθειαις εχρων- | 17 Which when they had taken |
| το, ὑποζωννυντες το πλοιον· | up, they used helps, undergirding the ship; |

---

* "An extensive reef, with numerous rocks, extends from Gozo to the N.W., which renders the passage between the two isles very dangerous." — *Sailing Direct.* p. 207. " On peut passer entre Gozo et Gozo Pulo; il faut de la pratique, et nous ne voyons pas la nécessité de s'engager dans un passage dangereux."—*Manuel de Pilotage,* p. 412.

† " I consider the ship to have drifted with her starboard side towards the wind, or on the starboard tack, as a sailor expresses it. When the south wind blew softly, the ship was slowly sailing along the coast of Crete with her starboard side towards the land, or towards the north. . . . The storm came on her starboard side, and in this manner she drifted." (Admiral Penrose's Observations). — *Conybeare and Howson,* vol. ii. p. 339.

which they had heard of its being done. The officer to whom I allude, Mr. Henry Smartley, who was master of the Royal Sovereign, was employed in 1815, to pilot the Russian fleet from England to the Baltic. One of the ships (the Jupiter) was frapped round the middle by three or four turns of a stream cable. Mr. Smartley is father to the talented marine painter, Mr. Smartley of Jersey; and it was under his direction that the undergirding is represented in the view which I have given of the ship anchored by the stern.

The mode in which ships are undergirded is thus described by Falconer, in his Marine Dictionary: —

"To frap a ship (*ceintrer un vaisseau*) is to pass four or five turns of a large cable-laid rope round the hull or frame of a ship, to support her in a great storm, or otherwise, when it is apprehended that she is not strong enough to resist the violent efforts of the sea; this expedient, however, is rarely put in practice."

It would not be difficult to multiply instances where this mode of strengthening ships has been put in practice in modern times*; I content myself with the latest I can find. Captain (now Sir George) Back, on his perilous return from his Arctic voyage, in 1837, was forced, in consequence of the shattered and leaky condition of his ship, to undergird her. It was thus done: —

---

* The Albion 74 encountered a hurricane on her voyage from India, and was under the necessity of frapping her hull together, in order to prevent her sinking. (*United Service Mag.*, May, 1846.) The Queen came home from Jamaica frapped or undergirded; and the Blenheim, in which Sir Thomas Troubridge was lost, left India frapped. See other instances in " Conybeare and Howson's Life of St. Paul," vol. ii. p. 337. note.

"A length of the stream chain-cable was passed under the bottom of the ship four feet before the mizen mast, hove tight by the capstan, and finally immovably fixed to six ring-bolts on the quarter-deck. The effect was at once manifested by a great diminution in the working of the parts already mentioned; and in a less agreeable way, by impeding her rate of sailing; a trifling consideration, however, when compared with the benefit received."*

We are told, that subsequent to this they met with a gale: —

"The water rushed in violently below, more especially about the sternpost and heel-hook, and oozing through different parts higher up, fell like a cascade into the bread-room and run .... while apprehensive that farther injury had been sustained about the keel, another length of chain was passed under the bottom and set well tight to a part of itself, across the after part of the quarter-deck."— p. 438.†

We are next told by St. Luke, that "being apprehensive of being driven towards the Syrtis, they lowered the gear." It is not easy to imagine a more erroneous translation than that of our authorised version: —

"Fearing lest they should fall into the quicksands, strake sail, and so were driven."—Verse 17.

It is, in fact, equivalent to saying that, fearing a certain danger, they deprived themselves of the only possible

---

| Φοβουμενοι τε μη εις την Συρτιν εκπεσωσι, χαλασαντες το σκευος, οὑτως εφεροντο. | And, fearing lest they should fall into the quicksands, strake sail, and so were driven. |

---

* Voyage, p. 433.
† See details of undergirding in dissertation on ancient ships.

means of avoiding it.* It is not by striking mast or sail that such dangers are to be avoided.

I have already shown that the same wind which drove them, " when yielding to it " (ἐπιδόντες), to Clauda, would, if they had continued to scud, have driven them directly towards the Syrtis. Under the circumstances in which they were now placed, they had but one course to pursue in order to avoid the apprehended danger, which was to turn the ship's head off shore, and to set such sail as the violence of the gale would permit them to carry. As they did avoid the danger, we may be certain, notwithstanding the silence of the historian, that this was the course which was adopted. I have already assigned my reasons for supposing that the ship must have been brought to on the starboard tack, under Clauda, for it was only on this tack that it was possible to avoid being driven on the African coast; when, therefore, they had taken every precaution against foundering which prudence and skilful seamanship could dictate, all that was required was to fill their storm sail, probably already set, and to stand on.

---

* Of course if any sail were set it could not be the mast which was lowered, as many commentators suppose; indeed it is not possible to suppose that the main-masts of large sailing ships were made to strike, like those of a Thames barge, although no doubt those of the row-galleys were:—

——Ἐν δὲ καὶ αὐτὸν
Ἱστὸν ἄφαρ χαλάσαντα.
APOLLONIUS RHODIUS, ii. 1267.

Juvenal tells us that the mast of the ship of Catullus was "cut away" (*Sat.* xii. 54.), and recommends his friends to provide themselves with hatchets before going to sea:

"Adspice sumendas in tempestate secures." *Sat.* xii, 61.

The question remains to be answered, What is the meaning of the expression "lowering the gear," "χαλασαντες το σκευος?" Σκευος, which I have translated "gear,"* when applied to a ship, means appurtenances of every kind, such as spars, sails, rigging, anchors, and cables, &c. Now, every ship situated as this one was, when preparing for a storm, sends down upon deck the "top hamper," or gear connected with the fair-weather sails, such as the *suppara*, or top-sails. A modern ship sends down top-gallant masts and yards†, a cutter strikes her topmast, when preparing for a gale. The author here, as elsewhere, states the fact, but gives no details; a seaman could scarcely have avoided doing so, if he had mentioned the circumstance at all. It is unnecessary to multiply instances which are so common as to occur in almost every account of a storm at sea; I content myself therefore, by giving a parallel case with the present, namely, that of one who was not a seaman, but was perfectly cognisant of nautical matters, Donald Campbell, of Barbreck.‡ On his passage from Goa to Madras he was shipwrecked on the coast of Malabar. Many of the events bear a striking resemblance to those recorded by St. Luke in his account.

---

* Rightly translated by Böckh "Geräthe;" Scotice, "Graith." "There I beheld a galeasse *gaily graithit for the weyr*, lyand fast at ane ankir."— *Complaynte of Scotland.* i. e. "Gallantly furnished for the war." M. Jal, whose courage as a translator is more conspicuous than his caution, amusingly renders it — "Qui virait gaiement sur l'ancre."

† Gower, in his Treatise on Seamanship, gives the following instructions for preparing for a gale: — "Let the top-gallant yards and masts, mizen-topsail yard, mizen yard, and cross-jack yard, be got down on deck, that the ship may be made as snug as possible."—P. 54.

‡ Journey to India, pt. iii. p. 16.

"Lowering the gear" is mentioned in the following terms: —

"Such exertions were made that, before morning, every stick that could possibly be struck was down upon the deck."

The only plausible conjecture I have met with respecting what was lowered, is that of Pricæus, who supposes it was "not the mast, but the yard with the sail attached to it."* This, indeed, is but a conjecture, but it is a probable one. We know from the representations on coins and marbles, that the ancients were in the habit of furling their sails aloft; and unless the main-yard was lowered when the ship was running before the wind, which we are not told was the case, it must have been done now. This, however, is but conjecture; and, in such an inquiry as the present, it is necessary to distinguish between conjecture and inference. We may conclude, with perfect certainty, that their object, in "lowering the gear," was to enable them to avoid the Syrtis; because we are, in effect, told that it was so, — "fearing lest they should be driven to the Syrtis, they lowered the gear." This alone, however, was not sufficient to have kept the ship off a lee shore. There were but two ways by which that could have been effected. She might have been anchored†, or her head might have been turned off shore and such sail set as the violence of the gale would permit her to carry. We know that the first of the alternatives was not adopted; we must,

---

* "Non malum, sed cum appenso velo antennam." — *Pricæus* in loc.

† There is an anchorage at Clauda; but it is open to the E. N. E., and therefore would have afforded no shelter in the present case.

therefore, conclude that the last was, for by no other way could she have avoided the apprehended danger.

A ship at sea, in a gale, must either scud or heave-to. In the present case, to have adopted the former alternative, would have been to have rushed on certain destruction. Falconer, in his notes on the shipwreck observes: —

> "The movement of scudding is never attempted in a contrary wind unless, as in the present instance, the condition of the ship rendered her incapable of any longer sustaining on her side the mutual effort of the wind and waves. The principal hazards incident to scudding are generally — a *pooping* sea; the difficulty of steering, which exposes the vessel perpetually to the risk of broaching-to; and the want of sufficient sea-room. A sea striking the ship violently on the stern may dash it inwards, by which she must inevitably founder; in broaching-to suddenly, she is threatened with being immediately overset; and for want of sea-room she is endangered with shipwreck on a lee shore, a circumstance too dreadful to require explanation."

This last must have been the inevitable consequence, had the ship been allowed to be driven at the mercy of the winds, as is generally supposed.

The only question which now remains to be answered is, Which tack was the ship hove-to upon? The answer is not difficult: if it had been on the port tack, that is, with her left side to the wind, she must have inevitably drifted upon the coast of Africa with the wind at E. N. E., as we have proved it to have been [*], and would, moreover, have been driven completely out of her course.

We are thus forced to the conclusion, when we are told that "they were thus borne along," οὕτως ἐφέροντο,

---

[*] See Dissertation on Euroclydon.

that it was not only with the ship undergirded and made snug, but that she had storm sails set*, and was on the starboard tack, which was the only course by which she could avoid falling into the Syrtis. With this notice concludes the first eventful day.

On the following day (τῇ ἑξῆς, ver. 18.), the gale continuing unabated, they lightened the ship.† Every step hitherto taken indicates skilful seamanship. In an old French work on maritime law‡ I find every one of these precautions pointed out as proper to be taken by able mariners under similar circumstances.

1st. With regard to undergirding, the author observes: —

"Il y a des mariniers habiles, lesquels prévoyantes les tourmentes, plongent en l'eau ceignent ou rident par bas tout le corps du navire avec des guerlins nommez en Levant *gomenes*, c'est à dire, grosses cordes, ce qui l'*assiste* et le rend plus puissant à résister aux secousses." — P. 528.

---

18 Σφοδρως δε χειμαζομενων ἡμων, τῃ ἑξης εκβολην εποιουντο.	18 And we being exceedingly tossed with a tempest, the next *day* they lightened the ship;

---

* "In a storm with a contrary wind or on a lee shore, a ship is obliged to lie-to under a very low sail; some sail is absolutely necessary to keep the ship steady, otherwise she would pitch about like a cork, and roll so deep as to strain and work herself to pieces."—*Encyc. Brit.*, Art. Seamanship.

† The technical terms for taking cargo out of a ship, given by Julius Pollux, are, εκθεσθαι, αποφορτισασθαι, κουφισαι την ναυν, επελαφρυναι, εκβολην ποιησασθαι των φορτιων. So that both here and afterwards in the 38th verse, when St. Luke says εκουφιζον το πλοιον, he uses appropriate technical phrases.

‡ Us et Coutumes de la Mer. Rouen, 1672.

2nd. " Lowering the gear :"—

"*Abaisser* les mats de hune ou *matereaux*.

3rd. " Heaving the ship to :"—

" Dans le péril convient caposer ou mettre le navire à la cape, c'est à dire, amarrer le gouvernail bien ferme et immobile pour suivre l'abandon du vent; trousser toutes les voiles sauf le pafi (mainsail, old French), qu'on laisse boursoufler, d'autant que le vent s'enfermant en iceluy pousse en haut le vaisseau le soulagent beaucoup au hurt et à la tombée."

4th. " Lightening the ship :"—

" Pour prévenir le malheur en ces occurrences et pour se conserver, le jet est nécessaire ' echason a la mar de lo qui viene en la nave para salvarla.' "

On the third day they threw overboard "the tackling of the ship" (ver. 19.). From the expression "with our own hands," αυτοχειρες, I suppose the mainyard is meant; an immense spar, probably as long as the ship, and which would require the united efforts of passengers and crew to launch overboard. The relief which a ship would experience by this, would be of the same kind as in a modern ship when the guns are thrown overboard.

A dreary interval of eleven days succeeds; the gale continues with unabated fury (σφοδρως δε χειμαζομενων); neither sun nor stars can be observed; and at length we

---

19 Και τη τριτη, αυτοχειρες την σκευην του πλοιου ερριψαμεν.

19 And the third *day* we cast out with our own hands the tackling of the ship.

20 Μητε δε ηλιου, μητε αστρων επιφαινοντων επι πλειονας ημερας,

20 And when neither sun nor stars in many days appeared,

are told that "all hope of being saved was taken away." But why was all hope taken away? An ancient ship, without a compass and without celestial observation, had no means of keeping a reckoning. This was, no doubt, a situation of danger, but not one of despair, for she might have been driven into safety. The true explanation I apprehend is this: their exertions to subdue the leak had been unavailing; they could not tell which way to make for the nearest land, in order to run their ship ashore, the only resource for a sinking ship; but unless they did make the land, they must founder at sea. Their apprehensions, therefore, were not so much caused by the fury of the tempest, as by the state of the ship.

We are now told that after much abstinence Paul addressed them; but before we hear his address the question occurs, what caused the abstinence? A ship with nearly three hundred people on board, on a voyage of some length, must have had more than a fortnight's provisions; in point of fact, the ship was loaded with wheat, as we learn afterwards; and it is not enough to say that, "worn out with their labours and fears, they did not think of eating."* Now, although the connection between heavy gales and

---

| χειμωνος τε ουκ ολιγου επικειμενου, λοιπον περιῃρειτο πασα ελπις του σωζεσθαι ἡμας. | and no small tempest lay on *us*, all hope that we should be saved was then taken away. |
| 21 Πολλης δε ασιτιας ὑπαρχουσης, τοτε σταθεις ὁ Παυλος εν μεσῳ αυτων, ειπεν· | 21 But after long abstinence Paul stood forth in the midst of them, and said, |

---

* "Continui labores et metus a periculis effecerant ut de cibo capiendo non cogitarent."—*Kuinoel.*

"much abstinence" is by no means obvious, yet we find it is one of their most frequent concomitants. The impossibility of cooking, or the destruction of provisions from leakage, are the principal causes which produce it. Breydenbach, the dean of Mentz, in his pilgrimage to the Holy Land, experienced two gales of wind [*], and very feelingly records the abstinence that ensued on each occasion. In one case a sea struck their vessel, and "destroyed their caboose or cooking-place, and broke every thing within it;"[†] in the other he tells us "there was no thought of eating or drinking, because the cooking-place was altogether under water." [‡]

John Newton, the celebrated vicar of Olney, in his interesting autobiography, relates a circumstance which occurred in his own experience of sea life; on a voyage from Cape Lopez a sea struck his ship, and strained her so much that she nearly foundered.

---

[*] Mentz, 1486. See account of this curious work in Dibdin's *Ædes Althorpianæ* and the *Journal of the Geographical Society*, vol. ix. p. 311.; as it is not paged, I count the leaves from the end.

[†] "Una vi ventorum acta ad latus nostræ galeæ grandi impetu impegit vehementer barcamque collateralem dirupit penitus, et destruxit nostram vero coquinam fregit earum et omnia quæ in ea erant."—19th leaf from the end. On the same leaf will be found the following invocation by the mariners to the Virgin, which I have not met with elsewhere:—

"Salve, Splendor Firmamenti!
Tu caliginosæ menti
Desuper irradia.
Placa mare, Maris Stella!
Ne involvat nos procella
Et tempestas obvia."

[‡] "Nec fuit memoria cibi aut potus hac tempestate, quia coquina erat in aquis tota."—*Ib.* 17th fol. from end.

"We found that the water having floated all our movables in the hold, all the casks of provisions had been beaten in pieces by the violent motion of the ship. On the other hand, our live stock, such as pigs, sheep, and poultry, had been washed overboard in the storm; in effect, all the provisions we saved . . . . . would have subsisted us but a week, at a scanty allowance." — *Omicron's Letters*, letter vii.

In the case of the Guipiscoa, the Spanish ship mentioned in Anson's Voyage, those who could work at the pumps were reduced to an ounce and a half of biscuit per diem; those who could not, were allowed an ounce of wheat. To some such cause the abstinence mentioned by St. Luke may, doubtless, be ascribed.

The hardships which the crew endured during a gale of such continuance, and their exhaustion from labour at the pumps and hunger, may be imagined, but are not described. Under these circumstances, St. Paul encourages them by the assurance that their lives would be spared. He thus addresses them: —

"Sirs, ye should have hearkened unto me, and not have loosed from Crete, and to have gained this harm and loss. And now I exhort you to be of good cheer; for there shall be no loss of *any man's* life among you, but of the ship. For there stood by me this night, the angel of God, whose I am, and whom I serve, saying, Fear not, Paul; thou must be brought before Cæsar: and, lo, God hath given thee all them that sail with thee. Wherefore, sirs, be of good cheer; for I believe God, that it shall be even as it was told me. Howbeit we must be cast upon a certain island."

Εδει μεν, ω ανδρες, πειθαρχησαντας μοι, μη αναγισθαι απο της Κρητης, κερδησαι τε την ύβριν ταυτην και την ζημιαν.	Sirs, ye should have hearkened unto me, and not have loosed from Crete, and to have gained this harm and loss.

At length, on the fourteenth night of their being " driven through " (διαφερομενων) the sea of Adria, towards midnight the seamen suspected (ὑπενοουν) that land was near (προσαγειν αυτοις, literally, was nearing them*). St. Luke does not tell us what the indications were; and the only

---

22 Και τανυν παραινω ὑμας ευθυμειν· αποβολη γαρ ψυχης ουδεμια εσται εξ ὑμων, πλην του πλοιου.

23 Παρεστη γαρ μοι τῃ νυκτι ταυτῃ αγγελος του Θεου, οὐ ειμι ᾧ και λατρευω·

24 Λεγων, Μη φοβου, Παυλε· Καισαρι σε δει παραστηναι· και ιδου κεχαρισται σοι ὁ Θεος, παντας τους πλεοντας μετα σου.

25 Διο ευθυμειτε, ανδρες· πιστευω γαρ τῳ Θεῳ ὁτι οὑτως εσται καθ' ὃν τροπον λελαληται μοι.

26 Εις νησον δε τινα δει ἡμας εκπεσειν.

27 Ὡς δε τεσσαρεσκαιδεκατη νυξ εγενετο, διαφερομενων ἡμων εν τῳ Αδριᾳ κατα μεσον της νυκτος ὑπενοουν οἱ ναυται προσαγειν τινα αὐτοις χωραν·

22 And now I exhort you to be of good cheer: for there shall be no loss of *any man's* life among you, but of the ship.

23 For there stood by me this night the angel of God, whose I am, and whom I serve,

24 Saying, Fear not, Paul; thou must be brought before Cæsar: and, lo, God hath given thee all them that sail with thee.

25 Wherefore, sirs, be of good cheer: for I believe God, that it shall be even as it was told me.

26 Howbeit we must be cast upon a certain island.

27 But when the fourteenth night was come, as we were driven up and down in Adria, about midnight the shipmen deemed that they drew near to some country;

---

* St. Luke here uses the graphic language of seamen to whom the ship is the principal object, whilst the land rises and sinks, nears, and recedes —

" Terræque urbesque recedunt."

The word χωραν evidently means the land as distinguished from the sea.

conjecture I have seen, is that of Calmet, that they became aware of it by the sense of smell. He says:—

"Ils soupçonnèrent l'approche de la terre, non par la vue, parceque c'était à minuit et qu'ils étaient dans des profondes ténèbres, mais apparemment par l'odeur de la terre, ou par la fraîcheur, ou par le vents."

But all these conjectures require off-shore winds. A storm on the face of a lee shore is not the time when —

> "Gentle gales,
> Fanning their odoriferous wings dispense
> Native perfumes, and whisper whence they stole
> Their balmy spoils."

The only other conjecture is, that they saw or heard the breakers on a rocky coast —

> "In dire amazement riveted they stand,
> And hear the breakers lash the rugged strand."
> FALCONER.

Such are the usual premonitory warnings to ships unexpectedly falling in with the land at night.

If we assume that St. Paul's Bay, in Malta, is the actual scene of the shipwreck, we can have no difficulty in explaining what these indications must have been. No ship can enter it from the east without passing within a quarter of a mile of the point of Koura; but, before reaching it, the land is too low, and too far from the track of a ship driven from the eastward, to be seen in a dark night. When she does come within this distance, it is impossible to avoid observing the breakers; for, with north-easterly gales, the sea breaks upon it with such violence, that Admiral Smyth in his view of the headland, has made the breakers its distinctive character.

By a singular chance I can establish an important link in the chain of evidence respecting the identity of this locality, namely, that the distance at which the breakers could be seen here is about a quarter of a mile, and that they are seen at this distance when the land itself is not seen.

On one of those rare occasions when there was no ground swell and a boat could land on the point of Koura, I landed with my friend the Rev. Mr. Robertson, of Saline, and was engaged in demonstrating to him, upon the spot, how rigidly every one of the conditions required to make it agree with the narrative were here fulfilled. To the east lay the low and receding shores of Malta, nowhere "approaching" within a mile of the track of a ship coming from Clauda, and which, therefore, could not be seen on a night such as that described in the narrative. In the opposite direction the shore, begirt with mural precipices ($\tau\rho\alpha\chi\epsilon\iota\varsigma\ \tau o\pi ou\varsigma$), where a ship would be dashed to pieces, but with "creeks with shores," into which she might be thrust; and on the rocks where we stood, not more than twenty feet above the surface of the sea, and totally destitute of vegetation, lay huge fragments of rock, forcibly torn up by the waves, and lodged at least twelve feet above the level of a tideless sea, affording no doubtful evidence of what must have been the force of the breakers in a gale from the Greco Levante, E.N.E. (Euro-aquilo), the point to which it is most exposed. One of our boatmen, who was listening attentively, said he knew what I was speaking about, and could point out the spot of the shipwreck; that he was a boy when it happened, and had gone to see the ship next day. This produced an explanation. He told us that thirty or forty years ago, the Lively, frigate, fell in unexpectedly with the point, in a dark night, and, missing stays, had run ashore at a spot which he showed us, and that, a gale coming on, she had gone to pieces.

Struck with the coincidence, on my return to England, I applied at the Admiralty, and examined the proceedings of the court martial held on the officers of the ship, from which it appears, that on the 10th of August, 1810, the Lively, frigate, coming from the westward with a fair wind, made the land of Gozo, and the west end of Malta, before it was dark. The weather, however, afterwards turned thick, and the land was lost sight of. When the captain (M'Kinlay) went below, he left orders with the master to heave the ship to at a certain hour, in order to get her put in order, before running into the harbour of Valetta next morning. This was accordingly done; but the ship was, unfortunately, and against the opinion of the lieutenant of the watch (Lieutenant, now Admiral Berkeley), brought to, with her head inshore. Soon afterward the quarter-master on the look-out gave the alarm of rocks to leeward.* He states, in his evidence,

* In reporting to the master, the quarter-master said there was neither room to tack nor wear, but "if all was thrown aback the ship might back out stern foremost." There can be no doubt but that if this plan had been adopted, the ship would have drifted clear of the point ; but the officers could not know how far the rocks extended, and there was no reason to fear that the frigate, *if properly* handled, would "miss stays ; " this was evidently the opinion of the court, who put repeated questions as to the cause of the ship's not coming round : one of the witnesses attributed it to the confusion caused by the captain's coming suddenly on deck, another to a brace being let go too soon. The master was reduced in rank for bringing the ship to with her head in-shore.

that he did not see the land, but "the curl of the sea" upon the rocks, at the distance of about a quarter of a mile. This was upon the point of Koura, the very spot where a ship driving from the east into St. Paul's Bay must have seen and heard the breakers, and the only spot where she could have done so. Upon perceiving the danger, the order, "ready about and *clear the anchor*," was immediately given by Lieutenant Berkeley; and as they were bracing round the maintop-sail to fill upon the ship, the man at the lead *sounded, and found twenty-five fathoms*. Before, however, she had sufficient way upon her, the helm was put down; but the ship missed stays, that is, they could not get her head round on the opposite tack. *The anchor was then let go* *; but before the ship brought up, she fell off broadside on the rocks, and a gale coming on she went to pieces.

Before proceeding to compare the notices in the narrative with the peculiarities of the supposed site, let us stop to inquire whether the data which this inquiry has furnished us will not enable us to ascertain, within certain limits, by *à priori* reasoning, whereabouts the ship was, that is, her longitude and latitude, when the "shipmen deemed that she drew near to some country."

I have already shown, from three independent sources, that the wind must have been ENE. $\frac{1}{4}$ N. to the nearest quarter of a point; and that the ship must have been on the starboard tack, that is, with her head to the north, in order to avoid the Syrtis. The first question which pre-

---

* This does not appear from the proceedings of the court; but one of our boatmen told us he assisted in sweeping for it, and that it was found many years afterwards.

sents itself is, what was the direction of the drift mentioned in the seventeenth verse, " so were driven " (οὕτως ἐφέροντο). The answer depends on the angle the ship's head makes with the wind and the lee-way. But an ancient ship could probably not lie nearer the wind than seven points, which, added to six points of lee-way, makes thirteen points, as the angle which such a ship would probably make with the wind.* ENE. ¼ N. is 2¼ points to the north of east: if we add thirteen to this, it makes the azimuth of the ship's course from Clauda W. ¾ N., or W. 8° N., *which is the bearing of Malta to the nearest degree.*

The next point to be ascertained is, how far would she have driven from Clauda about midnight " when the fourteenth night was come." The knowledge of this depends upon the rate of drift and the time consumed. The result which the calculation founded upon these data gives us is so very striking, that I feel called upon to state the elements on which it is founded at some length, lest I should be accused of " cooking " them, that is, of selecting those only which answered my purpose, and rejecting those which did not.

In order to ascertain what might be supposed to be the mean rate of drift of a ship circumstanced as that of St. Paul's was, I consulted two nautical friends, both of them at the time commanding ships in Valetta harbour, and

---

* I arrive at these results thus: ancient ships could sail on opposite tacks, "in contrariam" (Pliny, ii. 48.), hence they could lie with eight points of the wind, but they certainly could not lie so near the wind as modern ships, say six points; the mean, therefore, is seven points. The lee-way of a ship in a gale varies from 5½ to 6½ points (see Falconer's Marine Dictionary, article Lee-way); the mean of which is six points.

both of them familiar with the navigation of the Levant. To the first of these officers whom I met with (the late Captain W. M'Lean, R. N.), I put the question, "What would you say would be the probable rate of drift of a ship hove to in a gale of wind?" His answer was, "That depends on the force of the gale and the size of the ship." Upon explaining that I considered it a large ship, even as compared with modern merchantmen, and that the gale might be reckoned as one of mean intensity, he said, after considering the matter, that speaking in round numbers, forty miles in twenty-four hours might be reckoned a fair allowance. I put the same question to Captain Graves, R.N., who replied, "From three-quarters of a mile an hour to two miles an hour." The mean of these extremes is thirty-three miles in twenty-four hours, and the mean of both estimates is thirty-six and a half miles in twenty-four hours.*

I come now to the time elapsed. It is quite clear from the narrative, that St. Luke counts the time from the day the ship left Fair Havens. We hear of the "third day" (v. 19.); the preceding is termed "next day," which brings us to the first day, both of the gale and the voyage. It is also clear that the events of that day must have occupied a large portion of it. The time consumed in driving through the Sea of Adria, from the time they left the island of Clauda till they became aware of the vicinity of land at midnight of the fourteenth day, is, therefore, thirteen days complete, and a small fraction. But the distance from

---

* When Capt. Graves said from three-quarters of a mile to two miles an hour, I replied, "Very well, I may suppose a mile and a half an hour, about a mean rate," to which he assented.

Clauda to the point of Koura, where I suppose that this happened, is 476.6 miles*, which, at the rate as deduced from the information of Captains M'Lean and Graves, would take exactly thirteen days, one hour, and twenty-one minutes.

The coincidence of the actual bearing of St. Paul's Bay from Clauda, and the direction in which a ship must have driven in order to avoid the Syrtis, is, if possible, still more striking than that of the time actually consumed, and the calculated time.

The direction of the ship's course is inferred from that of the wind, from the angle of the ship's head with the wind, and from the lee-way. I have shown (see p. 98.) that the mean direction of the wind, as deduced from the notices in the narrative, was E. 26° 15′ N. In the dissertation on ancient ships I have assigned reasons for supposing seven points as the angle a ship's head would

---

* This distance is deduced from the position of the places by the following formula: —

	Lat., N.			Lon., E.	
Point of Koura,	35° 56′	mer. parts 2313		14° 25′	
Clauda,	34 52	mer. parts 2235		24 2	
Diff.	1° 4′ = 64′	Diff. 78		Diff. 9° 37′ = 577′	
As mer. diff. of		As rad.		-	10.000000
lat. 78 - log.	1.892095	is to diff. lat 64°		-	1.806180
is to rad. -	10.000000	so is sec. course			
so is diff., lon. 577	2.761176	82° 17′	-	-	12.872007
	12.761176				12.678187
	1.892395				10.000000
to tang. course 82° 17′ -	10.869081	to distance 476.6			2.678187

make with the wind, which, added to six points for leeway, makes an angle of 146° 15', which, added to the angle of the wind, makes the azimuth of the ship's course, as drawn from these data, E. 172° 30' N., or N. 82° 30' W., which agrees with the bearing of St. Paul's Bay, 82° 17', as drawn from the foregoing calculation to 13', which at the distance between Clauda and Malta is equivalent to about two miles and a half.

Hence, according to these calculations, a ship, starting late in the evening from Clauda, would, by midnight on the 14th, be less than three miles from the entrance of St. Paul's Bay. I admit that a coincidence so very close as this is, is to a certain extent accidental, but it is an accident which could not have happened had there been any inaccuracy on the part of the author of the narrative with regard to the numerous incidents upon which the calculations are founded, or had the ship been wrecked anywhere but at Malta, for there is no other place agreeing, either in name or description, within the limits to which we are tied down by calculations founded upon the narrative.

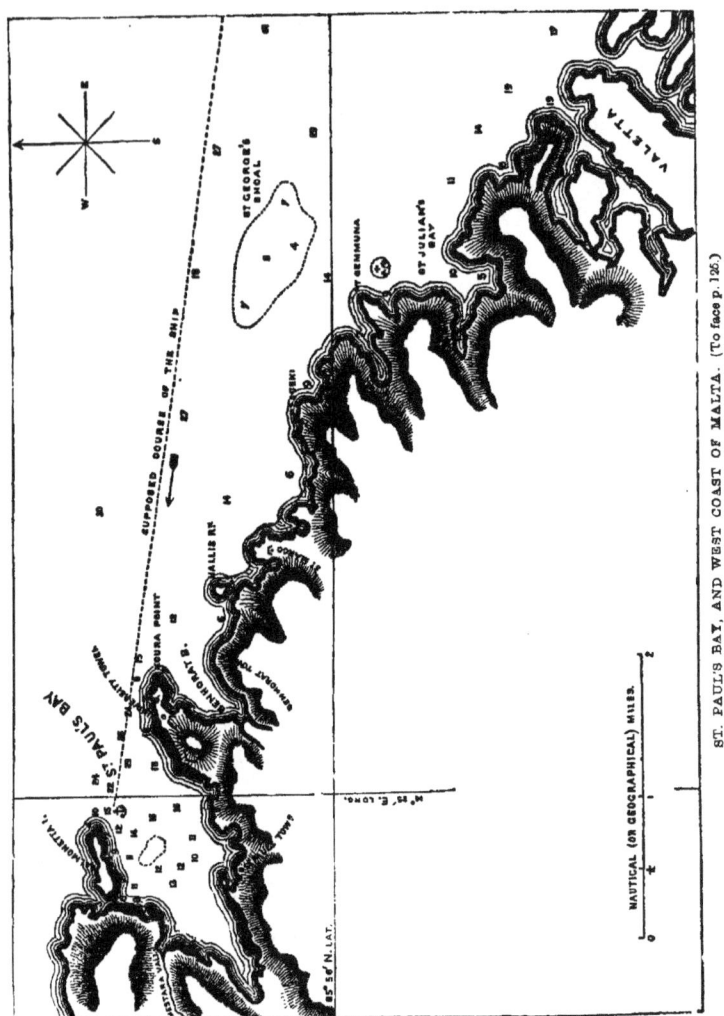

ST. PAUL'S BAY, AND WEST COAST OF MALTA. (To face p. 126.)

CHAP. IV.

THE SHIPWRECK.

THE ship now approaches the termination of her disastrous voyage. Land is not, indeed, in sight, but to the watchful senses of the "shipmen" the sound or appearance of breakers tells them that it is near, or, in the nautical language of St. Luke, that it is approaching. Such indications are the usual harbingers of destruction; here they call forth a display of presence of mind, promptitude, and seamanship, which could not be surpassed in the present day, and by which, under Providence, the lives of all on board were saved.

However appalling the alarm of breakers may be to a ship unexpectedly falling in with the land on an unknown coast, and in a dark and stormy night, it afforded in the present case a chance at least of safety. The hope which was taken away is restored. They can now adopt the last resource for a sinking ship, and run her ashore; but to do so before it was day would have been to have rushed on certain destruction. They must bring the ship, if it be possible, to anchor, and hold on till day-break, when they may perhaps discover some "creek with a shore," into which they may be able to "thrust the ship."

The progress of the narrative has brought us to the question, Whether the traditional locality is in reality that of the shipwreck? Now, if we attend minutely to the narrative, it will be seen that the number of conditions required to be fulfilled, in order to make any locality agree with it, are so numerous as to render it morally impossible to suppose that the agreement which we find here can be the effect of chance.

The first circumstance mentioned is, that at midnight the shipmen suspected the vicinity of land evidently without seeing it. The ship was driving from Clauda; her previous track must have been at such a distance from the land, and the land itself must be so low, as to prevent its being seen. Now, upon laying down the track of a ship driving in that direction to St. Paul's Bay, on Admiral Smyth's chart of Malta, I find that the land, which in that part of the island is very low, nowhere approaches within a mile of it*, but that it is impossible to enter the bay without passing within a quarter of a mile of a low rocky point, which juts out and forms its eastern entrance (the point of Koura). When the Lively, frigate, unexpectedly fell in with this very point, the quarter-master on the look-out, who first observed it, states, in his evidence at the court-martial, that at the distance of a quarter of a mile the land could not be seen, but that he saw the surf on the shore. Here, then, we establish the explanation of a hitherto unexplained passage of Scripture, by the oath of a competent witness. Till the ship arrived at the entrance of the bay they could not be aware of the vicinity of land; when they did come to it, they could

---

* Off Valetta the distance of the track of a ship from Clauda to St. Paul's Bay is three miles; it gradually diminishes to one mile.

ST. PAUL'S BAY, MALTA, FROM THE SOUTH. (To face p. 126.)

not avoid becoming aware of it. When they did so, they sounded, and found twenty fathoms.* But a ship coming from the eastward must, immediately after passing the point, pass over this depth.† It is quite true that every ship in approaching the land must pass over twenty fathoms and fifteen fathoms, but here not only must the twenty fathom depth be close to the spot where they had the indications of land, but it must bear E. by S. from the fifteen fathom depth, and at such a distance as would allow of preparation for anchoring, with four anchors from the stern; for we are not to suppose that ships from sea, unexpectedly falling in with land, can be prepared to anchor in an unusual manner on the instant. Now, about half an hour farther, estimating the ship's rate of progression by the time which had been hitherto consumed, we find the depth to be fifteen fathoms. Here we are told, " that fearing lest they should have fallen upon rocks‡,

---

28 Και βολισαντες, ευρον οργυιας εικοσι · βραχυ δε διαστησαντες, και παλιν βολισαντες, ευρον οργυιας δεκαπεντε.

28 And sounded and found it twenty fathoms, and when they had gone a little farther they sounded again and found it fifteen fathoms.

---

* The ancient fathom (οργυια) so nearly agrees with the English fathom, that the difference may be neglected. According to Hesychius, it is τα των αμφοτερων χειρων εκτασις, the space between both hands extended.

† See chart of St. Paul's Bay to the west of the point of Koura. I have given the soundings as they are laid down in Captain Smyth's chart. Although the depth of twenty fathoms is not marked, we know it must be between eleven and twenty-four.

‡ Τραχυς is mentioned as a hydrographic term by Julius Pollux, and

they cast four anchors out of the stern." This implies that there were rocks to leeward, on which, if they had not anchored, they must have fallen; but the fifteen fathom depth is as nearly as possible a quarter of a mile from the shore, which is here girt with mural precipices, and upon which the sea must have been breaking with great violence. Upon the former alarm the ship weathered the point; here it was impossible. From the position of the ship's head, the breakers must have been seen over the lee bow. Their only chance of safety, therefore, was to anchor, but to do so successfully in a gale of wind, on a lee shore, requires not only time for preparation, but holding-ground of extraordinary tenacity. In St. Paul's Bay the anchorage is thus described in the sailing directions: —

"The harbour of St. Paul is open to easterly and north-east winds. It is, notwithstanding, safe for small ships, the ground, generally, being very good; and while the cables hold there is no danger, *as the anchors will never start.*"— P. 161.

The proximate cause of anchoring was no doubt that assigned by St. Luke, namely, the fear of falling on the

---

29 Φοβουμενοι τε μηπως εις τραχεις τοπους εκπεσωσιν, εκ πρυμνης ῥιψαντες αγκυρας τεσσαρας, ηυχοντο ἡμεραν γενεσθαι.

29 And fearing lest she should have fallen upon rocks, they cast four anchors out of the stern and wished for day.

---

classed with the words δυσορμος, αλιμενος, &c., lib. i. 101. When Ulysses is wrecked on the coast of Phæacia,—

Τοφρα δε μιν μεγα κυμα φερε τ ρ η χ ε ι α ν επ' ακτην.
Ενθα κ' απο ρινους δρυφθη, συν δ' οστε' αραχθη,
Ει μη, κ.τ.λ.   Od. v. 425.

rocks to leeward; but they had also an ulterior object in view, which was to run the ship ashore as soon as daylight enabled them to select a spot where it could be done with a prospect of safety; for this purpose the very best position in which the ship could be, was to be anchored by the stern.

We have no occasion, therefore, to account for this proceeding, by showing that a certain class of vessels in the eastern seas anchor in this manner. To explain away the difficulty, is much the same as if the biographer of Lord Nelson were to explain away the well-known manœuvre of anchoring by the stern at the battle of the Nile*, by attempting to prove that this was a common practice with English ships. That of the ancients was the same as the moderns; except under particular circumstances, they anchored by the bow,—" Anchora de prora jacitur." The reasons for doing so are obvious; it is much easier to arrest a ship's way by the bow than by the stern.

It is proper, however, to observe, that from the very necessity of the case the antient navigators were forced to depend much more upon their ground tackle than the moderns. Ships constructed and rigged like theirs could

---

* Appian ascribes the success of a former naval victory on the coast of Africa to the manœuvre of anchoring by the stern, and for the same reasons as Lord Nelson's,—it obviated the necessity of exposing the weak points of the ships to the enemy in turning round. The ships of the Carthaginians were anchored along-shore, like the French fleet. The Romans attacked them from the sea, in the usual manner, but in turning round to repeat their blows, they received those of the enemy on their sides, till at last they let go their anchors by the stern, and with a long scope of cable hauled out their ships, κατα πρυμναν, by the stern. De Bell. Pun., edit. Stephani, p. 76.

not, when caught in a gale, work off a lee shore, they must of necessity anchor; hence they must have been very amply provided with anchors and cables, and habituated to the use of them in every possible contingency. I may also add, that, as both ends of their ships were alike, there was nothing in their form to prevent this mode of anchoring from being put in practice.

There is still one difficulty to be obviated, which I am indebted to a naval friend for starting. Upon pointing out to Captain M'Lean, R.N., whose authority I have already cited, the advantageous position in which it placed the ship for the purpose of running her ashore, he replied—"Very true; but were the ships of the antients fitted to anchor by the stern, had they hawse-holes aft? because if they had, we are only coming back to old practices."

This is the difficulty of a seaman, who immediately thinks of how the thing is to be done. I must admit myself too much of a landsman to have thought of it, otherwise I should have been able to have answered it, which I was not at the time; for I had copied from the "Antichità di Ercolano" the figure of the ship, in the picture of Theseus deserting Ariadne, which contains details showing, not only that they were so fitted, but the manner in which it was done; and that too, in a ship so strictly contemporaneous with that of St. Paul, that there is nothing impossible in the supposition, that the artist had taken his subject from that very ship, on loosing from the pier of Puteoli. A hawser is seen towing astern,—it passes through the rudder-port, and within board it is seen coiled round an upright beam or capstan, in front of the break of the poop-deck.

We see, therefore, that ships of the antients were fitted to anchor by the stern; and in the present instance that mode of anchoring was attended with most important advantages.

If St. Luke had been a seaman, we can scarcely suppose that he would have omitted to have mentioned the reasons for this particular mode of anchoring, or the precautions which were necessary in order to insure its being done with success; but, as usual, he is contented with a bare statement of facts, without assigning reasons or offering explanations. One most essential precaution in such a case, and probably, under the circumstances, a difficult one, was to lift the rudders out of the water, and secure them by lashings; we are not expressly told that this precaution was taken, but we learn afterwards, indirectly, that it was. Perhaps also the main-mast was cut away. Falconer, a seaman, contemplates the possibility of saving the ship by doing so,—

"The hull dismasted there awhile may ride,
With lengthened cables on the raging tide."
Shipwreck, canto ii.

The circumstance of the artemon having been hoisted * when they ran the ship ashore, lends probability to the conjecture, and nothing can be inferred from the author's silence, but it is nothing more than a conjecture; and I have not ventured, in the view of the ship anchored by the stern, to represent it so. (*See* Frontispiece.)

The advantages of being anchored in this manner are, that by cutting away the anchors (αγκυρας περιελοντες), loosing the bands of the rudder (ανεντες τας ζευκτηριας των πηδαλιων), and hoisting the artemon (επαραντες τον αρτεμονα), all of which could be, as they were in effect, done simultaneously, the ship was immediately under command, and could be directed with precision to any part of the shore which offered a prospect of safety. Whereas, if anchored in the usual mode, she might have taken "the wrong cast," or drifted on the rocks before she was under command.

The number of anchors which were let go shows that

---

* In the ship of Catullus, when the mast is cut away, they hoist the artemon,—"velo prora suo," which the scholiast explains "artemone solo velificaverunt."—Juv. Sat. xii. 69. See Dissertation on Ships for proof that the artemon was the foresail.

the able commander (ναυκληρος) left nothing to chance. The ship is now in a situation where escape is possible, but not certainly one in which it is probable. From the state of the ship, she may go down at her anchors, or the coast to leeward may be iron-bound, affording no beach (αιγιαλος) upon which they can land in safety. Hence their anxious longing for day; hence also the ungenerous but natural attempt of the seamen to save their own lives, by taking to the boat; an attempt not peculiar to ancient times.* They lower the boat under pretence of laying out anchors from the bow.† The design is penetrated and defeated by St. Paul. He tells the centurion, that unless they remain in the ship they cannot be saved. The soldiers cut the boat's hawsers, and allow her to go adrift.

During the interval which remained till day, Paul exhorted them to take food, saying,—

---

30 Των δε ναυτων ζητουντων φυγειν εκ του πλοιου και χαλασαντων την σκαφην εις την θαλασσαν προφασει ὡς εκ πρωρας μελλοντων αγκυρας εκτεινειν

30 And as the shipmen were about to flee out of the ship, when they had let down the boat into the sea, under colour as though they would have cast anchors out of the foreship,

---

* When the Athenienne, 64, was lost on the Skerki rocks, near Sicily, in 1806, two boats' crews deserted her. There were no officers in the boats. See United Service Magazine, February, 1845, p. 229.

† We hear of anchors being laid out from both ends of a ship (ἑκατερωθεν). Appian, B. C. 723.

It is to be observed, that casting anchors out of the foreship could have been of no possible advantage in the circumstances, and that as the pretext could not deceive a seaman, we must infer that the officers of the ship were parties to the unworthy attempt, which was perhaps detected by the nautical skill of St. Luke, and communicated by him to St. Paul.

This is the fourteenth day* that ye have tarried and continued fasting, having taken nothing, wherefore I pray you to take some food, for this is for your health, for there shall not a hair fall from the head of any of you.

They were now to eat in the ship for the last time, and needed no longer to stint themselves to an allowance; the apostle sets the example, and, giving thanks to God, takes a piece of bread, and breaking it, begins to eat;

31 Ειπεν ὁ Παυλος τῳ ἑκατονταρχῃ και τοις στρατιωταις· Εαν μη οὑτοι μεινωσιν εν τῳ πλοιῳ ὑμεις σωθηναι ου δυνασθε.	31 Paul said to the centurion and to the soldiers, Except these abide in the ship ye cannot be saved.
32 Τοτε οἱ στρατιωται απεκοψαν τα σχοινια της σκαφης, και ειασαν αυτην εκπεσειν.	32 And the soldiers cut off the ropes of the boat, and allowed her to fall off.
33 Αχρι δε οὑ εμελλεν ἡμερα γινεσθαι, παρεκαλει ὁ Παυλος ἁπαντας μεταλαβειν τροφης λεγων · Τεσσαρεςκαιδεκατην σημερον ἡμεραν προσδοκωντες, ασιτοι διατελειτε, μηδεν προσλαβομενοι.	33 And while the day was coming on, Paul besought *them* all to take meat, saying, This day is the fourteenth day that ye have tarried and continued fasting, having taken nothing.
34 Διο παρακαλω ὑμας προσλαβειν τροφης· τουτο γαρ προς της ὑμετερας σωτηριας ὑπαρχει· ουδενος γαρ ὑμων θριξ εκ της κεφαλης πεσειται.	34 Wherefore I pray you to take some meat, for this is for your health, for there shall not a hair fall from the head of any of you.
35 Ειπων δε ταυτα, και λαβων αρτον, ευχαριστησε τῳ Θεῳ, ενωπιον	35 And when he had thus spoken, he took bread, and gave

---

* Granville Penn thinks the reading ought to be τεσσαρας, και δε και σημερον ἡμερων, "four days even this very day," supposing that the apostle meant that they had literally taken nothing for so many days; but surely there is no difficulty in the case. St. Luke, when he speaks as a historian, terms their fasting "much abstinence" (πολλης ασιτιας, v. 21.). St. Paul uses the strong, but common, language, of calling taking very little taking nothing. It could not be mistaken by those to whom it was addressed.

inspirited by it, all of them partake a full meal, the first since the commencement of the gale; and with renewed strength make a last effort to lighten the ship*, not only by pumping, but by throwing the wheat † into the sea.

When day broke they did not know the land ‡; but it

παντων, και κλασας ηρξατο εσθιειν.

36 Ευθυμοι δε γενομενοι παντες, και αυτοι προσελαβοντο τροφης.

37 Ημεν δε εν τῳ πλοιῳ αἱ πασαι ψυχαι διακοσιαι ἑβδομηκοντα ἑξ.

38 Κορεσθεντες δε τροφης, εκουφιζον το πλοιον, εκβαλλομενοι τον σιτον εις την θαλασσαν.

thanks to God, in presence of them all, and when he had broken *it*, he began to eat.

36 Then were they all of good cheer, and they also took some meat.

37 And we were in all in the ship two hundred three score and sixteen souls.

38 And when they had eaten enough, they lightened the ship, and cast out the wheat into the sea.

---

* Εκουφιζον το πλοιον, they lighten the ship. Amongst the nautical terms of Julius Pollux we find κουφισαι την ναυν. (See note to verse 18.) The Septuagint has κουφισθηναι, Jonah, i. 5.

† Some suppose that by τον σιτον the remainder of the ship's provisions is meant; but to suppose that they had remaining such a quantity as would lighten the ship is quite inconsistent with the previous abstinence; and, besides, wheat was the staple commodity imported from Alexandria to Italy.

‡ It has been asked, if Malta was the island, how came it not to be known to some of the crew, for it is not to be supposed that Alexandrian seamen could be ignorant of that island? Major Rennel, with his usual candour, says: "It must be admitted, that, on a supposition that it was the island of Malta (as the author certainly concludes), it might appear extraordinary that it should not have been recognised by some of the crew of the ship, which belonged to Alexandria (chap. xxvii.), as it may be sup-

had certain peculiarities, and unless we can show that the shore to the west of the ship's supposed position possesses the same peculiarities, it will not agree with that mentioned in the text. The first of these is, " rocky places " (τραχεις τοπους); the fear of falling upon which at night had caused them to come to anchor. Now the shore here is skirted with precipices, against which the ship must have been dashed in pieces, had she not been anchored. The next is, a " creek with a sandy beach " (κολπον εχοντα αιγιαλον)*; and the third is, " a place of two seas " (τοπον διθαλασσον). It will be seen how perfectly these features still distinguish the coast.

Having observed from the ship a creek, such as we

---

39 Ὅτε δε ἡμερα εγενετο, την γην ουκ επεγινωσκον· κολπον δε τινα κατενοουν εχοντα αιγιαλον, εις ὁν εβουλευσαντο, ει δυναιντο, εξωσαι

39 And when it was day they knew not the land, but they discovered a certain creek with a shore, into the which they were

posed that Malta was well known to the navigators of that port. This, however, I cannot pretend to account for."—*Archæologia*, xxi. 103. But St. Paul's Bay is remote from the great harbour, and possesses no marked features by which it could be recognised.

* " A creek with a shore." Commentators tell us that every creek has a shore, and that it should be "a shore with a creek," vide Kuinoel ad loc.; but αιγιαλος, although it sometimes means the shore in general, in a restricted sense means a sandy beach, in contradistinction to a rocky coast. St. Luke here uses the correct hydrographical term. Arrian uses it frequently in this sense. Thus, in describing the shores of the Red Sea, he talks of a great and small beach, αιγιαλος και μικρος και μεγας, Perip. Mar. Eryth. p. 9.; and in the Periplus of Nearchus, we are told that the fleet was moved from one sandy beach to another, which was named Neoptana. Αλλα επλεον γαρ απο του αιγιαλου, αραντες, τῃ γῃ προσεχεες, και πλευσαντες σταδιους ὡς ἑπτακοσιους εν αλλῳ αιγιαλῳ ὡρμισαντο. Νεοπτανα ονομα τῳ αιγιαλῳ.—p. 23.

have described, they determined, if it were possible, to thrust the ship into it; they now cut their cables*, and left the anchors in the sea; and loosing (ανεντες) the lashings of the rudders †, and hoisting up the artemon ‡, or foresail (αρτεμονα), they made for the creek, which they had previously selected for the purpose.

The ship must have been driven to the west side of the bay, which is rocky, but has two creeks. One of these, Mestara Valley, has a shore. (See chart.) I am, how-

---

το πλοιον.	minded, if it were possible, to thrust in the ship.
40 Και τας αγκυρας περιελοντες ειων εις την θαλασσαν, άμα ανεντες τας ζευκτηριας των πηδαλιων, και επαραντες τον αρτεμονα τη πνεουση κατειχον εις τον αιγιαλον.	40 And when they had cut the anchors, they left them in the sea (marginal translation), and loosed the rudder bands, and hoised up the mainsail to the wind, and made towards shore.

---

* The marginal translation in our version is certainly the correct one, literally cutting off the anchors and leaving them in the sea.

† Antient ships were steered by two large paddles, one on each quarter. When anchored by the stern in a gale, it would be necessary to lift them out of the water and secure them by lashings or rudder bands, and to loose the rudder bands when the ship was again got under way.

‡ The artemon was certainly the foresail, not the mainsail. See Dissertation on antient Ships; see also frontispiece. A sailor will at once see that the foresail was the best possible sail that could be set under the circumstances. In the gale in the Crimea, in Nov. 1854, the captain of the ship the Lord Raglan, states that he cut away the main and mizen masts, but adds "*I held on the foremast in case of her parting, to carry her end on.*" . . . . "There was nothing left for us but to beach; accordingly we ran before it, trying to avoid running foul of the other ships on shore, which we fortunately managed. The foresail was blown adrift which helped her on. On striking, the sea swept over her," &c.—*Times*, Dec. 5. 1854.

ever, inclined to think that the point of appulse was in the creek, which has no longer a sandy beach, but which must have had one formerly, although now worn away by the wasting action of the sea; it is near the spot marked in the chart of St. Paul's Bay, as the traditional scene of the wreck. My chief reason for supposing that it was hereabouts that the ship was run ashore is its proximity to what St. Luke calls " a place of two seas " (τοπον διθαλασσον)*, or, as our authorised version renders it by a happy conjecture, "a place where two seas met." From the entrance of the bay, where the ship must have been anchored, they could not possibly have suspected that at the bottom of it there should be a communication with the sea outside; this unexpected circumstance naturally attracted the attention of the author, and served to mark the spot where the ship was wrecked. Selmoon Island, which separates the bay from the sea on the outside, is formed by a long rocky ridge, separated from the mainland by a channel of not more than a hundred yards in breadth.

Near this channel, which a glance at the chart will show must be where a ship from the eastward would be driven, they ran the ship ashore (επωκειλαν την ναυν) †; the

---

41 Περιπεσοντες δε εις τοπον διθαλασσον, επωκειλαν την ναυν· και

41 And falling into a place where two seas met, they ran the

* Εις τοπον διθαλασσον, in locum bimarem. It is generally supposed to mean an isthmus, which is no doubt dithalassic; but the interposition of land between the two seas is not necessary. Strabo calls the Bosphorus dithalassic. — Πελαγος δ καλουσι Προποντιδα· κακεινο εις αλλο το Ευξεινον προσαγορευομενον ποντον, εστι δε διθαλαττος τροπον τινα ούτος. — Lib. ii. cap. 5. 22. Oxford fol. vol. i. p. 164. The narrow sound between the island and the main in St. Paul's Bay is a Bosphorus in miniature.

† Julius Pollux has ωκειλεν ή ναυς, προσωκειλεν, εξωκειλεν. The word is used in the same sense as in the text by Arrian, Xenophon, Polybius, &c.

fore part stuck fast (ερεισασα), and remained entire; but the stern was dashed to pieces by the force of the waves. This is a remarkable circumstance, which, but for the peculiar nature of the bottom of St. Paul's Bay, it would be difficult to account for.

The rocks of Malta disintegrate into extremely minute particles of sand and clay, which, when acted upon by the currents, or surface agitation, form a deposit of tenacious clay; but, in still water, where these causes do not act, mud is formed; but it is only in the creeks where there are no currents, and at such a depth as to be undisturbed by the waves, that the mud occurs. In Admiral Smyth's chart of the bay the nearest soundings to the mud indicate a depth of about three fathoms, which is about what a large ship would draw. A ship, therefore, impelled by the force of a gale, into a creek with a bottom such as that laid down in the chart, would strike a bottom of mud, graduating into tenacious clay, into which the fore part would fix itself, and be held fast, whilst the stern was exposed to the force of the waves.

The ship has now reached the shore; but, before relating the escape of the passengers and crew, I shall endeavour to give the reader some idea of what must have been their privations and sufferings, and supply what is wanting in St. Luke's account, or merely hinted at, by

---

ἡ μεν πρωρα ερεισασα εμεινεν ασαλευτος, ἡ δε πρυμνα ελυετο ὑπο της βιας των κυματων.

ship aground, and the forepart struck fast, and remained unmoveable, but the hinder part was broken with the force of the waves.

citing examples of ships circumstanced as theirs was. I take the outline from the antient voyage, and fill up the details with "modern instances," limiting myself to two cases, that of a crazy ship, undergirded, and struggling with a gale, namely, Captain Back's; the other of a ship caught in a typhoon, namely the India Company's ship Bridgewater.*

I have already shown that the inevitable result of such a storm must have been to have strained the hull severely, and rendered the ship leaky to an alarming degree; and that the knowledge of this fact, which we only arrive at by inference, gives us a key which explains all the subsequent incidental notices which drop from the author. Such was the case both with the Terror and the Bridgewater. The leaks in the former ship were partly, no doubt, caused by the ice; in the latter case they were the effects of a typhonic gale. The officer who describes it says, they "found the ship had suffered severely in the hull."

After undergirding St. Paul's ship,—

Ver. 17. "They lowered the gear."

"Got our top-gallant masts and yards on deck."—*Bridgewater.*

Ver. 18. "Exceedingly tossed by a tempest."

"The unabated fury of the gale, strengthened by squalls, raised a long breaking sea, in which she plunged so heavily, that it was often unusually long before she recovered herself. It was evident she was getting more water-logged, and the straining and creaking of her whole frame, the working of the bulk-heads, which actually raised the officers' bed places, the rickety twisting occasioned by the fore and aft motion, and the prolonged dull roll to windward, to say

---

* From the United Service Magazine, 1831, part 2. p. 49. The ship encountered the typhoon, 4th March, 1829.

nothing of the cascade-like rushing of the water within; all these were certain indications of a consummation which no exertions of ours would probably be sufficient long to defer."—*Voyage of Terror*, p. 438.

"Next day they lightened the ship."

"It was determined that the guns should be thrown overboard, as well as part of the cargo."—*Bridgewater*.

Ver. 19. "Cast out . . . the tackling of the ship."

"Cut away the sheet and stream anchors."—*Bridgewater*.

Ver. 20. "All hope that we should be saved was then taken away."

"I confess that all hope of ultimate preservation entirely left me."—*Bridgewater*.

Ver. 21. "After long abstinence."

"To aggravate our disasters, the ship too laboured so as to make it impossible to light a fire, and thus deprived us of the nourishment essential to the restoration of our exhausted energies."—*Terror*, p. 440.

"With the exception of a biscuit and a glass of spirits occasionally, not a man in the ship had throughout three days either sustenance or sleep. Owing to this, together with the great exertions required of them at the pumps, they had become completely exhausted and dispirited."—*Bridgewater*.

Ver. 29. "They anchor the ship."

"Near midnight anchored safely in Loch Swilly."—*Terror*, p. 441.

Ver. 39. "They discovered a certain creek with a shore (beach), into which they were minded, if it were possible, to thrust in the ship."

"Finding that their united efforts were unable to keep her afloat it was determined to run her ashore on a small sandy beach, selected for the purpose."— *Terror*, p. 442.

I offer these extracts, not as curious coincidences, but that the reader may see from parallel cases what was the state of their ship, and the cause of their running her ashore.

They have now escaped the dangers of the sea; but other dangers await them: the guard, in conformity with the stern behests of Roman law, proposed to kill the prisoners, in order to prevent their escape. " But the centurion, willing to save Paul, kept them from their purpose; and commanded that they which could swim should cast themselves first into the sea, and get to land. And the rest, some on boards, and some on broken pieces of the ship. And so it came to pass that they escaped all safe to land."

---

42 Των δε στρατιωτων βουλη εγενετο, ινα τους δεσμωτας αποκτεινωσι, μη τις εκκολυμβησας διαφυγοι.

42 And the soldiers' counsel was to kill the prisoners, lest any of them should swim out and escape.

43 Ὁ δε ἑκατονταρχος, βουλομενος διασωσαι τον Παυλον, εκωλυσεν αυτους του βουληματος, εκελευσε τε τους δυναμενους κολυμβᾳν, αποῤῥιψαντας πρωτους επι την γην εξιεναι.

43 But the centurion, willing to save Paul, kept them from *their* purpose, and commanded that they which could swim should cast *themselves* first into the sea, and get to land.

44 Και τους λοιπους, οὑς μεν επι σανισιν, οὑς δε επι τινων των απο του πλοιου· και οὑτως εγενετο παντας διασωθηναι επι την γην.

44 And the rest, some on boards, and some on *broken pieces* of the ship. And so it came to pass that they escaped all safe to land.

CHAP. V.

MELITA TO ITALY.

(Chap. xxviii. 1.)

AFTER reaching the shore, they learnt, for the first time, that the name of the island was Melita. Their previous ignorance of this has been adduced, as an argument * that this could not be a place so well known as the African Melita, now Malta. Major Rennel, with his usual candour, states the difficulty, and admits that he cannot remove it. This circumstance, however, will not be felt as a difficulty by any one acquainted with the locality; the sailors were, probably, little acquainted with any part of the island, except the great harbour (of Valetta) and the coast near it — the scene of the shipwreck lies remote from it, and it is out of the usual track of ships approaching the harbour; and there is no marked feature in the configuration of the land which could make it known even to a native, if he came unexpectedly upon it.†

---

1 Και διασωθεντες, τοτε επεγνωσαν ὁτι Μελιτη ἡ νησος καλειται.

1 And when they were escaped, then they knew that the island was called Melita.

---

* Georgi, p. 191. See note at p. 100.
† Admiral Smyth makes use of the buildings, Selmoon palace and the university tower, as land-marks.

The natives* received the unfortunate voyagers with kindness, and kindled a fire, because of the rain, and because of the cold.

These meteorological remarks prove that the wind was to the north of east, for if it had been a Scirocco wind (S.E.), as Bryant and others contend, it would have been hot and sultry, for such is the character of that wind in the Mediterranean even so late as the month of November. I may add, that the scirocco seldom or ever lasts more than three days.†

---

2 Οἱ δε βαρβαροι παρειχον ου την τυχουσαν φιλανθρωπιαν ἡμιν· αναψαντες γαρ πυραν, προσελαβοντο παντας ἡμας δια τον ὑετον τον ἐφεστωτα, και δια το ψυχος.

2 And the barbarous people showed us no little kindness, for they kindled a fire, and received us every one, because of the present rain, and because of the cold.

---

* In the Dissertation on the Island of Melita, I have answered the arguments of Bryant, founded on the term βαρβαροι, applied by St. Luke to the natives.

† Gales, in other directions, are of much longer continuance. Mr. Greswell cites a case which agrees in a remarkable manner with that of St. Paul. Aristides (the orator) encounters a gale in the Ægean Sea, and is driven through it for fourteen days and nights. Τετταρες παλιν αυται προς ταις δεκα ἡμεραι και νυκτες χειμωνος κυκλῳ δια παντος του πελαγους φερομενων.— Dissertations, vol. iv. p. 197. Professor Newman met with a continuous easterly gale on the coast of Cyprus, in Dec. 1830. He writes: "We were bound for Latakia in Syria, the course almost due east; but were driven back and forced to take refuge in the port of Famagousta, the antient Salamis. Here we lay wind-bound for days. Owing to our frequent remonstrances, the captain three times sailed out . . . but was always driven back, and once after encountering very heavy seas and no small danger. It was finally the 1st January when we reached the Syrian coast."

MELITA TO ITALY.

A circumstance now occurs which has given rise to much discussion:—

"When Paul had gathered a bundle of sticks, and laid them on the fire, there came a viper out of the heat and fastened on his hand; and when the natives saw the venomous beast hang upon his hand, they said among themselves, no doubt this man is a murderer, whom, though he hath escaped the sea, yet vengeance suffereth not to live. He, however, shook off the beast into the fire, and felt no harm. But they expected that he would have swollen, or fallen down dead suddenly; but after they had looked a great while, and saw no harm come to him, they changed their minds and said he was a God."

The difficulty here is, that although there are serpents

---

3 Συστρεψαντος δε του Παυλου φρυγανων πληθος, και επιθεντος επι την πυραν, εχιδνα εκ της θερμης εξελθουσα καθηψε της χειρος αυτου.

4. Ὡς δε ειδον οἱ βαρβαροι κρεμαμενον το θηριον εκ της χειρος αυτου ελεγον προς αλληλους· Παντως φονευς εστιν ὁ ανθρωπος οὑτος, ὁν διασωθεντα εκ της θαλασσης ἡ δικη ζῆν ουκ ειασεν.

5 Ὁ μεν ουν αποτιναξας το θηριον εις το πυρ, επαθεν ουδεν κακον.

6. Οἱ δε προσεδοκων αυτον μελλειν πιμπρασθαι, η καταπιπτειν αφνω νεκρον· επι πολυ δε αυτων προσδοκωντων και θεωρουντων μηδεν ατοπον εις αυτον γινομενον, μεταβαλλομενοι ελεγον Θεον αυτον ειναι.

3 And when Paul had gathered a bundle of sticks, and laid them on the fire, there came a viper out of the heat and fastened on his hand.

4 And when the barbarous people saw the *venomous* beast hang upon his hand, they said among themselves, No doubt this man is a murderer, whom though he hath escaped the sea, yet vengeance suffereth not to live.

5 And he shook off the beast into the fire, and felt no harm.

6 Howbeit, they looked when he should have swollen, or fallen down dead suddenly: but after they had looked a great while, and saw no harm come to him, they changed their minds, and said he was a God.

L

in Malta, they are not venomous, as the term εχιδνα (viper) implies. Upon this point I would merely observe that no person who has studied the changes which the operations of man have produced on [the Fauna (animals) of any country, will be surprised that a particular species of reptiles should have disappeared from that of Malta. My lamented friend the late Rev. Dr. Landsborough, in his interesting excursions in Arran, has repeatedly noticed the gradual disappearance of the viper from that island since it has become more frequented.

In the statistical account of the parish of Urr, the writer informs us that "The small deadly coluber, said to be found in Galloway, has very probably existence; though this animal be rare. This probability is admitted not only from numerous traditions, but because the writer of this account has once or twice met with a copper-coloured worm or little serpent, differing greatly from both the viper and the common blind worm (*Anguis fragilis*)."—Stat. Acc. vol. xi. p. 67. The reasoning is not conclusive; but it proves that there is a tradition of the former existence of vipers in Galloway, although now unknown.

Mr. Lyell, in quoting the travels of Spix and Martius in Brazil, observes,—

"They speak of the dangers to which they were exposed from the jaguar, *the poisonous serpents*, crocodiles, scorpions, centipedes, and spiders. But with the increasing population and cultivation of the country, say these naturalists, these evils will gradually diminish; when the inhabitants have cut down the woods, drained the marshes, made roads in all directions, and founded villages and towns, man will by degrees triumph over the rank vegetation and the noxious animals."*

------

* Principles of Geology, seventh edition, p. 655. The evidence of Pliny has been adduced to show that when he wrote there were no noxious

Perhaps there is nowhere a surface of equal extent in so artificial a state as that of Malta is, at the present day, and nowhere has the aboriginal forest been more completely cleared; but it by no means follows that this was the case when St. Luke wrote. Indeed there are traditions and other indications of former woods in the island. We need not, therefore, be surprised that with the disappearance of the woods, the noxious reptiles which infested them should also have disappeared.

We are now told, that " In the same quarters were the possessions of the chief man of the island, whose name was Publius, who received us and lodged us three days courteously."

The term πρωτος της νησου, "the chief or first of the island," may mean either that Publius was the principal person in the island, as our translators have understood it; or it may be an official title. There are several reasons for supposing that it is in the latter sense that St. Luke uses it. The word in the plural, οἱ πρωτοι, is elsewhere appropriately used to designate the principal men of a place, Mar. vi. 21.; Acts, xiii. 50., xxviii. 17.; but it is no-

---

7 Εν δε τοις περι τον τοπον εκεινον ὑπηρχε χωρια τῳ πρωτῳ της νησου, ονοματι Ποπλιῳ, ὁς αναδεξαμενος ἡμας, τρεις ἡμερας φιλοφρονως εξενισεν.

7 In the same quarters were possessions of the chief man of the island, whose name was Publius, who received us and lodged us three days courteously.

---

animals in the African islands. The passage is as follows: "Mox Gaulos (Gozo) et Galata cujus terra scorpionem dirum animal Africæ necat."— Lib. v. c. 7. Answer: Melita is not mentioned; scorpions are not vipers; there are scorpions both in Gozo and Malta.

where in the New Testament used in this sense in the singular, and it is difficult to suppose that in a populous island there was any one who, independently of official rank, was so prominent as to be mentioned, by his position, even in preference to his name. It is also to be observed, that the father of Publius was alive, and it is unlikely that, except by official rank, the son should have been so emphatically styled the chief man of the island in his life-time.

But we have nearly conclusive proof that πρωτος was an official designation, in two inscriptions, one in Greek and the other in Latin, still, or lately *, in Malta. In the

---

* These interesting and important inscriptions were certainly seen and carefully copied by Ciantar, from whose work I give the Greek inscription, as being probably the most correct copy. He says,—" Questo marmo si trova oggi posto alla pila d' un fonte che scaturisce nel fosso sotto la mura e alla porto della Citta Notabile (Citta Vecchia)."—T. i. p. 515. The inscription is as follows · —

A. K...ΚΙΟΣ ΚΥΡ ΠΡΟΥΔΙΝΣ ΙΠΠΕΥΣ ΡΩΜ ΠΡΩΤΟΣ ΜΕΛΙΤΑΙΩΝ
ΚΑΙ ΠΑΤΡΩΝ ΑΡΞΑΣ ΚΑΙ ΑΜΦΙΠΟΛΕΥΣ Α Σ ΘΕΩ ΑΥΥΟΥ
..... ΣΤΩ ... ΕΣΧ .... Ν .. Ε .. Ι .. ΝΕ

which has been restored conjecturally thus,—

Α(υλος) Κ(αστρι)κιος Κυρ Προυδυς Ιππευς Ρωμ Πρωτος Μελιταιων και Πατρων αρξας και αμφιπολευς Α(υγουστψ) Σ(εβαστψ) Θεψ αυτου (Σέβα)στψ.. κ.τ.λ.

It is supposed to form a votive inscription by a Roman knight, named Aulus Castricius, chief of the Melitans (Πρωτος Μελιταιων), to the emperor. The Latin inscription was discovered at Citta Vecchia, in excavating the foundation of the Casa del Magistrato, in 1747; it is inscribed on the pedestal of a column, and is said by Ciantar to be preserved in the hall of that building.

I was unable to find either of these inscriptions. It is to be hoped that they will be brought to light, and preserved in the valuable collection of Maltese antiquities, in the Knights' Library.

former, a certain Roman knight, A.K . . . κιος, is styled by the same title as Publius, chief of the Melitans (πρωτος Μελιταιων); and in the Latin inscription subsequently discovered, the same title occurs, MEL. PRIMUS.

I conclude, therefore, that πρωτος here is an official title.*

We come now to the miraculous cure of the father of Publius. His disease is mentioned in the accurate and professional language which distinguishes the writings of St. Luke: it is stated that he lay, seized with, or labouring under (συνεχομενον)†, fevers and dysentery (πυρετοις και δυσεντερια).

"To whom Paul entered in and prayed, and laid his hands on him and healed him. So when this was done, others also which had diseases in the island came and were healed."

Here we have the evidence of a medical man distin-

| 8 Εγενετο δε τον πατερα του Ποπλιου πυρετοις και δυσεντερια συνεχομενον κατακεισθαι προς ον ὁ Παυλος εισελθων, και προσευξαμενος, επιθεις τας χειρας αυτω ιασατο αυτον. | And it came to pass, that the father of Publius lay sick of a fever and of a bloody flux: to whom Paul entered in, and prayed, and laid his hands upon him, and healed him. |

---

* Schaeffer, in his "Dissertatio de Publio Πρωτῳ Melitensium" (4to., Jena, 1755), arrives at the same conclusion. His labour, however, is chiefly bestowed upon the attempt to prove that Publius was of a Roman family.

† "In speaking of Simon's wife's mother, who was taken with a great fever, he uses the term συνεχομενη in the same sense that the Greek (medical) writers do."—*Walker* "on the Medical Language of St. Luke," *Gent. Mag.* June, 1841. And Hippocrates uses the term πυρετοι (fevers) in the plural.—Epid. iii.

guished for his caution, upon a point upon which he could not be mistaken, and where he was an eye witness.

But this was not the only miraculous cure wrought by the apostle; for "others also, which had diseases in the island, came and were healed, who also honoured us with many honours, and when we departed, they loaded us with such things as were necessary.

"And after three months we departed in a ship of Alexandria, which had wintered in the isle, whose sign was Castor and Pollux.

"And landing at Syracuse, we tarried there three days."

After leaving this port, which is not more than a day's sail from Melita, they proceeded circuitously (περιελθοντες), towards Rhegium. The meaning of the expression is not

---

9 Τουτου ουν γενομενου, και οἱ λοιποι οἱ εχοντες ασθενειας εν τῃ νησῳ προσηρχοντο, και εθεραπευοντο.

9 So when this was done, others also, which had diseases in the island, came and were healed:

10 Οἱ και πολλαις τιμαις ετιμησαν ἡμας, και αναγομενοις επεθεντο τα προς την χρειαν.

10 Who also honoured us with many honours; and when we departed they laded us with such things as were necessary.

11 Μετα δε τρεις μηνας ανηχθημεν εν πλοιῳ παρακεχειμακοτι εν τῃ νησῳ Ἀλεξανδρινῳ, παρασημῳ Διοσκουροις.

11 And after three months, we departed in a ship of Alexandria, which had wintered in the isle, whose sign was Castor and Pollux.

12 Και καταχθεντες εις Συρακουσας, επεμειναμεν ἡμερας τρεις.

12 And, landing at Syracuse, we tarried there three days.

13 Ὁθεν περιελθοντες κατηντησαμεν εις Ῥηγιον· και μετα μιαν

13 And from thence we fetched a compass, and came to Rhegium;

very clear. I am inclined to suppose that the wind was north-west, and that they worked to windward, availing themselves of the sinuosities of the coast; but with this wind they could not proceed through the Straits of Messina, from the tendency which the wind always has to blow parallel to the direction of narrow channels; they were therefore obliged to put into Rhegium, at the entrance of the strait. But after one day the wind became fair (from the south); and on the following they arrived at Puteoli, having accomplished a distance of about 180 nautical miles in less than two days.*

Puteoli was then, as it is now, the most sheltered part of the Bay of Naples. It was the principal port of southern Italy, and, in particular, it was the great emporium for the Alexandrian wheat ships. Seneca, in one of his epistles, gives an interesting and graphic account of the arrival of the Alexandrian fleet.† All ships entering the bay were

---

ἡμεραν επιγενομενου νοτου, δευτε-   and after one day the south
ραιοι ηλθομεν εις Ποτιολους.   wind blew, and we came the next day to Puteoli.

---

* See remarks on the Rate of Sailing of Ancient Ships, in the Dissertation on the Ships, &c. of the Ancients.

† " Subito nobis hodie Alexandrinæ naves apparuerunt, quæ præmitti solent et nuntiare secuturæ classis adventum. Tabellarias vocant. Gratus illarum adspectus Campaniæ est. Omnis in pilis Puteolorum turba consistit, et ex ipso genere velorum, Alexandrinas quamvis in magna turba navium intelligit, solis enim licet supparum intendere quod in alto omnes habent naves. Nulla enim res æque adjuvat cursum, quam summa pars veli, illinc maxime navis urgetur. Itaque quoties ventus increbuit majorque

obliged to strike their topsails (suppara), except wheat ships, which were allowed to carry theirs. They could therefore be distinguished whenever they hove in sight. It was the practice to send forward fast-sailing vessels (tabellariæ), to announce the speedy arrival of the fleet; and the circumstance of their carrying topsails, made them distinguishable in a crowd of vessels. The supparum, therefore, was the distinguishing signal of the Alexandrian ships.

The farther proceedings of the apostle, till his arrival at Rome, I give in the words of our Authorized Translation. At Puteoli, St. Luke says (v. 14.),—

"We found brethren, and were desired to tarry with them seven days; and so we went towards Rome; and from thence when the brethren heard of us, they came to meet us as far as Appii Forum, and the Three Taverns, whom, when Paul saw, he thanked God and took courage. And when we came to Rome, the centurion delivered the prisoners to the captain of the guard; but Paul was suffered to dwell by himself, with a soldier that kept him."

We learn, in the thirtieth verse, that St. Paul hired a house, and dwelt in it for at least two years. During this period, St. Luke wrote the Acts of the Apostles. This must have been in the third year of the governorship of Festus, the Roman procurator of Judea, an impor-

---

est quam expedit, antenna submittitur, minus habet virium flatus ex humili; cum intrare Capreas et promontorium ex quo

> Alto procellas speculatur vertice Pallas —

cæteræ velo jubentur esse contentæ, supparum Alexandrinarum insigne est."
—*Epist.* 77.

tant date, for it establishes the still earlier date of his gospel.

That work, in its turn, proves the previous existence of written accounts of the transactions of our Saviour, by eye-witnesses and ministers of the word.*

* See Dissertation on the Life of St. Luke.

DISSERTATION I.

ON THE WIND EUROCLYDON.

BRYANT, in his dissertation on the wind Euroclydon, contends for the common reading of the word, in opposition to Dr. Bentley, who defends the reading Euro-aquilo on etymological grounds, considering it to be a compound of Eurus and Aquilo, taking Eurus as Gellius and the Latin poets use it, for the middle equinoctial east, and Aquilo as north-east; hence the intermediate point between these two winds is E. N. E., which Dr. Bentley considers to be the true direction of the wind.*

Bryant thus meets his argument: —

"The learned writer whose opinion I am controverting takes uncommon pains to remove Eurus from the point where it is ever stationed, in order to compound it with a wind that it is really incompatible with. And how does he effect it? By means the most extraordinary; no less than by making Gellius and the Latin poets, whose authority he does not produce, the best judges to determine the establishment of the Greek winds, *in contradiction to the Greeks themselves*. All which labour is undertaken to introduce a reading as new and uncommon as that which he repudiates. And in making use of Roman authority, he confessedly sets aside the evidence of the best and most respectable writers, and founds his opinion on the report of a single person, who will at the last turn out a confused

---

* See Dr. Bentley's observations on this subject, extracted from " Remarks on a late Discourse on Free Thinking," Appendix, No. 2.

and second-hand voucher. But let us attend to his words,—' 'Tis true according to Vitruvius, Seneca, Pliny (he might have added Varro, Columella, —and of the Greeks, who were the best judges, —Aristotle, Timosthenes, Bio, Posidonius, Strabo, &c.), according to the opinion of these, there could be no such wind or word as Euroaquilo; but Eurus is here taken, as the Latin poets use it, for the middle equinoctial east.' As to the poets, he does not produce their evidence, nor is it worth producing ; they write always so indeterminately, and with such a latitude. The whole of the argument, then, rests upon Gellius : let us turn to him, and see what he says. He tell us nothing of himself, but only *Favorinus ita fabulatus est*. Being at dinner with one Favorinus, that person discoursed at large about the winds, and ran counter to the best writers that preceded him. Among other things that he determined, was the place of the wind Eurus, which, as far as we can understand him, he would fain remove from the eastern winter solstice, and make it the same as the *Solanus* and Αφηλιωτης, that is, in place of the south-east, he would place it in the eastern *equinoctial point*. But this *Favorinus* is not of sufficient consequence to be *opposed singly* to the group of illustrious writers before mentioned. He was a sophist, and does not, in the present affair, acquit himself with proper precision. The words of his commentator upon this very passage will give one a just idea what his authority merits: '*Intricate hic loquitur* Favorinus, *et dubito an seipsum intellexerit; vel per Eurum Euronotum sive Volturnum denotaverit. Sed quid commune Volturno cum Aquilone*,' &c. Thus all this laboured evidence vanishes in smoke ; and it is the real opinion of his scholiast that the sophist did not understand himself any more than he is understood of others. So much for *Favorinus Fabulator*."

I have given Bryant's answer to Bentley at full length. His argument, if argument it can be called, is, first, that Bentley uses *Latin* authorities to overset the *invariable practice of Greek writers*. Bentley mentions the Latin poets and Aulus Gellius. Bryant evades the argument drawn from the meaning attached to the word by the poets, by observing that Bentley " does not produce his authorities;" but this is a task which any school-boy, who had read Virgil or Ovid * would be competent to perform. He confines himself to discuss the evidence of Gellius, which it seems is brought forward to remove " Eurus from the point where it is *ever* stationed ... and in the place of the *south-east* he would place it in the eastern equinoctial point."

It is difficult to understand how any person who has read the Noctes *Atticæ* of Aulus Gellius could argue thus; for the authority brought forward by that writer is, in fact, that of the celebrated *Greek* philosopher Favorinus †, who is the

---

* " Confligunt Zephyrusque Notusque, et lætus Eois
  Eurus equis."—*Æn.* ii. 417.

" Eurus ad Auroram, Nabathæaque regna recessit,
Persidaque, et radiis juga subdita matutinis.
Vesper, et occiduo quæ littora sole tepescunt,
Proxima sunt Zephyro; Scythiam septemque trionem
Horrifer invasit Boreas; contraria tellus
Nubibus assiduis, pluvioque madescit ab Austro."
            OVID. *Met.* i. 61.

" Nam modo purpureo vires capit Eurus ab ortu,
  Nunc Zephyrus sero vespere missus adest,
  Nunc gelidus sicca Boreas bacchatur ab Arcto,
  Nunc Notus adversa prælia fronte gerit."
            Amor. lib. ii. eleg. xi.

† Favorinus is the philosopher who allowed himself to be overcome in argument by the Emperor Adrian, excusing himself by saying—"Would you have me pretend to be wiser than the master of thirty legions?"

Lucian mentions him by name in "Damonax;" and alludes to him in "Eunuchus," in a way that cannot be mistaken, as " celebrated amongst the Greeks." Ακαδημαικος Ευνουχος εκ Κελτων ολιγον προ ημων ευδοκιμησας εν τοις Ἑλληνεσιν. Philostratus quotes him as a *Greek* authority, lib. iv.

principal personage of the Noctes. Let us enquire into the *invariable* practice of the Greeks. I admit that some Greek authorities did place Eurus in the south-east, others at the point of the horizon where the sun rises at the winter solstice; but it is quite easy to show that this was anything but the invariable practice of Greek writers. In point of fact it is rather the exception than the rule.

Homer places Eurus in the eastern cardinal point.* Strabo quotes Homer as an authority, and adds that " he keeps the proper order" (φυλαττει την οικειαν ταξιν, L. G. i. c. 2.). Strabo also makes it the opposite to west, speaking of a ship " sailing from west to east," he says, απο της δυσεως Ευρῳ πλεων. (lib. ii. c. 3.) Aristotle says it is the general name for easterly winds; οἱ ανεμοι απο Ανατολης συνεχεις Ευροι κεκληνται. (*De Mundo*, c. iv.) Musæus makes it one of the cardinal winds, and opposed to the west wind, Ζεφυρῳ δ' αντεπνεεν Ευρος. (v. 316.) Dionysius, the geographer, says, " Italy is bounded on the eastern side (Ευρον) by the Adriatic." Stobæus follows Aristotle (lib. i.); and Arrian, in his Periplus of the Euxine, uses it to express the wind at due

---

c. viii.) ; he is also quoted by Diog. Laert. as a *Greek* author; Gellius repeatedly mentions him as thinking, speaking, and writing in *Greek*. See lib. xvi. c. iii.; xiii. c. xxiv.; xiv. c. i., &c. "So much for Favorinus Fabulator," as Bryant says.

* Συν δ' Ευρος τε Νοτος τ' επεσε Ζεφυρος τε δυσαης,
Και Βορεης.   Odys. v. 295.

And

Αλλοτε μεν τε Νοτος Βορεη προβαλεσκε φερεσθαι,
Αλλοτε δ' αντ' Ευρος Ζεφυρῳ ειξασκε διωκειν.
Ib. 331.

DISSERTATION II.

ON THE ISLAND MELITA.

I now proceed to notice the arguments brought forward by Bryant and others in support of the opinion that it was the Illyrian, and not the African, Melita upon which St. Paul was shipwrecked.

Bryant, after concluding his remarks on the wind Euroclydon, proceeds thus : —

"Having thus dispatched, and I hope satisfactorily, what I first premised to take in hand, I come now to the second part, which was to ascertain the particular island upon which the Apostle Paul was shipwrecked. This, one would imagine, could be attended with no difficulty; for it is very plainly expressed that, after being tossed for some time in the Adria, they were at last cast upon the island Melite. The only question is, which is the sea called Adria, and what island can be found *in that sea* mentioned by such a name?" (p. 23.)

This is not a fair statement of the question; the author of the narrative does not say Melita was in Adria, but only that the ship was *driven through* Adria ($\delta\iota\alpha\phi\epsilon\rho\rho\mu\epsilon\nu\omega\nu$), after leaving Clauda, before she reached Melita. The real question is this. Was the sea which is interposed between Crete and Malta termed Adria when the narrative was written? for it is not denied by Bryant that this sea was known by the name of Adria afterwards. It is only necessary to cast a glance at the map of the Mediterranean to see that this part of it forms a natural geographical division. Major Rennel terms it, with much propriety, "the middle basin of the Mediterranean."* Now, this sea, as well as the gulf at present known by the same name, was then known as the Adriatic. The proof of this is very easily established. Ptolemy, who flourished immediately after St. Luke, describes this sea so often and so particularly by this name, as to leave the point without a shadow of doubt. With the accuracy of a geographer he distinguishes the *Gulf* of Adria from the *Sea* of Adria; thus, in enumerating the boundaries of Italy, he tells us that it is bounded on one side by the shores of the Gulf of Adria, and on the south by the shores of the Adria†, (lib.

---

* Humboldt calls it the Syrtic Basin. "More to the west we have the Ionian Sea, or the Syrtic Basin, in which Malta is situated."—*Kosmos, Sabine's Translation*, ii. 118. Procopius calls this basin the Adriatic Sea, and places Gaulos and Melita (Gozo and Malta) upon the verge of it, making them the boundary between it and the Tyrrhenian Sea on the west. "αραμενοι τε κατα ταχος τα ιστια, Γαυλῳ και Μελιτῃ ταις νησοις προσεσχον αἱ το τε Αδριατικον και Τυρρηνικον πελαγος διοριζουσιν." *Bel. Vand*, i. 14. Commentators gravely tell us that because Ptolemy calls Melita an African island it cannot be in the Adriatic sea.

† The only perplexing circumstance connected with Bryant's speculations on this subject is the fact, that he should have succeeded in persuading himself that St. Paul's ship was driven into the Gulf of Venice, as I believe he did. That he should have persuaded others by an array of one-sided evidence is not wonderful. Macknight, who has adopted his views, assigns this as his reason : he says, " In support of his opinion, Bryant cites ancient authors, who, in enumerating the Adriatic islands, mention Melite very particularly." (note, p. 128.) Mason the poet thus accounts for his self-deception: "He had been much engaged in antiquities, and consequently had imbibed too much of the spirit of a professed antiquary. Now we know from a thousand instances that no set of men are more willingly duped than these, especially by any thing that comes to them under the fascinating

iii. c. 1.) "ἀπο δε μεσημβριας τῃ τε του Αδριου παραλιῳ;" and that Sicily is bounded on the east by the sea of Adria, (Ib. cap. 4.) "απο δε ανατολων ὑπο του Αδριου πελαγους." He further informs us that Italy is bounded on the south by the Adriatic Sea" (Ib. c. 15.), that the Peloponnesus is bounded on the west and south by the Adriatic Sea (Ib. cap. 16.), and that Crete is bounded on the west by the Adriatic Sea (Ib. cap. 17.).

Here, then, we have the bounds of this sea, which Ptolemy sometimes calls Adria, sometimes the sea of Adria, and sometimes the Adriatic Sea, laid down with such precision, that it is difficult to understand how it could be made a question; and those who have not read Bryant's work must be puzzled to guess how he disposes of such proofs. The answer is that, although he adduces the authority of Ptolemy often enough when it answers his purpose, he passes over those parts of the work which bear directly on the question in total silence! I will, as in the case of his observations on Euroclydon, allow Bryant to state his own case: —

"The grand difficulty, and, indeed, an insurmountable one, lies here; that, as *St. Paul says* expressly that the island he was cast upon was in the *Adria, Malta*, to be proved the place spoken of, must be made an *Adriatic* island. To effect this the learned *Bochart* labours hard. He shows that the sea we are speaking of encroached upon the *Ionian*, — that it extended itself to the *Sinus Corinthiacus;*

---

form of a new discovery." The patronising manner in which Bryant excuses the erroneous views, as he holds them to be, of such writers as Bentley, Grotius, Beza, Bochart, Cluverius, is amusing: the field they were conversant in was so ample, that "a person of the most extensive knowledge might sometimes be bewildered and lost " (p. 65.) It is to be hoped that the school of antiquarians to which he belonged has now passed away.

then, in order, it engrossed the Sicilian sea and the Cretan: and thus, advancing step by step, he includes Malta within its verge; makes the coast of Africa washed by its waves, and would persuade you that Leptis, in Agro Tripolitano, was situated upon the Adriatic coast. All this he does upon the authority of the poets and a few later historians.

"As for the poets, their evidence is not worth taking notice of; they make every thing subservient to measure. Yet, even of these, nothing he quotes comes up to his purpose. The learned writer makes use of their trespasses, merely to prepare the reader for what is to come, that he may not be too much shocked by the violence of the after evidence. What Ovid and Tibullus say is only preparative. Philostratus and Pausanias come but half way; those that speak to the purpose are Procopius, Orosius, and Æthicus. These are they that advance the Adriatic to the confines of Barca; and by the same proceeding might make Carthage itself, if they pleased, an appendage to Ragusa.

"But we ought to enquire of what rank and of what age the writers are whose authority he appeals to; * * * doubtless writers of some eminence in their several times, so let them have their due; who lived, however, many centuries after the fact we are determining; so that all you can learn from their evidence in respect to St. Paul and his shipwreck, is how things were called four or five hundred years afterwards; this is the utmost it will amount to."— (P. 26.)

It would be difficult to string together a greater tissue of blunders even from Bryant's writings. Yet, with the exception of those mentioned in the foregoing paragraphs, he has not noticed one of the authorities adduced by Bochart*, whom he undertakes to refute.

Let us examine his statement in detail. It begins with the double blunder of supposing St. Paul the author of the Acts, and that it is expressly said in the narrative

---

* See Bochart's observations on this subject, Appendix

" that the island he was cast upon was in the Adria; the next assertion is that Bochart confines his authorities to the poets and a few later historians. The poets are easily disposed of, " they make everything subservient to measure." Let us, therefore, pass to the later historians. He says in one place that they are not to be believed because they " lived four or five hundred years," in another, " many centuries," after the fact.

The first question to be determined here, is the date of the fact, When did St. Luke write the account of the shipwreck? Without entering very minutely into the inquiry as to its date, I think it probable that it was written A. D. 63. Now two of Bochart's authorities, Ptolemy and Pausanias *, were contemporaries of Adrian, who was born A. D. 76. We do not know the dates of their births, but the chances are two to one against the supposition that they were both younger than the emperor. One of these authors, and it is immaterial which, was probably born about the time when St. Luke wrote, or very soon afterwards. The supposition that either of them invented the

* Ptolemy has recorded an eclipse observed by him in the eighth of Adrian (A. D. 125.), (Almagest, lib. iv. c. 9.): and Pausanias speaks of that emperor as living when he wrote. He relates the legend of the fountain of Arethusa, which is said to be the river Alpheus, which flows under the Adria from Greece to Ortygia (Syracuse), μηδε Αδριας επισχησειν αυτον του προσω, " Nor can the Adria restrain its flowing on; " (Arcadica, lib. viii.) and speaks of the Straits of Messina as communicating with the Adriatic and Tyrhenian seas (Eliaca, l. v.). Solinus does the same; he says, " sunt et alteri montes duo (in Sicilia) Nebrodes et Neptunus, e Neptuno specula est in pelagus Tuscum et Adriaticum " (Polyhistor, 6. xi.). Camertinus thinks that this author was a contemporary of Pliny, whom he abridged: " suspicor vivente adhuc Plinio opusculum hoc suum scripsisse " (Vita Solini).

name does not require notice. But in point of fact there is ample evidence that this name was given to the lower sea, between Crete and Malta, long before either of them wrote. Like the seas in modern times, this sea had different names. It was called the Ionian, the Sicilian, and the Adriatic. Bryant is at pains to extract passages from ancient authors, who used other names than the Adriatic, and, as might have been expected from such a line of argument, proves a great deal too much. If his arguments be good for anything, there was no such sea at all as the Adria. This he admits in a note, apparently unconscious that it destroys his own case. The note is as follows:—

"The truth is, Appian calls the whole sinus the Ionian Gulf: and not only Appian, but Dio, in lib. 41., and Herodian do the same; so far from extending the Adriatic to Sicily or Malta, they do not seem to allow that such a sea existed."—Note, p. 33.

I proceed to Bryant's next argument, which I will state in his own words:—

"It is observable, that in speaking of the natives, the sacred writer never calls them Μελιταιοι or Νησιωται, but βαρβαροι. The ancient Greeks called all nations that were not of Grecian origin indiscriminately *barbarians*. This continued for a long time; but after they had been conquered by the Romans, and, as it were, beat into good manners, they by degrees laid aside their saucy distinction, and were more complaisant to their neighbours. Hence we find that Polybius, Diodorus, and others, who wrote after the decline of the Grecian power, seldom made use of the distinction, unless the people they treat of are notorious for their ferity or rudeness. But supposing a Grecian writer might continue this partial distinction, and look upon every country but his own as barbarous, yet St. Paul cannot be supposed to have acted so. He was no *Greek*, but a *Jew* of *Tarsus*, and in the same predicament as those that are spoken of.

"Whenever the Apostle calls a people barbarous, you may be sure it was the real character of the nation."—(P. 39.)

We have here again the blunder of supposing St. Paul the author of the Acts, and the still greater one of supposing that St. Paul would only have applied the term barbarian to people " notorious for ferity and rudeness." St. Paul repeatedly uses the word; but upon no one occasion does he use it in the sense which Bryant supposes he would, or in a sense inapplicable to the ancient inhabitants of Malta in contradistinction to the Greeks. The Melitans were not Greeks, therefore they were barbarians. (Rom. i. 14.) If they did not understand the language of him who addressed them, then each party would be barbarous to the other. (1 Cor. xiv. 11.) The natives would not understand their visitors, therefore they were barbarians.

Bryant is at great pains to contrast the civilisation of the antient inhabitants with that of the Illyrian Melitans. He tells us, that according to Diodorus Siculus, and others,

"*Melite Africana* was first a colony of *Phœnicians*, and was afterwards inhabited successively by Carthaginians, Greeks, and Romans. Who will be so hardy as to denominate any of these nations barbarous?"

The answer to this question is not difficult; nobody called the Greeks barbarians, but Scylax calls the Phœnicians barbarous*, and Polybius makes one of his speakers, a

---

* Scylax places the Phœnicians amongst the inhabitants of Sicily, who are barbarians. "Εν δε Σικελια εθνη βαρβαρα τα δε εστιν, Εδυνοι, Σικανοι, Σικελοι, Φοινικες, Τρωες."—*Periplus*, p. 4.

Greek, call both the Carthaginians and Romans barbarians.*

In his anxiety to vindicate the ancient Maltese from the charge of barbarism he actually quotes the Acts to show that the term did not even apply to the lower orders — again unconscious that he was overturning his own argument, by admitting that it was the Maltese who received them hospitably.

"But it is said that some of the lower sort might still be rude and savage, though the people of rank were otherwise. But St. Paul experienced nothing but civility from the lower sort, nay, ου την τυχουσαν φιλανθροπιαν, uncommon civility, as *he himself witnesses*. Therefore, if the common people are civil and humane, and their superiors polite and ingenious, a general imputation of barbarism can never square with that nation. In short, take them separately or collectively, this stain is incompatible with the natives of Malta."— (P. 42.)

The next argument is, that there are no vipers in Malta; but St. Luke mentions that one fixed itself on St. Paul's hand. (v. 3.) Bryant does not dwell much upon this, but Giorgi lays considerable stress upon it, and Dr. Falconer † does the same. Both of these writers attribute the pre-

---

* Agalaus of Naupactus advises the Greeks not to fight with each other, but unite to resist the barbarians (the Romans and Carthaginians). Hist. lib. v. 104.

† "The circumstance of the viper or poisonous snake that fastened on St. Paul's hand merits consideration. Father Giorgi, an ecclesiastic of Melita Adriatica, who has written upon that subject, suggests very properly that as there are now no serpents in Malta, and as it should seem were none in the time of Pliny, that there never were any there. The country being dry and rocky, and not affording shelter or proper nourishment for animals of that description. But Meleda abounds with these reptiles, being woody and damp, and favourable to their way of life and propagation."—*Falconer*

sence of these animals in Meleda to the moisture of the climate, caused by its woods, "densissimas habet silvas," (Giorgi)* and their absence from Malta to its aridity. I am not disposed to call this in question.

At present Malta is entirely clear of wood, and its surface is in the most artificial state; but when St. Paul visited the island this was not the case, for there are still a few ancient carouba trees — evidently the remains of former woods. We have therefore sufficient cause for such a change in the Fauna as will account for the disappearance of this species of reptiles, as already noticed in the account of the voyage.

Bochart says, that as the ship in which St. Paul sailed from Melita was on her voyage from Egypt to Puteoli, we cannot suppose she would winter at the Illyrian Melita, if she did, she must have gone much out of her way, "toto salo aberrasse." Bryant meets this with the case of Lucian's ship which was driven to Athens. He says,

"Upon Bochart's principle one might argue that this ship, coming to Africa and the Piræeus must be a mistake, for it was certainly Malta that it arrived at, because Attica is quite out of the way for any ship to touch at that is bound from the Nile to the Tiber, — 'Toto cœlo et toto salo errant,' &c. But ships that lose their passage cannot always choose their retreat, they are at the will of the winds, and are sped in all directions."—8vo. edit. p. 412.

But there is no parallelism whatever in the cases: ships crossing the Ægean, as this ship was, may meet with a southerly gale and be driven to the north. Every reader

* Giorgi consulted Vallisneri, a celebrated naturalist, who proved by experiment that the earth of Malta was no protection against the bite of a viper.

of Falconer's Shipwreck must be familiar with such a case;
the ship was driven from Crete towards Athens: —

"Now, through the parting waves, impetuous bore,
The scudding vessel stemmed the Athenian shore;"

but, less fortunate than that of Lucian, was wrecked on
the coast of Attica. But if we are to believe that Adria
means the Gulf of Venice, then we must suppose that by
some means or other almost every ship coming from the
Levant, to the west side of Italy, found its way into it.
We hear of four cases of ships in this predicament all about
the same time, possibly in the same year:— 1st. St.
Paul's ship. 2nd. The Castor and Pollux. 3rd. The ship
of Josephus which sank in Adria. 4th. The ship of
Cyrene which picked him up and carried him to Puteoli.*

The only other argument against the supposition that
Malta was the scene of the shipwreck which remains unanswered, is brought forward by Dr. Falconer, he says—

"The disease with which the father of Publius was affected (dysentery combined with fever) affords a presumptive evidence of the nature of the island. Such a place as Melita Africana (Malta), dry and rocky, and remarkably healthy, was not likely to produce a disease which is almost peculiar to moist situations." (P. 21.)

It is obvious that the answer to the former argument
applies also to this one; but in point of fact, Dr. Galland
of Valetta informs me that the disease is by no means uncommon in Malta.

L'Avocat†, a French writer, merely repeats without

* Josephi Vita, edit. Hudsoni, p. 905.
† Dissertation Historique et Critique sur le Naufrage de St. Paul, dans laquelle on examine si c'est dans l'isle de Meleda qu'il fut mordu d'une vipère, et qu'il guérit miraculeusement le père de Publius.—1745.

adding anything to the arguments of Giorgi. He does not, however, as Bryant and Falconer have done, pass over the unequivocal testimony of Ptolemy in silence; he says—

"Ptolomée, qui n'a vécu que plus de 80 ans après St. Luc, est le premier qui a donné plus d'étendue á la Mer d'Adriatique au Golfe de Venise."—(P. 40.)

The answer to this is, that we do not know that Ptolemy lived even one year after St. Luke; neither was he the first who used it. I have already noticed his contemporary Pausanias, who also used it, and, as Major Rennel observes, "changes of names in geography take place very gradually, and almost imperceptibly."* But Josephus who made the same voyage, and probably in the same year, if not the year before, tells us in his life that his ship sank in the Adria †, and that he and others were picked up by a ship of Cyrene and carried to Puteoli. The events related by Josephus could not have happened in the Gulf. Ovid repeatedly calls this sea Adria ‡, and Horace places Actium on Adria.§

* Father Giorgi admits that after the time of Ptolemy the name of Adria was almost universally adopted; he answers the question: ' Cur autem, si universi antea geographi secus docuerat, nova hæc atque insolens opinio non per gradus sed quasi uno impetu deinceps apud scriptores invaluerit?" by attributing it to the celebrity of Ptolemy.

† Dr. Gray supposes that Josephus was in St. Paul's ship! Connection of Sacred and Profane Literature.—i. 362.

‡ Adriacumque patens late bimaremque Corinthum.
Fasti, lib. iv. 501.

Aut hanc me, gelidi tremerem cum mense Decembris,
Scribentem mediis Adria vidit aquis;
Aut, postquam biinarem cursu superavimus Isthmon,
Alteraque est nostræ sumta carina fugæ.
Trist. lib. i. Eleg. 12.

§   Actia pugna,

There is another modern writer who takes the same side of the question who is entitled at least to the merit of originality. In a modern French work entitled, "L'Univers," M. La Croix, the author of the account of Malta, tells us —

"Qu'on remarque bien qu'il avait fait halte dans un port de la côte *septentrionale* de Candie : "

that the wind Euroclydon is —

" suivant Pline, Vitruve, Aristotle, et Strabon, un vent qui tient le milieu entre le midi et le levant; c'était donc, pour parler le langage moderne, un vent de sud-est, ou ce qu'on nomme dans la Méditerranée le sirocco. Sur ce point il ne peut y avoir un ombre de doute."

He then asks,

" Dira-t-on que l'Ecriture Sainte a pu confondre la mer de Sicile, où est située Malte, avec la Mer Adriatique? Une telle supposition est inadmissable. D'abord, Malte est très-eloignée de la Mer Adriatique; ensuite cette mer n'a jamais eu d'autres bornes que celles que les géographes lui assignent aujourd'hui ; elle a toujours été deux cents lieues de longueur sur quarante dans sa plus grande largeur; dimensions sur lesquelles s'accordent Pline, Strabon, et Thucydide."

The information that Fair Havens is on the *north side* of Crete; that Pliny, Vitruvius, Aristotle, and Strabo tell us the direction of Euroclydon; and that Pliny, Strabo, and Thucydides tell us that the Adriatic never had other boundaries than its present, requires confirmation. M. La

Te duce, per pueros hostili more refertur ;
Adversarius est frater; lacus, Adria.
Epist. lib. i. Ep. xviii. ver. 61.

Croix cannot understand how, if Malta had been the island, St. Paul could have been delayed three months. The island, wherever it was, he says, must have been "bien peu frequentée par les navigateurs, ce que n'a jamais été vrai pour Malte;" he should have added, not even in winter. It would be a waste of words to answer such arguments.

DISSERTATION III.

ON THE SHIPS OF THE ANTIENTS.

THERE are few branches of classical antiquity of which so little is known as that which relates to ships, navigation, and seamanship; no work written expressly on those subjects by any antient author has come down to us [*], and the scattered notices which we meet with in historians and poets often tend to mislead. The representation of antient ships are in a great measure confined to coins and marbles, where we cannot expect to find accuracy of detail, except in detached parts, such as the aplustra or head and stern ornaments, rudders, anchors, &c.

There are, however, two circumstances to which we are indebted for much valuable information respecting the very class of ships with which we are at present chiefly concerned.

The Emperor Commodus, during a season of scarcity, imported grain from Africa; in commemoration of which a series of coins (great and middle brass) was struck, bearing upon the reverse figures of ships under sail; and one of the Alexandrian wheat ships was driven, by stress

---

[*] The Emperor Leo, in his Tactics, in treating περι ναυμαχιας, makes the same complaint. He says he could find nothing written on the subject by the antients.

of weather, into the Piræus. The extraordinary size of this vessel excited much curiosity on the part of the Athenians; and Lucian, who visited her, lays the scene of his dialogue, entitled "The Ship or Wishes" (Πλοιον η Ευχαι), on board of her; in the course of which we learn, incidentally, many interesting circumstances regarding the ship, her voyage, and management.

The marbles and paintings of Herculaneum and Pompeii also afford valuable details, and have the advantage of synchronising perfectly with the voyage of St. Paul, the catastrophe to which they owe their preservation having happened less than twenty years after his shipwreck.

As all these authorities agree very well with each other, we can derive from them what we may consider a tolerably correct idea of a merchant ship of the period.

The forepart of the hull below the upper works differed but little in form from that of the ships of modern times; and as both ends were alike, if we suppose a full built merchant ship of the present day cut in two, and the stern half replaced by one exactly the same as that of the bow, we shall have a pretty accurate notion of what these ships were. The sheer or contour of the top of the sides was nearly straight in the middle, but curving upwards at each end, the stem and stern posts rising to a considerable height, and terminated by ornaments which were very commonly the head and neck of a water-fowl bent backwards. This was called the cheniscus (χηνισκος). It forms the stern ornament of the ship on the tomb of Nævoleia Tyche at Pompeii, the stern post of which terminates with the head of Minerva. Lucian, in describing the Alexandrian ship, mentions that the stern rose gradually in a curve surmounted by a golden cheniscus, and that the prow was elevated in a similar manner. In the coins of Commodus we find the cheniscus, in some instances, at the head, and, in others, at the stern.

The bulwarks round the deck appear to have generally been open rails. There were projecting galleries at the bow and stern. The stern gallery is often covered with an awning, as in the ship on the tomb of Nævoleia. The galleries at the bow served, as it would appear from Lucian's description, as places where to stow the anchors and also the στροφεια and περιαγωγεις. The exact meaning of these terms is not clear. Some think they meant instruments for heaving up the anchors, others for helping the ship round. I think it not improbable that both were meant. The στροφεια, "winders," were probably windlasses or capstans. We have evidence that both were used by the antients, for in the ship of Theseus, represented in one of the paintings found at Herculaneum, we see a capstan with a hawser coiled round it*; and in a figure of the ship of Ulysses, said to be taken from an ancient marble, in the edition of Virgil, 3 vols. fol., Rome, 1765, we see the cable coiled round a windlass. The περιαγωγεις, "drive abouts," were probably paddles for the purpose of helping the ship round, when "slack in the stays."

The ancient ships were not steered, as those in modern time are, by rudders hinged to the stern-post, but by two great oars or paddles (πηδαλια), one on each side of the stern: hence the mention of them in the plural number by St. Luke; a circumstance which has caused, as Dr.

---

* See figure of this ship, *ante*, page 95.

Bloomfield observes, "no little perplexity to commentators."* But no sea-going vessel had less than two rudders, although small boats and river craft, such as those on the Nile, were sometimes steered by one. Dr. Bloomfield is at the very unnecessary trouble of quoting a

* Note to Acts xxvii. 40. This is scarcely to be wondered at, at least by those who have had recourse to the most obvious sources of information —the writers de re navali antiquâ. Berghaus, the most voluminous, and, I believe, the most laborious writer on the subject, has given a restoration of the after-part, "Hintertheile," of St. Paul's ship, with a square stern, a single hinged rudder, with the tiller pointing aft, and with rudder bands with dead eyes spliced into the ends! about as like an ancient ship as a Chinese junk is to an English yacht. The work of this author, which is entitled "Geschichte der Schiffartskunde der Vornehmsten der Alterthums," 8vo. Leipzic, 1792, is in three ponderous volumes (1670 pp.), scarcely a page of which is not fortified by an array of authorities, all of which, he tell us, he has verified ("habe ich meines Wissens kein Citatum von andern auf treu und glauben unternommen, ohne von der Richtigkeit desselben überzeugt zu seyn." Vorrede, xxiv.). As may be supposed, he has carefully preserved all the blunders of his predecessors; his anchors have no stocks, and the artemon is set at the mast-head. This author is fairly outdone in absurdity by M. le Roy, author of "Mémoires sur la Marine des Anciens," Hist. de l'Acad. des Inscript., tom. xxxvii.; of "Nouvelles Recherches sur les Navires des Anciens," Mém. de l'Institute, tom. i.; and of "Les Navires des Anciens considérés par rapport à leurs Voiles," 8vo, Par. 1783. M. le Roy has undertaken to explain the difficulties attending the description of the ship of Ptolemy Philopator, given by Athenæus; amongst others we are told by that author that she took twelve hypozomes (undergirders) with her (ὑποζώματα δε ελαμβανε δωδεκα); this he renders, "Il avoit douze ponts ou étages," twelve decks or platforms! but the most amusingly absurd part of his writings is his work on the sails of antient ships,—a full-rigged ship. according to him, had a lateen sail at the bow (le dolon); the main-sail (l'acatian) is, in his representation, triangular with the apex below; farther aft than this was another lateen sail (l'artemon), and at the stern another lateen sail (l'épidrome). M. le Roy had a boat rigged in this manner, and found she could both tack and turn to windward. Probatum est.

passage from Orpheus to prove, what was in fact the universal practice, that large ships had two rudders, and that it is —

"Probable they were regularly taken off when the ship was in port and laid in dock. But the question is, *how* and *where* were they fixed on? Many (as Alberto, Bishop Pearce, and Kuinoel) think that the rudders were one at the stern and the other at the bow of the ship; while others suppose both to have been at the stern. I know not, however, of the numerous passages cited by the above commentators, any one that *determines* this point; but that which I have adduced from Orpheus undoubtedly does — namely, as we have seen that they were both at the stern."

Writers are not in the habit of telling what every one knows. I question if I could prove, by a quotation, that the rudders in English ships are at the stern; but every representation — and they are numerous — shows us that those of the antients were there. Commentators who suppose that the two rudders in sailing ships were, one at the head and one at the stern ("unum in prora alterum in puppi" — *Kuinoel*), have been misled by a passage in Tacitus (An. ii. 6.) who is not describing sailing vessels, but flat-bottomed boats on the Rhine, which were to be moved by the current, and had a rudder at each end, just as river boats of the same description have at the present day, in which the antient paddle rudders are retained. With regard to the question how they were fixed, the answer is, that they were not fixed any more than other oars are. In small vessels they rested in a notch, or rowlock, in the upper gunwale, and were secured by a tropoter, or leathern thong, or by an iron clamp. Instances of both modes of retaining the rudder in its place may be seen on Trajan's Column. In those vessels which had projecting gangways, or stern galleries, the rudders were often passed through them.* Some larger vessels had a rudder case fixed on the outside, on each quarter. In others the wales of the ship projected far enough from the side at the stern to allow space for the rudder to pass through them. This may be observed in the ship on the Tomb of Naevoleia Tyche at Pompeii †; but the most common way was to have rudder ports at each quarter, as in the ship of Theseus (see figure at page 131.). These also served for hawseholes, when the ship was anchored by the stern.

This mode of steering was retained till a comparatively late period. In a bass-relief over the doorway of the leaning tower of Pisa, built in the twelfth century, ships are represented with the paddle rudders, as are those in the Bayeux tapestry, representing the Norman invasion. They must have been in use till after the middle of the thirteenth century, for in the contracts to supply Louis IX. with ships, the contractors are bound to furnish them with two rudders (duos timones).‡ This may no doubt mean a spare one, but we learn from Joinville that the

---

* There is a bronze model of a ship under sail in the Grand-ducal gallery at Florence, with the rudders fitted in this manner. See also the figures of galleys on the coins of Adrian, *post*.

† In the Peregrinatio ad terram Sanctam of Breydenbach, Ven. 1486, in which the details of the figures of ships are extremely correct, we have the figure of a ship in the transition state, in respect to her rudders. She has a hinged rudder, but she has also a paddle rudder slung at her side, passing through the wales, as in the above example. See View of Modon.

‡ Archæologie Navale, ii. 388.

king's ship had rudders expressed in the plural "Gouvernaus" (ch. 78.).

By the middle of the following century we find the hinged rudders on the gold noble of Edward III. The change in the mode of steering must, therefore, have taken place about the end of the thirteenth, or early in the fourteenth century.

With regard to the dimensions of the ships of the antients, some of them must have been quite equal to the largest merchantmen of the present day. The ship of St. Paul had, in passengers and crew, 276 persons on board, besides her cargo of wheat; and as they were carried on by another ship of the same class, she must also have been of great size. The ship in which Josephus was wrecked contained 600 people. But the best account we have of the size of some of these ships is that which I have already alluded to as given by Lucian, on the authority of the carpenter ($ναυπηγος$) of the Isis, the Alexandrian wheat ship, which was driven by contrary winds to Athens. Both Bryant* and Dr. Falconer adduce this ship as an example of the great size of vessels of the class to which she belonged; but both of them exaggerate her dimensions to an absurd degree. Bryant compares her with the Royal George, which was at that time probably the largest ship in the British navy, the dimensions of which he gives; but, with his usual inaccuracy, he makes the breadth of the antient ship one third, in place of one fourth of her length, or nine feet broader, instead of six feet narrower, than the Royal George. Dr. Falconer

---

* Bryant's Observations, p. 16.

corrects this error, but falls into one nearly as great; for, in calculating her tonnage, he multiplies by the length given by Lucian, which is evidently the extreme, instead of by the length of the keel, which was till lately the rule, and is the only one applicable in cases where the only dimensions given are length and breadth. The consequence of calculating in this manner is, that he increases her tonnage by at least one half, making it more than 1900 tons, whereas it must have been less than 1300. The rule by which the tonnage of the Royal George was computed, was to multiply the length of keel* by the extreme breadth, and the product by half the breadth for depth, and divide the whole by 94. Dr. Falconer has made the ship of Lucian to measure 1938 tons. Her length, according to Lucian, was 120 cubits, which, at a foot and a half each, is 180 feet; her breadth one fourth, or 45 feet. Now, it is evident, that Dr. Falconer has calculated in the manner I suppose: for if we take the extreme length, 180 feet, as the multiplier, the tonnage is exactly what he makes it, $\frac{180 \times 45 \times 22.5}{94} = 1938$ tons.

Although we have no means of knowing the length of this ship's keel, we may, from the dimensions given by Lucian, form an estimate of her relative size, as compared with any other ship, the dimensions of which are known. I take the Royal George, as the ship these authors compare her with, and the dimensions of that ship, as given by Bryant, which appear to be correct; but as the height is given in one case to the taffrail, and in the other to the

* As the fore part of the keel joins the stem-post in a curve, in order to obviate uncertainty it was measured as far as the perpendicular of the length on deck, and three-fifths of the breadth of beam deducted for the fore-rake

upper deck, I take one half of the breadth for the depth, which is the usual rule for computation, in both cases. Hence,

$$\text{Royal George } 212\cdot75 \times 51 \times 25\cdot = 276681$$
$$\text{Isis, Lucian's ship, } 180 \times 45 \times 22\cdot5 = 182250$$

This is in the ratio of 2000 tons to 1320; if, therefore, the keel of the antient ship was as long in proportion to her extreme length as that of the Royal George, she would measure upwards of 1300 tons, but we know that the antient ships had projections at each end, much greater than in modern ships, and, as they are not included in the measurement for tonnage, they must be deducted: that at the prow of the one in question is distinctly mentioned by Lucian. In the Navicella at Rome the keel is only about half the extreme length.

Perhaps an early built English ship, when the antient " beak head," or projection forward, was still retained, will give the most correct idea of her proportions. We have a very particular account of the Royal Sovereign [*], or, as she was called during the Commonwealth, " The Sovereign of the Seas." Her length is stated to be " a prora ad puppim, 232 foote," the length of the keel 120 feet.

---

[*] See account of her, bearing the title, " The Commonwealth's great ship, commonly called the Sovereign of the Seas, built in the year 1637, with a true and exact account of her bulk and burden, and those decorements which beautify and adorn her, with the carving work, figures and mottoes upon them. She is besides her tonnage, 1637 tons in burden; she beareth five lanthorns, the biggest of which will hold ten persons to stand upright, without shouldering or pressing on one another, with the names of all the ropes, masts, sails, and cordage that belong unto a ship." 4to. Lon. 1653.

If the keel of the antient ship bore the same proportion to her length, "a prora ad puppim," which this one did, it would be only 99 feet, and the tonnage, calculated by its length, instead of the extreme length, would be 1015 tons. Taking the mean of the two results, it is probable that the ship of Lucian would measure between eleven and twelve hundred tons. Although, therefore, her dimensions are not so wonderful as former calculations make them, they were equal to those of a large modern merchant-vessel. We need not, therefore, be surprised at the numbers we sometimes hear of as being carried in antient ships.

From every representation which has come down to us, as well as from every notice in authors, they appear to have been rigged with extreme simplicity. They depended for progression upon a single square sail, all the other sails which we hear of being subsidiary. It is evident that this was the case in Lucian's ship, notwithstanding her unusual size. We hear of his friends looking up with wonder on the magnitude of the mast and yard; the sail therefore must have been furled aloft. We hear, indeed, in another part of the same dialogue, of ships with three sails ($\tau\rho\iota\alpha\rho\mu\epsilon\nu\alpha$*), but we are not told whether they

---

* Lucian has mentioned a circumstance which has perplexed commentators, and which I do not pretend to explain: he speaks of "looking up and counting the piles of hides" ($\alpha\nu\alpha\beta\lambda\epsilon\pi o\nu\tau\epsilon s\ \alpha\rho\iota\theta\mu o\upsilon\nu\tau\epsilon s\ \tau\omega\nu\ \beta\upsilon\rho\sigma\omega\nu\ \tau\alpha s\ \epsilon\pi\iota\beta o\lambda\alpha s$), or rather the rows of hides placed above each other. Scheffer supposes that by hides the author means sails, which, he says, "ex corio pellibusque primum facta videntur. Nomen indicare potest, est enim velum a vellere, id est pelle, ut Varro docet." (p. 141.) He translates the above passage "sursum spectantes numerantes vela alia aliis imposita," adding

OF THE ANTIENTS. 183

were set upon separate masts, or one above another. From the manner in which they are mentioned, it is obvious that these three-sailed ships were of the largest size; we must conclude, therefore, that it was not a common circumstance to have so many as three principal sails. What may be considered, therefore, as the plain sails of an antient ship consisted of one great square sail, with a small one at the bow.

The following figure, taken from the Archæologie

Navale of M. Jal, from a marble in the Borghese collection at Rome, appears to give a good idea of the relative size

the following criticism on the Latin translation: "interpres ibi coria scripsit quod nullum habet sensum."

Captain Spratt, R. N., supposes, with Scheffer, that sails are meant: he writes me, "That passage of Lucian, ' looking up and counting the hides,' may be explained by supposing the sails to have been sometimes made of light hides sewn together . . . the thin flexible goat skins now tanned in the Levant would form excellent sails."

and position of the sails, except that the mainmast is evidently placed too near the bow.

We hear of other sails, but from the manner in which they are mentioned by Pliny*, we must suppose that they were considered as extra sails. Julius Pollux calls " the great and proper mast " (ὁ μεγας και γνησιος ἱστος) the acatian: he adds, however, that some give that name to the smallest. Xenophon †, on the other hand, calls the principal sails " the great sails," τα μεγαλα ἱστια, and the small ones acatia. The propriety of Xenophon's terms is confirmed by the Attic Tables, which speak of the acatia, in contradistinction to the great sails.

The name of the small sail at the bow of the vessel, or the fore-sail, has very generally been supposed to be the dolon. I believe, however, that this is a mistake, and that the name of this sail was the "artemon." As

---

* "Jam nec vela satis esse majora navigiis. Sed quamvis amplitudini antemnarum singulæ arbores sufficiant, super eas tamen addi velorum alia vela præterque alia in proris et alia in puppibus ac toto modio provocari mortem."—*Proem.* in lib. xix. This is surely a non sequitur; it could be no good reason for not setting more sail that single spars were sufficient for the size of the yards. Instead of "quamvis," the reading "cum vix" has been suggested. I am, however, satisfied that the word "non" has been dropped out, and that it ought to be read, " singulæ arbores *non* sufficiant." In point of fact, single spars are *not* sufficient for the great yards of the single-masted Mediterranean vessels of the present day; and we find, wherever the details are correctly given, that the same was the case in the middle ages, and in antient times. See the views in Breydenbach, and the ship on the tomb at Pompeii. Pliny's dislike of additional sails does not say much for his seamanship, although he died in command of a fleet; it proves, however, that they were only occasionally used.

† Xenophon, in the Hellenica (lib. vi.), speaking of the manner in which Iphicrates exercised his crews, says, he left "the great sails," τα μεγαλα ἱστια, and took the small ones, ακατια.

this is the name of the sail stated by St. Luke to have been hoisted when the ship was run ashore, and as lexicographers and translators differ as to the meaning of the word, I shall endeavour to ascertain what is its true meaning, by adducing all the evidence I have been able to discover on the subject.

The word artemon (αρτεμων) does not occur in any antient Greek author, except in St. Luke's account of St. Paul's voyage; neither does it occur in any mediæval Greek author. It is, however, still used in the French nautical vocabulary, to designate the sail at the stern (the mizen, or, in modern language, the mizen trysail). Hence the French translators, by using the word " artimon," give it that meaning. In our authorised version it is rendered " mainsail." In Wyclif's it is " a litil sail." Dr. Bloomfield considers it to be " the foresail." It is, however, most commonly supposed to be the same as the supparum or topsail.* Böckh supposes it to be the highest of all the sails, equivalent to the modern top-gallant-sail. He says, "there was also, above the upper sail (obern Segel), a third smaller sail, which is doubtless the artemon."† Alciati supposes it " the bonnet," or addition to a sail, which can be removed. Papias Vocabulista makes it a storm-sail ‡, &c. It has also been supposed to mean the

* Αρτεμων, Supparum das ober am Mast hing."—*Berghaus.* See also Schneider, ad verb.; Scheffer, p. 140, &c.

† "Ausser der untern und obern Segeln der beiden Masten liess sich gewiss auch ein drittes kleineres anbringen; und dieses ist ohne Zweifel der Artemon."—p. 140.

‡ " Artemon, velum navis breve, quod quia melius levari potest in summo periculo extendit malus et antenna."

mast, the yard, the rudder, the vane at the mast head, the main block, &c.; but it is unnecessary to take these latter suppositions into consideration, as they are manifestly untenable. We learn from Isidore of Seville that the artemon was a sail, and the question is which sail was it? I shall endeavour, in the first place, to point out what sails it was not.

Professor Böckh says very decidedly (ohne Zweifel) that it was the highest sail of all, but does not give his reasons, as being foreign to his object, the artemon not being mentioned in the Attic Tables (p. 140.) I presume, however, he derives them from the following passage in Scheffer:—" Nomina eorum (velorum) ex Polluce hæc sunt . . . artemon quod in fuso supra antemnam suspenditur."— *Milit. Naval.* (p. 140.)

Now, there can be no doubt but that if the artemon be suspended from the spindle at the mast-head, it must be the highest sail. Scheffer gives Pollux as his authority; but, upon turning to Pollux, we find that it is the *vane* (επισειων) at the mast-head he is speaking of, and not the artemon. Scheffer had looked at the Latin translation, which is, " Et quod supra antemnam est fusus nominatur, a qua parte *artemonem* suspendunt," and not at the original, which is τον επισειοντα, the streamer or vane, so called from its fluttering motion. The translator, ignorant of the meaning both of this word and artemon, has chosen to translate the one by the other, and Scheffer has adopted his blunder, and from him it has become traditional, and has been adopted by every succeeding writer " de re navali." Scheffer himself, however, became aware of his blunder, and explains it away, ingeniously, if not ingenuously, in the Addenda to his work. He says—

"Επισειων, id est tænia, seu velum ludens in aere . . . forte hoc este quod Artemona Isidorus ait, quia απαρτωσι του ατρακτου, ut Pollux loquitur, dirigit sane navem quia ex ejus situ gubernatores ventum cognoscent!"

which is as much as to say that because the vane or streamer shows the direction of the wind, it must be synonymous with the artemon, which Isodore says was principally useful in directing ships. We may very safely reject this explanation of the word, which takes its rise in a blunder.

I come now to those who translate it the mizen or sail at the poop. The cause of this is obvious enough: the word artimon still exists in the French nautical vocabulary, and translators, not competent to determine whether it retains its original signification or not, have very naturally left the word unchanged. They have committed the same error which an English translator would do who should render the French word "misaine," the foresail, into "mizen," for there can be no doubt but that, in this case also, the words in both languages are originally the same, coming from the Italian mezzana*, middle size, in contradistinction to vela grande, although the mât de misaine has changed its place as well as the mât d'artimon. Before I show that such a change has taken place, I shall consider our English translation where it is rendered main-

---

* In Italian the mast at the stern (mizen) is Albero de mezzana.

sail, because the evidence which clears up this mistranslation explains the other also.

The English translators naturally consulted Bayfius, or De Baif, the earliest of the modern writers " de re navali," and probably the only one when the translation was made; he thus explains the word:

"Est autem artemon velum majus navis, ut in Actis Apost. xxvii. . . . etenim etiam nunc nomen Venetis vulgo retinent et Artemon vocant."

It appears, therefore, that, when this author wrote in the middle of the sixteenth century, the word was still in use at Venice as a marine term, and that it meant the velum majus, or *largest sail* in the ship. De Baif is good authority, because it appears that he had spent the three years preceding the publication of his work at Venice. But the largest sail of the Venetian vessels of the time was the *foresail.* The error, therefore, does not lie with him, but with the translation of velum majus into *mainsail.* The mainsail was at first, no doubt, the largest sail; but, in very many vessels, it has ceased to be so. In modern ships, it is smaller than the maintop-sail, and in many two-masted vessels, it is smaller than the foresail. Dr. Bloomfield, in his Note on the subject, states that "Bayfius, Junius, Alberti, and Wolf, explain it as the large sail of the poop, answering to our mizen-sail, and even yet called by the Venetians artemon." (Note on v. 40.) This, however, is a mistake: it was the largest sail in two-masted vessels of the period; but, instead of being at the poop, it was at the prow; it was in reality the *foresail.* The word, although formerly an Italian nautical term, has now become obsolete in that language. The Vocabolario della Crusca calls it

" la maggior vela che abbia la nave," and quotes Dante *
and Ariosto † as authorities. There is nothing in Dante
but a mere enumeration of terms ; but in the Commentary
of Landino upon that author, printed at Venice in 1493,
we find the following remark on the passage : " La minore,
terzeruolo, et una in mezzo delle due lequale si chiama la
mezza." This at least shows that it was not in the
middle of the vessel, or the mainsail, but at one end. The
terzeruolo is said to be the smallest sail ; in the modern
Italian nautical nomenclature, it means " a reef," or the
part of a sail tied up to reduce it. It is clear, then, that
if the artemon was neither the sail in the middle
nor the smallest sail, it must have been the foresail,
which was the largest sail in the vessel when Landino
wrote.

Ariosto, in the passage quoted in the Vocabolario, says
the artemon was cut away : —

> " Il padrone
> Fatto l' arbor tagliar dell' Artimone."

He says afterwards that, when the storm subsided,

> " La disiata luce di Sant' Ermo,
> Che *in prua* su un cocchina a por si venne,
> Che più non v' erano arbori nè antenne."—xix. 50.

---

* " Chi ribatte da proda, e chi da poppa,
Altri fa remi, et altri volge sarte ;
Chi terzeruolo et Artimon rintoppa."
Inferno, canto xxi. st. 5.

† " Di cui per men travaglio avea il padrone
Fatto l' arbor tagliar dell' artimone."
Orlando Fur. c. xix. st. 48.

> "Saint Ermo's light
> Low settling *on the prow* with ray serene
> It shone, for masts or sails no more were seen."
> *Hoole.*

The artemon was, therefore, according to Ariosto, the mast of the prow, for it was that mast which had been cut away.

The latest authority which I can find for the meaning of this word in Italian is in the " Dizionario di Marina," Venice, 1769. It does not occur in the dictionary itself; but, in the index, the reader is referred to " Trinchetta " as its synonyme. Now the trinchetta, in modern Italian, is the foresail; in the dictionary it is described as " vela triangulare che in alcuni bastimenti si pone nel davanti o a prua." I think this passage explains the reason why the French term artimon is applied to the sail at the stern. The foresail, antiently, was very often a triangular or lateen sail.* Latterly, and up till the end of the eighteenth century, the mizen was a triangular sail; when, therefore, the triangular sail was placed at the stern by the French, it retained the name which had been given to the triangular sail when placed at the bow. From the dimensions of the sails taken from the contracts of the Genoese with Louis IX. of France, to be afterwards quoted, it will be seen that the artemon, although placed at the bow, was in fact the largest sail. This is confirmed by one of the figures in the views of Breydenbach.† The ship in question is a

---

* " Artimon c'est une voile latine ou faite en tiers pointe à la difference des autres voiles qui sont quarées."—*Aubin, Dict. de Marine,* 1702.

† This ship is figured in Creuze's article on Ship-building, Encyc. Brit. 4th edit. See also another ship taken from the same view in Dibdin's Ædes Althorpianæ. Vol. iii. p. 222.

two-masted vessel, with the sails furled on the yards, the foremast being the largest. De Baif was, therefore, correct in saying that the artemon was the largest sail in the ship.

I come now to the ships of the middle ages, and avail myself of the documents published by M. Jal in his Archæologie Navale. From the Capitulaire Nautique, 1255, we have the following list of sails of ships of certain dimensions: —

"Navis de milliariis ccc usque DC in proda ita sit contata in velis, habeat artimonem terzarolem et dolonum, unum de fustagno vel de bombasio, et parpaglonem unum de canaveza. In medio habet majorem et dolonum de bombasio."— t. ii. p. 434.

Here we find the artemon at the prow (proda). The dolon is not, as generally supposed, confined to the prow, as we find one "in medio," on the middle or main-mast.

This is confirmed by certain contracts, entered into by the Genoese, to provide ships for Louis IX. In one of these, given by Jal (ii. 388), they are bound to supply two ships, each to have —

"Arborem unam de prorra (*sic*) longitudinis cubitorum quinquaginta unius, grossitudinis palmorum tredecem minus quarta . . . item arborem unam de medio longitudinis cubitorum quadraginta septem . . . Item debet habere vela sex cotoni infra scrip-tarum mensurarum, videlicet, *pro artimono* cubitorum sexaginta sex . . . . item velum unum de medio cubitorum quinquaginta octo."

Here the artemon is the largest sail, and belongs to the largest mast, which is the *foremast*, "arbor de prora."

According to Wetstein, there is in the " Versio Syra Posterior," on the margin, " artemon est stipes in capite," *i. e.* the mast at the head of the vessel; and in the antient Scholia on Juvenal, in the passage in the 12th satire, where he describes the disabled state of the ship of Catullus.

> "Vestibus extentis et quod superaverat unum
> Velo prora suo."

The scholiast observes, " Artemone solo velificaverunt." The artemon is not mentioned by Julius Pollux.

There is a passage in Isidore of Seville which would seem to imply that the name of the sail at the prow was dolon; and we are told by many writers that Pliny and Pollux give this sail the same name; but Pliny does not mention the dolon at all, and Pollux merely says that it is the smallest sail ($ὁ\ δε\ ελαττων\ δολων$.—i. 91.). The meaning of the passage in Isidore depends on the punctuation. It is as follows:—" Dolon est minimum velum et ad proram defixum. Artemo dirigendæ potius navis causa commendatum quam celeritate."—*Origines*, xix. 3. As it is pointed, this means that " the dolon is the smallest sail, and placed at the bow. The artemon rather for the purpose of directing the ship than for speed." I suspect, however, that it should be read thus—" The dolon is the smallest sail; and, placed at the bow, the artemon rather for directing the ship than for speed: " and that the authority of Isidore may be added to the others, to show that it is the foresail. It is, at all events, not contradictory to that of the authors I have quoted. Isidore is, however, by no means high authority on such a subject.

According to etymologists [*], the word is derived from αρταω, appendere, or αρτημα, an appendage. Now, knowing as we do, that the antients depended for speed upon one principal sail, an appendage or additional sail at the bow of the ship was required for the purpose of directing the vessel when in the act of putting about; for, although there could be no difficulty in bringing the ship's head to the wind with the great sail alone, a small sail at the bow would be indispensable for making her "pay off," that is, bringing her head round, otherwise she would acquire stern-way [†], and thereby endanger the rudders, if not the ship itself.

The annexed figure of an African corn-ship, from the reverse of a coin of the emperor Commodus, appears to give a good idea of the relative size and position of the two principal sails.[‡]

I am inclined to think that the etymology is a correct one, as Vitruvius uses the word to denote the "leading block" in a system of pullies. But this block forms no part of the purchase, but is a mere appendage used for the purpose of changing the direction of the force.

The sails were strengthened by bands of rope sewed

---

[*] See Calepenius, ad verb.

[†] If any of my readers have tried to heave a cutter to, with her square-sail set and kept aback, they will understand this; — haud inexpertus loquor.

[‡] Taken from a coin in the Museum at Avignon, by the author.

across them; so that if one part was rent, the injury would be confined to one compartment. This mode of strengthening sails appears to have been continued till a late period, as we find it in one of the figures in Breydenbach.*

In one of the coins of the emperor Commodus, representing a wheat-ship, we have this mode of strengthening the sails clearly expressed.†

The sail at the stern (ὁ κατοπιν) is called by Pollux, "epidromus" (ἐπίδρομος); and by Hesychius, "pharos,

---

* The modern practice of using canvas bands is, perhaps, no improvement on the ancient practice of using rope bands. A correspondent of the Nautical Magazine (1834, p. 87.), who signs himself Master of a British Merchant Ship, states, that in a long voyage his stock of spare canvas was expended, and he was forced to employ rope bands instead. This he found to answer perfectly well, and thinks it an improvement.

† Admiral Smyth observes with regard to this coin, that it "was struck, A. D. 186, and it testifies the care of Commodus in the frumentarean supply. He established a company of merchants, and a fleet for conveying corn from Africa to Rome, to guard against any misfortunes that might befall the ships which transported it from Egypt. As this was a good act, his inflated vanity on the occasion shall pass uncensured."—No. 294. of *Admiral Smyth's Collection*, p. 161. of his Catalogue.

and the smallest" (φαρον και ελασσον, art. επιδρομον). Pliny also mentions that there was a sail at the stern, and we frequently see a mast there, as in the above figure; but I have seen no representation of one with a sail set upon it.

The next class of sails are the Suppara, or topsails. Isidore describes them as having only one sheet*, *i. e.* the rope which extends the foot of the sail, and named in Latin pes veli (Gr. πους)†. This would imply that the sail was triangular, attached to a yard with the apex undermost. This seems so strange a mode of setting a triangular sail as to be almost incredible. It would appear, however, that in the middle ages such topsails were actually in use; for in an old collection of views in the Knights' Library, at Malta, printed about the beginning

---

* "Siparum, genus veli unum pedem habens, quo juvari navigia solent in navigatione quoties vis venti languescit; de quo Lucanus:—

'Summaque pandens
Suppara velorum perituras colligit auras.'"
Origines, lib. xix. c. iii

† Commentators and translators have no difficulty as to the meaning of πους, or pes veli, the rope which extends the lower corner of the sail to the side of the ship, Anglicè, "the sheet;" but they are puzzled with προπους, or "propes." Böckh supposes it the lower end of the rope, or that which was fastened to the ship's side: "Untern Ende der Schote, und wurden am Schiffe befestigt."—*Urkunde*, p. 154. I can see no difficulty in the matter; all large square sails must have two ropes at each lower corner of the sail, one to draw it aft, and the other to draw it forward; the former is called the *sheet*, the latter the *tack*. Now προπους, or "propes," is obviously the *tack*, it would naturally be called the fore-sheet, but that is appropriated to the sheet of the foresail: with the antients, both ropes were called ποδες, "sheets;" thus Aristotle, describing the shifting of a sail, says, το δε προς την πρωραν ποδιαιον ποιησαμενοι εφιασιν (Mechan. 8.), hence what the antients called the fore-sheet is now called the tack.

of the sixteenth century, there is one of "La Città di Trepani," with a topsail agreeing with the description of Isidore. I have not, however, seen any which belong to the classical period. There are, indeed, triangular topsails upon the ships in some of the coins of the Emperor Commodus; but the apex, instead of being the foot of the sail (pes veli), is the head, whilst the base of the triangle is extended on the main-yard. This, at least, is a shipshape way of setting a sail, as no additional spars are required for it.

When we read of at least three tier of sails above each other, we must be certain that they had topsail-yards. Montfauçon has given a figure of a coin of Nero, representing the port of Ostium (vol. iv. pl. 143.), in which one of the ships has top and top-gallant yards across: but the details of his figures, at least those from coins, are not to be depended upon. I have a sulphur impression from the same type, from a coin in the British Museum, in fine condition, in which there is no appearance of yards above the great sail. But in one of the antient paintings which illustrate a MS. of Homer, supposed of the fifth century, preserved in the Ambrosian Library, which was published at Rome, 1835, the ships are represented with topsail-yards across, with the sails furled on them. (Pl. 32.)

In addition to the three lower sails, and the suppara or topsails, we hear of Acatia and Dolones. The meaning of both terms has hitherto been misunderstood,—the acatium is not the mainsail, nor is the dolon the foresail. It is not, however, so easy to say what they were, as what they were not. We have sufficient proof that both the acatia and dolones were small sails. Now, small sails may be either set in addition to large sails in fine weather, or substituted for them in bad weather, — *i. e.* " storm sails." It would appear from the passage from Xenophon (cited at p. 183.), that the former were substituted for the great sails: all we can learn with regard to the dolones is, that they were the small masts or sails in ships (οἱ μικροι ἱστοι εν τοις πλοιοις, Hesych.: τα μικρα ἱστια, Suidas). Suidas quotes a passage from Procopius, which shows that they also were occasionally substituted for the great sails: χαλασαντες τα μεγαλα αρμενα τοις μικροις ἁ δη δολωνες καλουσιν, ἑπεσθαι. I must say, therefore, with Dindorf, " manemus igitur incerti." In one of the paintings from Herculaneum, representing a galley under sail, two triangular sails are seen attached to the main-yard, with the apices below.* I suspect that in stormy weather the great sail was furled, and triangular sails substituted; two of these would reduce the sail to one half, and one to one fourth: by bringing down the fore yard-arm to the deck, and leading aft the sheet, we have the modern lateen sail.

The spars and wooden gear (σκευη ξυλινα) are, with the exception of the hinged rudder, precisely the same as we see in the coasting craft in the Roman states and Tuscany at the present day. They consisted of a strong and rather short mast, placed a little before the centre of the

---

* Böckh supposes this a mistake, and that it is a square sail, with the middle drawn up (p. 141.). I can scarcely suppose that the engraver could have given the details, unless warranted by the original; he has represented "the ear-rings" or upper corners overlapping each other. After a century's exposure, the original is much faded; it is in the Museo Borbonico at Naples, but, at such a height, I could not make out the details.

vessel. In the following figure, taken from the tomb of Nævoleia Tyche, at Pompeii, the mast is hooped, which would seem to indicate that it was built of several pieces. The foremast (artimonium) rakes over the bow, and the main-yard, which is fully as long as the vessel, is composed of two pieces, doubled in the centre, exactly as the lateen yards of large sails are at present; the main halyard block, which does not differ in any respect from that of the modern Italian craft, is formed by a large block of

wood, not strapped, but at the upper end of it there is a hole, through which the pendant of the halyard is passed.

We have no means of knowing with accuracy the internal arrangements or manner in which the decks were laid with respect to breaks or hatchways. In the ship of Theseus we observe a break in the decks at the poop. Lucian mentions cabins near the stern in the Alexandrian ship, which he describes in his dialogue of the ship. In the following figure, taken from the Antichità di Ercolano (tom. ii. pl. xiv.), we see the roof of one of these cabins (οικησεις).

This is an interesting fragment, because the artist, although evidently quite ignorant of the details, must have had an accurate prototype to copy from. The subject is Theseus abandoning Ariadne.* In order to give it the air

of rude antiquity the mast is formed by the trunk of a tree inverted; a rope, thrown carelessly over the yard, is seen to pass between it and the sail, which the wind blows in one direction, whilst it fills the sail in another; another rope passes between the sail and the bolt-rope, and the feather ornament at the stern is absurdly exaggerated. In spite of all these blunders, this is, perhaps, the most

* I was unable to discover the original when at Naples.

instructive representation of an antient ship which has been preserved; and, when we remember that it was painted within sight of the port to which the Alexandrian wheat ships resorted, and probably at the time when St. Paul's ship was in existence, we are warranted in supposing that many of the details agree with the class of ships to which she belonged. In the account of the voyage, I have referred to this painting for evidence to prove that the ships of the antients were fitted for anchoring by the stern as well as to show the manner in which it was done. The rudders, in such a case, were necessarily lifted out of the water, or unshipped; in either case, the rudder-port, or rudder-case, served the purpose of a hawse hole. In the ship of St. Paul we know that the rudders were secured.

In a vignette to the splendid copy of Virgil, printed at Rome, 1761, we have the figure of a ship anchored by the stern, taken from an antient marble. In this case the rudders are unshipped; the cable is passed through the rudder-case, and is seen within board, coiled round a windlass.

We have ample evidence, therefore, to prove that the ships were fitted for this manner of anchoring. I have already stated the reasons why it was put in practice in the case of St. Paul's ship.* The success with which it was

---

* The anchoring by the stern has always been a stumblingblock to the sailor only acquainted with ships of the present day. I have heard it called "lubberly," and an old Scotch sailor, who had made many voyages with me on the west coast of Scotland, declared that "there was just ae thing in the Scriptures he could na quite gae alang wi'—St. Paul's anchoring by the stern; nae doubt the Apostle was an inspired man, *but he should hae keepit*

done, under circumstances of no ordinary difficulty, affords convincing proof of the superiority of the antients in this important branch of seamanship. The anchors differed but little from those of the present day, except that they do not appear to have had palms, or triangular plates of iron (flukes) attached to the extremities of the arms. It is by no means certain that this addition increases the holding powers of anchors. The Dutch anchors, which have no palms, but merely the extremities of the arms flattened, are known to hold remarkably well.* The following extract from a recent newspaper † is interesting both in an antiquarian and geological view, and shows that Ovid was quite correct in referring to anchors for proofs of geological changes : —

"A few days ago, as some parties were employed in trenching a piece of moss on a hill in the vicinity of Kishorn, Lochcarron, some miles from the sea, they found the stock and flues of a rudely-constructed anchor situated between the moss and a substratum of clay. The part which appeared to have been imbedded in the clay was wholly eaten away, and only distinguished by a rusty outline; that which lay in the moss only remains. The stock is furnished with an inside and outside ring, and must have been used according to some method now unknown. The flukes are sharp at the ends, some-

---

her head ti'l't." John Auld's sole difficulty in the Scriptures would, I think, have been removed, could the friend to whom he confided it have explained to him, that the ship was alike at both ends, had only paddle rudders which could be triced up, had hawse-holes at the stern, was not running, but hove-to, when she anchored, and finally, that the object was to cut the cables, and beach the ship at daylight.

* Rodger's patent, which have very small palms, or rather none, but the extremities of the arms flattened and barbed, have also great powers of holding, as I can testify from experiments I witnessed near Portsmouth.

† Glasgow Courier, 8th Aug. 1846.

what like the blade of a penknife, and the very nature of the metal seems changed into a substance more resembling lead than iron."

In the above description the *stock* is evidently mistaken for the *shank*: the two rings are very often seen in antient anchors, in fact the description corresponds exactly with the anchors of the Romans. Modern writers *de re nautica* tell us that the anchors of the antients were without stocks *: this is one of those traditional blunders which have been handed down from Scheffer. The antients did not excel in perspective, and very often omitted the stock, which is at right angles with the arms; but there are several antient coins which represent it, such as the annexed of Antoninus Pius †, which will show how perfectly it resembles the modern anchors: —

The next point which requires elucidation in our present

---

* Berghaus, v. ii. p. 432. *Böckh:* "Uebrigens fehlt allen Ankern der Alten bekanntlich der Stock oder das an dem Schafte befindliche Querholz." (p. 166.) *Scheffer:* "Nullis in transversum lignis sicut hodie consuevit, vulgo apud veteres inveniri instructas, sive pictorum incuria, sive quod magis credo quoniam in usu non fuerant." *Beechey:* "The transverse piece or anchor-stock is found wanting in all of them." (xxii.)

† From the British Museum.

inquiry is the mode of undergirding the ships. Here also we have to clear away a considerable mass of error, resting in a great measure on the remarks of a scholiast evidently ignorant of the subject, as to the meaning of a word in Aristophanes. In the Knights, an informer accuses a person of stealing the " zomeumata" (ζωμευματα) of the Peloponnesian galleys*, an intentional misnomer for hypozomata (ὑποζωματα); " and the question is, What were the hypozomata?" The explanation given by the scholiast is that they were the timbers (τα ξυλα) of ships. Scheffer, Le Roy, and Bloomfield contend that they were of wood. According to Scheffer, the hypozomata were the wooden bends (ζωστηρες), or belts, which encircle the ship externally. Le Roy supposes they were the decks†, and Bloomfield wooden stays to be applied internally.‡ It is not now necessary to discuss these explanations, because we learn from the Attic Tables, an authority quite conclusive in this case, that the hypozomata did not form part of the wooden gear (σκευη ξυλινα). What, then, were they? In the first place, they were external, as the name implies, "under zones." Plato, in his legend of the Vision of Eros, compares the most distant starry zone to the hypozomata of galleys, binding the whole together.§ It is

---

* Τουτονι τον ανδρ' εγω δεικνυμι, και φημ' εξαγειν
ταισι Πελοποννησιων τριηρεσι ζωμευματα.'
'Ιππεις, v. 278.

† Le Roy translates the Hypozomata of the ship of Ptolemy Philopater, " Il avoit douze ponts ou étages " !—*Hist. de l'Acad. des Inscriptions*, tom. xxxviii. p. 589.

‡ Note upon Acts xxvii. 17. Taylor also, the translator of Plato, renders them the "transverse beams of ships."—Vol. i. p. 471.

§ De Republic lib. 10. sec. 13. Και ιδειν αυτοθι κατα μεσον το φως εκ του

probable that ships were occasionally undergirded with wooden planks; but this could only be done in harbour. In the Louvre there is a statue of a marine goddess standing upon a galley, upon the sides of which planks are seen placed vertically. Polybius talks of ships being "undergirded"* before putting to sea, evidently meaning that they were to be repaired in a temporary manner; but this can have no reference to the "helps," which were carried with the ships for the purpose of being applied at sea, when required, which were necessarily flexible. Isidore of Seville mentions "the mitra" as a *cable* by which a ship is bound round the middle.† Hesychius says, also, that they were "cables binding ships round the middle."‡

The next question to be considered is, How were they applied? One would have thought this easily answered,— that the hypozomata should be bound round the middle of the ship, at right angles to the length, and not parallel to it. As, however, Böckh endeavours to prove that they were applied lengthways §, and as this view is adopted by

---

ουρανου τα ακρα αυτου των δεσμων τεταμενα· ειναι γαρ τουτο το φως ξυνδεσμον του ουρανου, οιον τα υποζωματα των τριηρων ουτου πασαν ξυνεχον την περιφοραν.

* ναυς συμβουλευσας τοις Ῥοδιοις υποζωννυειν.—Leg. 64. This mode of strengthening old ships is still in use. The Rainha, an old Portuguese line-of-battle ship, was very successfully fitted with external braces and girders, and sent to sea during the late civil wars.

† "Mitra, funis qua navis media vincitur."—*Orig.* lib. xix. c. 4.

‡ Ζωμευματα, υποζωματα σχοινια κατα μεσον την ναυν δεσμευομενα. Scheffer refers to "Boysii Roma Subterranea" for a figure of the application of the hypozomata. I searched through the work twice, but could not discover it; Böckh makes the same remark (p. 135.).

§ Urkunden, p. 134.

others,—see Smith's Dictionary of Greek and Roman Antiquities (p. 880.),—it is necessary to examine their arguments. Böckh, in the first place, quotes a passage in Vitruvius, who describes certain ropes as being attached to the beam of a battering ram in the same manner as " a ship is kept from head to stern." " Quemadmodum navis a puppi ad proram continetur." After searching for the passage, which is erroneously cited*, I found that the important word "malus," mast, was omitted, and that the meaning was, that the ropes were attached to the beam in the same way as the standing rigging was attached to the mast, which is intelligible. The next quotation is from Isidore, and is more to the purpose, because it does appear that ropes were occasionally applied in a longitudinal as well as in a transverse direction, to prevent ships from straining. "The tormentum is a cable in *long* ships, which is extended from stem to stern, in order to bind them together." †

Isidore mentions two kinds of cables for the purpose,— the mitra, to bind them round the middle, and the tormentum: this, he says, is so called because it is twisted.

---

* Erroneously cited, in both the works referred to, as x. 15. 6., in place of x. 21. This is one of the annoyances to which a person determined to examine authorities for himself is subjected to; but a proof of the necessity of the task. The passage is as follows: "A capite autem ad imam calcem tigni contenti fuerunt funes quatuor, crassitudini digitorum octo, ita religati quemadmodum *malus* navis a puppi ad proram continetur." The word "malus" is omitted in the edition of Schneider, but is retained in the later carefully edited edition of Poleni, Utini, 1829.

† "Tormentum, funis in navibus longis quo prora ad puppim extenditur quo magis constringantur, tormentum autem a tortu dicta."— *Orig.* xix. 4.

There is nothing which implies that it was passed round the ship externally; and it is not clear how a ship could be bound together in the mode supposed: the "naves longæ," from the weight of the rostra and towers at the extremities, and from their great length, must have been extremely apt to "hog," or fall down at each end; but as the stem and stern posts rose above the rest of the vessel, a simple way of preventing this would be to pass a rope round them, and heave a strain upon it by twisting the parts together, as was done in the military engines called tormenta; and Isidore's etymology of the name "tormenta, a tortu dicta," seems to confirm this. Böckh also notices the hypozomata of the great ship of Ptolemy Philopater. I agree with him that the word ελαμβανε (took) shews that they were not fixed to the ship; but I do not see anything in the account of Athenæus to prove that they were meant to be applied lengthways, and still less that this was the only mode.

The last proof which he adduces in favour of this hypothesis, is taken from a bronze relief in the public museum at Berlin. It is figured in the Thesaurus Brandenburgicus of Beger (vol. iii. p. 406.), and in Montfauçon.* I have not seen the original bronze, but the figures do not warrant the inference. The rope mouldings are evidently ornamental, and three out of the four do not go round the vessel, but are interrupted by the stem-post. The Victoria and Albert royal yacht has also a rope moulding exactly where the antique has it; it would scarcely be a fair inference to suppose that it was meant to hold a crazy

* Antiquité expliquée, tom. iv. pt. 2. p. 214. pl. cxxxiv.

vessel from falling to pieces. I cannot, therefore, see any reason for supposing that ships were undergirded lengthways, a mode which must have been as impracticable as it would have been unavailing for the purpose of strengthening the ship. It would appear from the Attic Tables that the hypozomata formed a regular part of the gear of every ship, and that they were laid up in the magazines.

In the account of St. Paul's Voyage, I have adduced examples to show that the practice of undergirding ships is still occasionally resorted to.

I have only a few remarks to offer on the capabilities of the antient ships in working to windward. Paul Hoste has observed that no person could infer *à priori* that a vessel impelled by the wind could sail to a place which, in respect to that from which it started, was directly to windward. This may be true, but on the other hand no person who tried to impel a vessel by sails could avoid making the discovery — for on the most unfavourable supposition, that of a sail set at right angles to the keel, it would be discovered — that even though the wind did not blow directly upon it, so long as the sail was full, the vessel would go a-head, and of course, if the yard could be braced, that she could go nearer to the wind than at right angles to it, or within eight points. We have no information as to the exact angle with the wind which an antient ship could sail. It must, however, have been less than eight points, but more than six, the usual allowance for a modern merchantship in moderate weather. I have, therefore, in my calculations taken seven as the mean between these extremes; and I cannot suppose it would be much greater or less.

Notwithstanding the imperfect manner in which the ships were rigged, they appear to have made excellent passages. Pliny has enumerated several which would be considered respectable in modern times. Thus he tells us that the prefects Galerius and Babilius made quick passages from the Straits of Messina to Alexandria; the former arrived on the seventh, the latter on the sixth day; that in the following summer Valerius Marianus made the passage from Puteoli, on the ninth day, " lenissimo flatu ": he also mentions passages from the Straits of Hercules to Ostia, in seven days; from the nearest port of Spain, in four; from the province of Narbonne, in three; and from Africa, in two.* Upon these passages Admiral Beechey offers the following remarks : —

"It does not appear that there is any mistake in the numbers here mentioned by Pliny; for the instances are all of them consistent with each other, one only being below 140 M. P. per day, and another 143; two examples afford 160; two 175 and 185. The lowest of these rates of sailing may be reckoned at between six and seven M. P. per hour, and the highest at something less than eight; giving a mean of seven M. P. per hour, which would be reckoned a good one for ships of the present day."— *Appendix to Trav. in Africa*, p. xxxviii.

The most rapid run which I have met with is mentioned by Arrian, in his Periplus of the Euxine (p. 5.), who stated that " they got under weigh about daybreak," αραντες μεν ὑπο την ἑω; and that by mid-day they had come more than 500 stadia, και ηλθομεν προ της μεσημβριας

---

* Hist. Nat. Procem. ad lib. xix.

σταδιους πλειονας η πεντακοσιους, that is, more than fifty geographical miles, which is at least eight miles an hour.

Major Rennel, in his Observations on the Geography of Herodotus (p. 678.), supposes that the average rate of a day's sail was only thirty-seven miles. Vessels navigating unknown coasts, such as those of Africa when Herodotus wrote, and putting into port at night, may not have made more in a day; and it would be no objection to the credibility of a narrative, were this stated to be the case: but it is absolutely impossible that ships four times as long as they were broad, with a large square sail, could make so little progress with a fair wind; and the foregoing examples prove that they did not. When St. Luke states that the ship sailed from Rhegium on one day and arrived at Puteoli on the following, he tells us that the wind was south (xxviii. 13.). Now, as the course is nearly due north, the vessel was running right before the wind, which to a single-masted vessel is the most favourable point of sailing. The distance is about 182 miles. If we suppose she sailed at the rate of seven miles an hour — the mean of the foregoing examples, the time consumed would be about twenty-six hours, which agrees perfectly with St. Luke's account.

The passage, therefore, from Rhegium to Puteoli, which terminated on the day following that upon which they left it, although a quick one, was by no means unprecedented.

We are apt to consider the antients as timid and unskilful sailors, afraid to venture out of sight of land, or to make long voyages in winter. I can see no evidence that this was the case. The cause of their not making voyages after the end of summer arose, in a great measure, from the comparative obscurity of the sky during the winter, and not from the gales which prevail at that season. With no means of directing their course, except by observing the heavenly bodies, they were necessarily prevented from putting to sea when they could not depend upon their being visible.

In what manner they calculated the distance, as well as the direction of their course, is uncertain. Vitruvius describes what may be termed a perpetual log; that is, a mode of estimating the distance passed over by the revolutions of a wheel (x. 14.). From the manner in which he speaks of it, it appears rather to be a scheme which might be adopted, or the tradition of one which had been in use, than the description of an instrument actually in use. The wheels were, or supposed to be, fixed to the sides of the ships. It appears to be one of those plans that look well in theory; but which the disturbing causes, arising from the inclination of the vessel or the violence of the sea, would render of little value.

The internal arrangement of the rowers in the war galleys of the antients is a problem of great difficulty, as to the true solution of which much difference of opinion exists. No work expressly describing the arrangement is extant, and it is one not well fitted for graphic representation. The incidental notices of antient writers, and the representations on coins, marbles, bronzes, and pictures, however, in a great degree limit the problem, and, as appears to me, when combined with the essential condition of practicability, lead us to the true solution.

I shall, in the first place, notice the solutions which have been proposed by other writers.

, M. Jal, the latest writer on the subject, cuts the knot, by disbelieving the possibility of three ranks being placed one above the other. Speaking of the figures on Trajan's column he says—

"La colonne représente des navires à trois rangs de rames superposés et d'autres à deux rangs. Pour les birèmes, bien qu'elles soient mal rendues, pas de difficulté : j'admets les birèmes ; le texte des Tactiques de l'empereur Léon est trop clair, trop positif pour me laisser un doute. Quant aux trirèmes, c'est différent. La longueur de la rame supérieure aurait dû être telle qu'il n'y a ni bois assez long pour la faire, ni bras assez forts pour la mouvoir."—*Archæol. Nav.* i. 34.

M. Jal in this passage apparently proceeds upon the assumption that the calculations of Lescallier, the author of *Vocabulaire des Termes de Marine*, are correct. That author supposes that the lower oars were 44 feet long, and that each rank of oars was separated by a deck, like the tiers of guns in a line of battle ship, both of which suppositions are in direct opposition to the evidence which has come down to us. According to his calculation, the oars of the second rank must have been 77 feet in length, of the third 110 feet, &c. Such oars could not be pulled by one man; but it is clear from the description of the bireme, given by the Emperor Leo, which M. Jal admits as authority, that there was only one rower to each oar. According to the emperor, there were two ranks, one above and one below, seated upon benches, of which there were twenty-five above, and as many below—fifty in all. Upon each bench were seated two rowers—*one* upon the right side, and *one* upon the left, so that in all, both rowers and soldiers, above and below, there were a hundred men.* With regard to the triremes there is no point better established than this, that their oars were pulled by one man each; and the late discovery of the Attic tables proves that the longest oars in this class of vessels did not exceed in length those of an ordinary row boat of the present day. (I. 9. 14. &c.)

De Baif and others suppose that the ranks were not placed directly one above and overlapping the other, but that the thranites or highest rank were placed at the stern; that the zygites were placed in the middle of the ship, lower than the thranites; and the thalamites at the bow, and lower than the zygites.

The only authority which is cited for this arrangement is a passage in the antient scholia on the Ranæ of Aristophanes, which is to the following effect:—

"Thalamax, one who rows in the lower part of the trireme. The thalamaces receive low pay on account of their using short oars compared with the other three ranks of oars, because they are nearer the water. There were three ranks of rowers; the lowest rank were called thalamites, the middle zygites, and the upper thranites. The thranite, then, is placed towards the stern, the zygite in the middle, and the thalamite towards the bow." †

---

* Εχων μεν τας λεγομενας ελασιας δυο, την τε κατω, την ανω, εκαστη δε εχετω ζυγους, το ελαχιστον πεντε και εικοσι, εν οις οι κωπηλαται καθεσθησονται, ως ειναι ζυγους τους απαντας, κατω μεν εικοσι και πεντε, ανω δε ομοιως εικοσι και πεντε, ομου πεντηκοντα, καθ' ενα δε αυτων δυο καθεζεσθωσαν οι κωπηλατουντες εις μεν δεξιᾳ εις δε αριστερᾳ, ως ειναι τους απαντας κωπηλατας ομου και τους αυτους και στρατιωτας τους τε ανω και τους κατω ανδρες εκατον.— *Tactica, Meursii Opera*, t. vi. 829. It has been doubted whether this description applies to the war galleys of the period when Leo wrote (ninth century), but it is evident that it did, for they were fitted with a siphon (σιφωνα κατα την πρωραν) for darting Greek fire.

† Θαλαμακι τῳ κωπηλατουντι εν τῳ κατω μερει της τριηρους. οι δε θαλα-

This passage has always been understood, both by those who with De Baif suppose that the three classes of rowers were placed as last mentioned, and by those who suppose that they were placed directly one above the other, to mean that the thranites as a body were placed at the stern of the ship, the zygites as a body in the middle of the ship, and the thalamites as a body next the bow; and those who suppose that the ranks were placed directly one above the other, accuse the scholiast of having committed a blunder. But were such the meaning of the scholiast, the last part of the passage would be alike inconsistent with the first, and with the jest, such as it is, which it is meant to illustrate. The words thranite, zygite, and thalamite, in the last part of the passage, are in the singular; and the true meaning of the passage appears to me to be that each thranite was placed nearer the stern than, and therefore in front of and above, a zygite; and each thalamite nearer the bow than, and therefore behind and below, a zygite and a thranite. This mode of arrangement is actually figured on a coin of Adrian, of which I have given an engraving on a subsequent page, and by this construction the passage from the scholiast becomes sensible and an authority for an arrangement different from that in support of which it has been cited.

General Melville supposes that the sides of the galleys formed an angle of 45° with the water.* Such an over-

μακες ολιγον ελαμβανον μισθον, δια το κολοβαις χρησθαι κωπαις παρα τας αλλας τρεις ταξεις των ερετμων, ὁτι μαλλον εγγυς εστι του ὑδατος. ησαν δε τρεις των ερετμων. και ἡ μεν κατω Θαλαμιται, ἡ δε μεση ζυγιται, ἡ δε ανω Θρανιται. Θρανιτης ουν ὁ προς την πρυμνην, ζυγιτης ὁ μεσος, Θαλαμιτης ὁ προς την πρωραν.—*Schol. ad Ranæ*, v. 1074.

* Pownall on the Study of Antiquities, p. 119., and Appendix, 235.

hang would admit of several ranks of rowers, without adding much to the height of the vessels; but it would be destructive of their stability, and is unsupported by evidence.

The most general explanation given is, that the oar-ports were arranged diagonally in echelons along the sides of the vessel, thus:—

Isaac Vossius* and others estimate the rate of the ship from the number of oars in each echelon. According to him, a ship with oar-ports arranged as above would be a trireme. Mr. Howel† adopts the same arrangement, but estimates the vessel's rate from the number of echelons. According to him the above figure represents a portion of the oar-ports of a quinquereme. The oar-ports of a trireme he supposes to have been arranged in the following manner:—

But this mode of arrangement is unsupported by any antient authority, and would not admit of the number of oars which we know triremes carried; some of them, as we learn from the Attic tables, having 170. (Böckh, Urkunden, p. 119.)

---

* De Triremium Constructione.

† Essay on the War Galleys of the Antients. Edin. 1826.

The arrangement of the oar-ports, according to Vossius, does not differ materially from what I conceive to have been the true arrangement, except as to their mutual distances. His internal arrangement of the rowers makes it necessary to suppose that the distance between two oar-ports of the same rank was seven feet, even allowing scanty room for the rowers. This distance between the oar-ports would not admit the requisite number of oars. A trireme carrying 170 oars must, on this arrangement, have been considerably more than 200 feet long, a length which is quite out of the question.

It will be convenient, before I offer any conjectures of my own, to state what are the well-established facts respecting the mode by which the antient galleys were impelled by oars. They are—

1st. The oars were ranged in horizontal tiers; those in each tier being so near each other as just to admit of the rowers pulling without interfering with those immediately before and behind them. This appears to me to be evident from every representation which has come down to us, and is confirmed by a passage in Vitruvius, who calls the interscalmium, or space on the ship's side between the oar-ports, διπηχαικη, or two cubits length (navibus interscalmio quod διπηχαικη dicitur, i. 2.). Now two cubits, or three feet, is the smallest space which will allow rowers in the same rank to pull with facility.

2d. That the ranks were arranged one directly above the other, the vertical distance of two adjoining ranks not being more than one-half of the distance of the two adjoining oar-ports of the same rank. On this point all the representations agree.

3d. The oars, at least in the triremes and all below that rate, were pulled by one man; this is proved by the extracts of the Emperor Leo's work, already quoted; by the account given by Thucydides of the night march of the Peloponnesians, in which each man carried his oar (see note, Appendix, No. 4.); and by the dimensions of the spare oars, given in the inventories of the Attic navy, none of which are more than $9\frac{1}{2}$ cubits, or 14 feet 3 inches. (Böckh, Urkunden, p. 123.)

4th. The fighting-men, epibatæ, pulled, when not engaged in combat, on platforms or gangways laid along the sides of the vessels.

Having premised these established facts, I shall now proceed to explain what I conceive to have been the arrangement of the rowers in the trireme, showing the considerations by which I have been guided, and comparing the result with the notices in antient writers, and with antient representations which have come down to us.

The row-boats to which we are accustomed, have only one rank of rowers. Such boats are not adapted for the antient mode of fighting at close quarters. The oars would impede the free motion of the soldiers on the decks. To allow of this, a platform or gangway must be laid above the oars and along each side of the vessel. This may be a complete deck, in which case it must be higher than the heads of the rowers; or it may only extend a short distance from the side, not covering the rowers, in which case the height need only be such as to allow free motion to the handles of the oars; or it may partly or wholly project over the side of the vessel, in which case it need be a very little higher than the row-locks or oar-ports. That the war-galleys of the antients must have had such gangways we might have inferred from the necessity of the case; but it also distinctly appears from antient coins, pictures, and medals.*

From these it appears that the gangways generally projected to some distance over the side of the vessel. In combat this gangway or platform must have been cleared of oars; but this was the exceptional case. When not actually engaged in combat, the gangways were disposable for the purpose of rowing; and if oars were placed so as to dip into the water in the intervals between the oars of the men below, they would not interfere with those; and here again we might have inferred, independently of antient authorities, what however is amply confirmed by them, that when the ships were not engaged in combat, and particularly when speed was of vital consequence, as in pursuit or flight, there was a second tier of oars pulled from the gangways. Thus, then, we arrive at the conclusion, almost independently of antient authorities, that war-galleys must have been fitted to row with at least two tiers of oars; the upper tier, or thranites, being em-

---

* Montfaucon has given a representation of a naval combat (vol. iv. pl. 142.), copied from a marble at Seville, in which soldiers are seen fighting from the gangways. Winkelman, in his Antichite Inedite (vol. ii. fig. 207.), has figured a trireme in action, the soldiers engaged in combat, with two ranks of oars pulling below. In Smith's Dictionary of Greek and Roman Antiquities, one of the galleys from Montfaucon and the galley from Winkelman are figured (p. 877.). In Piranesi's great work on antient vases, marbles, &c. (vol. i.), will be found a large and accurate representation of the galley first figured by Winkelman; it is now in the Vatican. In the coins of Adrian, figured p. 193., the upper ranks are seen pulling from the gangways.

ployed in rowing when not engaged in combat; the lower row, or zygites, rowing at all times.

In the case we have supposed, each thranite is placed above, and nearer the side of the vessel than the corresponding zygite. It will, however, be easily seen that two tiers of oars may approach still nearer to each other, when the rowers in the lower tier are nearer the side of the vessel than those in the upper tier. They may then be placed so that the handle of an oar of the upper tier may work as it were in the lap of a rower of the lower tier; and as the oars are moved in the same direction at the same time, a comparatively small vertical and horizontal distance of the row-locks will keep the handle of the oar of the rower of the upper tier from striking the arm or face of the rower of the lower tier who is behind his oar, or the back of the rower of the lower tier who is before it. Thus, then, a third tier of rowers, the thalamites, may be added at a very small distance below the zygites; and if the zygites are supposed to sit on benches placed on the deck, and the thalamites on the deck itself, the height of the vessel would not be increased by the introduction of the thalamites.

The thalamites will be placed immediately under the thranites, but covered by the platform or gangway, on which the thranites sit. These ranks do not therefore interfere with each other within the vessel: and if the oar-ports are so placed that the oars of one rank dip into the water in the intervals between the oars of the other, they will not interfere externally.

Of the practicability of this arrangement I satisfied myself by actual trial. I cut two oar-ports to represent the row-locks of the zygites, at a distance of 3 feet 6 inches from centre to centre, which is the distance allowed in launches of a man-of-war which are pulled " doubled banked," or with two rowers on each bench, as in the antient galleys; and I found that by cutting an oar-port 14 inches below those of the upper tier, and at about one-third of their horizontal distance, reckoning from bow to stern, a rower seated on the deck, and rowing in the lower oar-port, was not interfered with by the rowers seated on benches nearer the centre of the vessel, and rowing in the upper oar-ports. It was unnecessary to make a similar experiment with regard to the thranites. Sitting on the gangway they could not interfere internally with the zygites or thalamites; and in order that they should not interfere externally, it would only be necessary that the horizontal distance of the oar-port of a thranite from the oar-port of the zygite next before him, should be one third of the distance between two consecutive oar-ports of the zygites.

Such, then, I suppose to have been the arrangement of the rowers in a trireme, which I will shortly recapitulate. The thalamite I suppose to have sat on the deck, not far from the side of the vessel, and to have rowed with a short oar in an oar-port little higher than the deck, and probably little more than two feet above the water; and the distance between two successive oar-ports of the same tier, I suppose to have been about 3 feet 6 inches. About 14 inches nearer the bow, and about 14 inches higher than the oar-port of a thalamite, was the oar-port of a zygite, who sat on a bench or stool placed on the deck, on the inner side of the thalamite, about 14 inches behind his seat, and whose oar worked in the angle made by the head and arms of the thalamite. Immediately over the heads of the thalamites a platform extended from the side of the vessel, probably not extending so far inwards as the zygites, but reaching to their shoulders; and this platform projected a short distance over the side of the vessel. On this platform, the thranites sat and rowed. Their oar-ports were arranged along the outer edge of the platform, each oar-port being about 14 inches nearer the bow than the nearest oar-port of a zygite, and 14 inches nearer the stern than the nearest oar-port of a thalamite, and being about 3 feet higher from the water than the oar-ports of the thalamites and 1 foot 9 inches higher than the oar-ports of the zygites. The highest oar-port was, therefore, probably not more than 5 feet above the water; a height not too great for the use of the oars mentioned in the Attic tables, viz. 9 or $9\frac{1}{2}$ cubits, or about 14 feet.*

The general external agreement of the arrangement I have supposed with that of antient ships will appear from the annexed engravings of two coins of the Emperor

---

* Mitford cites the bouanga of the Philippine Islands, described by Pagés (Voyages, i. 169.), as a case in point of an existing trireme; but as the

Hadrian. One represents a bireme; the other, a trireme.

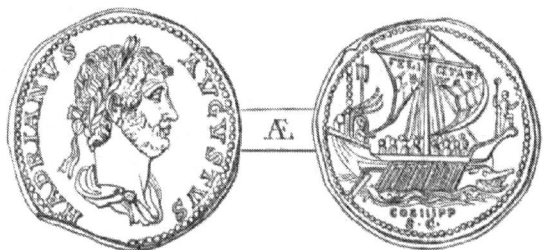

We have no similar means of testing what I have supposed to be the internal arrangement; and I shall, therefore, examine some of the passages in antient authors which most directly bear on this point; and to assist my readers in this examination, I annex a diagram (see p. 222.) drawn to a scale, of the transverse section of a trireme; the oars on one side dipping into the water, the oars on the other side lifted out of it.

It will be observed that I have represented the oars of the different tiers as dipping into the water at the same distance from the side of the vessel, and the middle oar, that pulled by the zygite, to be the longest. This appears to have been the case from several passages in antient authors. Galen says, speaking of the human hand, that, although the fingers are of unequal length; yet, when the

bouanga has an outrigger upon which rowers are seated, it may be called a double vessel. The main body of the vessel is a bireme, with a tier of oars pulled from a projecting bamboo gallery. The corcore of the Moluccas is, however, a regular bireme, not depending on an outrigger for stability (in which the upper or outer oars are pulled from a projecting gallery). Freycinet, Voyage, ii. 11. pl. 37.

hand is shut, their extremities come together, "just as in triremes the ends of the oars extend to an equal dis-

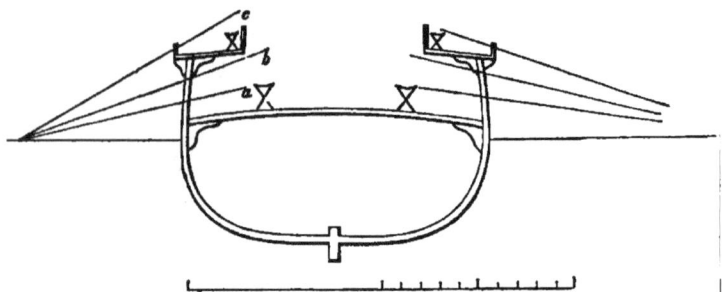

a, oar of thalamite seated on deck. *b*, oar of zygite seated on stool on deck. *c*, oar of thranite seated on stool on gangway.

tance, although they are not all of equal length, but in that case also the middle ones are longest."*

It is only necessary to look at the diagram to see that the comparison is by no means a far-fetched one Aristotle, also, observes, that, "the middle finger, like the middle oar, is the longest."† The longest oars, in the above diagram, are of the length indicated in the Attic tables.

I am aware that Professor Böckh, who is high authority in matters of Grecian antiquity, differs from the explanation I have given of the passages from Aristotle and Galen, and supposes that the "middle oars," which these

---

* Καθαπερ οιμαι κἀν ταις τριηρεσι τα πειρατα των κωπων εις ισον εξικνειται, τοι γ' ουκ ισων ἁπασων ουσων, και γαρ ουν κἀκει τας μεσας μεγιστας.—Galen, De Usu Partium Corporis Humani, lib. i. cap. 24.

† Και ὁ μεσος μακρος, ὡσπερ κωπη μεσονεως.—De Partibus Animalium, iv. 10.

authors said were the longest, were in the middle of the vessel with respect to length, and not with respect to height, and supports this construction of the passages by an entry in one of the Attic tables (ii. 56. Urkunde, p. 288.), from which it appears that out of forty-eight damaged thranitic oars, ten might serve as zygitic, implying that the thranitic oars were at least as long as the zygitic. It may, indeed, be true that the oars in the centre of the vessel were longer than those near the bow and stern, and we may perhaps thus explain the passage in the Attic tables; for it might well be that the longer of the thranitic oars might serve for the shorter of the zygitic; but the difference of adjoining oars of the same rank must have been imperceptible, and could scarcely have suggested the comparison of Galen.

Eustathius tells us that the thalamites rowed under the thranites.* Julius Pollux tells us that the part of the ship where the thalamites rowed, was called the thalamus *i.e.* sleeping-place.† A glance at the foregoing diagram will explain the propriety of the appellation; it is the only part of deck sheltered from the weather. He also tells us that the middle of the ship was called zyga, or the beams, where zygites sat; and that the seat round the gangways or platform (καταστρωμα ‡) was called thranos, where the thranites sat.

* Ὅθεν μεταφορικως και θαλαμιται και θαλαμακες ερεται οἱ ὑπο τους θρανιτας.

† Καλοιτο δ᾽ αν και θαλαμος, οὑ οἱ θαλαμιοι ερετουσι· τα δε μεσα της νεως ζυγα, οὑ οἱ ζυγιοι καθηνται· το δε περι το καταστρωμα θρανος, οὑ οἱ θρανιται.— Julius Pollux, lib. i. 87.

‡ "Καταστρωμα, tabulatum quo navis superiore ex parte striata est, quodque nautas discurrentes aut milites propugnantes sustinet."—*Scapula*.

I shall now consider whether this mode of arrangement could be extended beyond three tiers of oars. The antients, we know, had quinqueremes, or galleys with five banks of oars. Of these we have no graphical representations, and are left still more to conjecture than in the case of triremes. The quinquereme must, of course, have been larger than the trireme. A vessel twice the size of another, if the proportions are the same, is one-fourth larger in every dimension. If the height of the gangway of the one is 5 feet above the water, the gangway of the other will be 6 feet 3 inches. If the deck remains at the same height as before above the water, the additional height of the gangway will allow space for an additional tier of oars under the gangways, the oar-ports of which must be placed in the same position relatively to the oar-ports of the zygites, as the latter are relatively to the oar-ports of the thalamites. This third rank of rowers must be placed nearer the middle of the vessel than the zygites, either standing on the deck or sitting on seats more elevated than those of the zygites. But the oars of this third rank of rowers would interfere externally with the oars of the thranites, if these remained as before. This may be remedied by increasing the length of the oars of the thranites, or by making the gangway project further from the side of the vessel, so that the oars of the rowers on the gangways may always dip into the sea, outside of the oars of those who row below the gangways.* This being done,

---

* Lucan notices the greater distance from the ship's side at which the oars struck the water in a sexireme :—

it will be evident that one or even two additional ranks of rowers may be placed on the gangways, without interfering with the other rowers, and we thus obtain a quinquereme or a sexireme. This arrangement of the oars of a quinquereme is shown in the annexed figure, which is drawn to a scale.

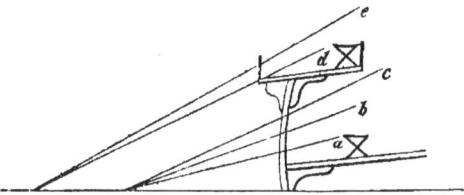

The longest oar in the case here represented is 20 feet, a length quite within the power of one man.*

I do not consider it necessary to inquire how far the mode of adding to the number of ranks can be carried. Meibomius†, and after him Witsen‡, have arranged the alternate ranks nearer and farther from the side, as I have done; but, instead of placing the upper rower, when there are three ranks, either upon a projecting gangway or nearest the middle of the ship, they place him next

"Celsior at cunctis Bruti prætoria puppis
Verberibus senis agitur, molemque profundo
Invehit, et summis longe petit æquora remis."

Phars. iii. 533.

* The sweeps used in decked boats are sometimes 22 feet long, and are pulled by one man.

† Meibomii de Fabrica Triremium, Amst. 1671, p. 1.

‡ Aeloude en Hedendaegsche Scheeps-bouw en bestier. door N. Witsen, fol. Amst. 1671. Appendix, p. 4.

the side: hence according to their representation, he is obliged to grasp his oar at one-twelfth of its length from the fulcrum; but no oar could be rowed in this manner.

I shall, now, offer a few remarks on the galley of Ptolemy Philopator, which, according to Plutarch [*] and Athenæus [†], had forty ranks of oars, and, according to Pliny [‡], fifty. The dimensions given by the two former authors are the same; and as the account of Athenæus is the most particular, I shall offer some remarks upon it. It is said to have been 280 cubits, or 420 feet, in length; and 38 cubits, or 57 feet, in breadth. I see no impossibility in the size. The breadth is less than that of some of our line-of-battle ships. If we suppose that the length of the keel bore the same proportion to the extreme length, as in the Sovereign of the Seas already mentioned, her measurement would be about 4000 tons, or about one-third more than our first rates.[§] There is certainly nothing improbable in the supposition, that a despotic prince could construct such a vessel. Plutarch says that it was little better than an immovable building, more calculated for show than use. It was so constructed, that it could be moved with either end first, having rudders and rostra at each end.[||] The oars of the highest ranks were 38 cubits,

---

[*] Vita Demetrii.   [†] Lib. v. c. 37.
[‡] Hist. Nat. lib. vii. c. 56.
[§] The Persia steamer measures 3600 tons.
[||] The rostra are described as having seven beaks, one principal one in the centre, and three on each side, gradually shorter (εμβολα ειχεν επτα τουτων εν μεν ηγουμενον, τα δ' υποστελλοντα). The two prows, two sterns, and four rudders of this ship have occasioned much needless perplexity to commentators and nautical antiquaries. M. Jal, who never believes what he does not understand, and is, it must be allowed, exceedingly sceptical

or 57 feet, in length. These are certainly not very extraordinary dimensions — not longer than the sweeps formerly used in our sloops of war, or in the Maltese galleys. They are, however, obviously too large to be pulled by one man. If we deduct from the length of the oar what must have been in the inside of the vessel, which cannot be less than one-fourth, and allow at least 10 feet to be dipped in the water, such an oar could not be pulled with advantage, were the oar-ports more than 25 feet above the

in treating of antient ships, does not believe in the double prow, because the shocks of the sea in the re-entering angle would strain the ship and impede her sailing; nor in the seven beaks; nor in the length of the oars, 57 feet, when the height of the ship was 72. It does not appear to me that any of these points present difficulties. Athenæus does not say that the two prows were at the same end. The ship was evidently built so that she could move with either end first. M. Jal's own explanation of Tacitus is quite applicable to Athenæus: — "Ce vaisseau, qui a une proue à chacune de ses extrémités (utrimque), pour être toujours prêt à donner ou à recevoir l'abordage." (i. 122.) Such a vessel must have had four rudders, two at each end. Dion Cassius describes similar vessels fitted with rudders at each end, ἑκατερωθεν και εκ της πρυμνης και εκ της πρωρας πηδαλιοις ησκητο, and states as the reason that they were so, that they did not require to be turned, ὁπως αυτοι μηαναστρεφομενοι, κ. τ. λ. (ii. 1252.)

With regard to the rostra, that of every ship had a principal beak, and at least two shorter ones, one on each side: —

"Totumque dehiscit,
Convulsum remis rostrisque tridentibus, æquor."

Æn. 5. 142.

That a ship of this size and power should have three on each side, can excite no surprise. As to the height mentioned by Athenæus, it is to the top of the acrostoleum, or bow or stern ornament, which rose much above the other parts of the ship. M. Jal thinks it would take an hour to get such a ship round — a very sufficient reason for having her fitted so as not to require turning.

water. Now, it is obviously impossible to arrange forty tiers of oars above each other in this space, nor can we see what object would be gained by such an arrangement. I do not pretend to explain the meaning of the forty ranks here; but it does not follow that, because we cannot explain this particular case, we are to doubt the fact so clearly established by antient authorities respecting the arrangements of the galleys with fewer tiers of oars. It appears, from Athenæus, that the very large galleys had several gangways, one above the other: thus the great galley of Hiero, king of Syracuse, had three gangways (τριπαροδος), the lowest, the middle, and the upper one.* I have shown that it is quite possible to arrange three ranks upon each deck or gangway. This ship, therefore, might have had three tiers of oars from each of her gangways, and three from the deck below them, or twelve in all.

I conceive it quite possible that six tiers might be pulled by oars, with one man at each; and certainly there is no difficulty in supposing that triremes could be pulled by such oars.

Dio Cassius states that some of the ships of Antony, at the battle of Actium, had ten ranks; and Polybius (lib. xvi.), that there were ships of that size at the naval battle at Chios. But ships with so many ranks are always noticed as being of extraordinary magnitude. I therefore conceive that their oars may have been arranged and their rates reckoned on the same principles as those of the triremes and quinqueremes. But in ships of forty ranks of oars, the rate must have been reckoned on some other principle as yet unknown.

* Athen. lib. v. cap. 41.

EDITIONS OF AUTHORS REFERRED TO IN THE DISSERTATION ON THE SHIPS OF THE ANTIENTS.*

Appiani Opera. Tollii. 8vo. Amst. 1670.
Arriani Expeditio Alexandri. Raphelii. 8vo. Amst. 1757.
——— Periplus Euxini Ap. Geog. Min. 8vo. Oxon, 1707.
——————— Maris Erythrei, Ibid.
——— Epictetus. 8vo. Leips. 1799.

> Arrian writes like a seaman, and even in his Epictetus uses sea phrases.

Athenæi Deipnosophistæ. 8vo. Arg. 1801.
Aubin, Dictionnaire de la Marine. 4to. Amst. 1702.

> See page 190.

Bayfius, De Re Navali. 4to. Par. 1536.
———, ib. ap. Gronovii Thes. Græc. xi. 567.

> This author supposes, but with doubt, that the three ranks of oars were on the same deck. He says: "Nec tamen verebor ingenue fateri mihi adhuc non liquere an hæc nostra conjectura vera sit." See Dissertation on the Ships of the Ancients, for his remarks on Artimon, 208.

Bechi, Istoria dell' Origine e Progressi della Nautica Antica. 8vo. Firenze, 1785.
Beechey (Capt. F. W.) R. N., Expedition to the North Coast of Tripoli. 4to. Lond. 1828.

> In the Appendix there is an article on ancient ships avowedly taken from Potter: it contains, however, some good remarks on the rate of sailing of ancient ships. See page 208.

Begeri Thesaurus Brandenburgicus. Fol. Col. 1696.

> See page 206.

---

* This list contains the titles of some works consulted, although not quoted in the text.

Berghaus, Geschichte der Schiffartskunde bey der vornehmsten Volkern des Alterthums. 8vo. Leips. 1792.

See remarks on this work, note to page 176.

Böckh (Aug.), Urkünden über das Seewesen des Attischen Staates. 8vo. Ber. 1840.

In excavating the foundation of a building in the Piræus in 1834, a number of inscriptions were discovered, which proved to be inventories of the appurtenances (σκευη ξυλινη and σκευη κρεμαστη) of each ship of the Attic navy, which were laid up in store-houses, specifying those which were serviceable and those which were not. We have thus, in the most authentic form, a great mass of information respecting the ships of the ancients.

Breydenbach (Erhard), Peregrinatio in Terram sanctam. Fol. Mogunt. 1486.

The earliest printed voyage which is illustrated with prints. The figures of shipping are correct in the details. The most important will be found in the article " Ship-building " in the Encyclopædia Britannica, 4th edit.

Bushnell (Edmund), the Compleat Shipwright. 4to. Lond. 1554.

Calcagninus, De Re Nautica, ap. Thes. Græc. Gronovii, xi. 758.

Carli (Il Conte), Delle Triremi, Quinqueremi, ec. Opp. t. ix.

Count Carli takes nearly the same view as Bayfius respecting the arrangement of the rowers.

Charnock (John), History of Marine Architecture. 4to. Lond. 1801.

Gives the lines of the Navicella at Rome.

Complaynt of Scotland. 16mo, 1542 ; reprinted and edited by Leyden. 8vo. Edin. 1802.

Contains a curious description of a ship weighing anchor and setting sail.

Crescentio (Bartolomeo), Nautica Mediterranea, nella quale si mostra la Fabbrica delle Galee, Galleazze, e Galèone. 4to. Rom. 1607.

<small>A correct description and representation of the ships of the period.</small>

Creuze (A.), On Ship-Building. 8vo. Edin.

<small>From the Encyclopædia Britannica.</small>

Description of an antient Galley. United Ser. Mag. May, 1831.

<small>This is evidently the Palestrine galley, figured and described by Winkelmann, Ant. ined. ii. pl. 207. The author supposes the rowers stood side by side on external gangways, and pulled with the oar vertical.</small>

Deslandes, Essai sur la Marine des Anciens. 8vo. Par. 1768.

Desroches, Dictionnaire des Termes de Marine. 4to. Par. 1687.

Doletus (Steph.), De Re Navali, Gronovii Thes. Græc. xi. 628.

Falconer (William), Marine Dictionary, by Burney. 4to. Lond. 1815.

―――― Shipwreck. 8vo. Lond. 1810.

Fabretti, De Columna Trajana Syntagma. Fol. Rome, 1683. Cap. V. De remorum ordinibus in veterum triremibus et aliis multiremibus navigiis.

<small>Excellent illustrations from an ancient marble in the church of S. Lorenzo fuori le Mure, which have been copied by Montfaucon and subsequent writers.</small>

Gyraldi (Lylii), De Re Nautica. 12mo. Bas. 1540.

―――――― Idem. Opera, fol. Amst. 1696, p. 601.

<small>Explains ancient terms, but offers no conjecture respecting the arrangement of the rowers.</small>

Hasæus, De Navibus Alexandrinis, Crit. Sacra, tom. xii. p. 717.

Howel (John), Essay on the War Galleys of the Antients. 8vo. Edin. 1826.

<small>See page 214.</small>

Jal (A.), Archæologie Navale. 8vo. Par. 1840.
> The chief value of this work is derived from the original documents inserted in it. M. Jal, as he informs us, was educated at a naval school; he therefore understands his subject. See page 191, &c.

Isidori Hispalensis Opera. Fol. Par. 1601.

Leo Imperator, Tactica ap. Meursii Opera, fol. Flor. 1745, tom. vi. p. 828.

Lescallier, Vocabulaire des Termes de Marine. 4to. Par. 1777.

Manwayring (Sir Henry), The Seaman's Dictionary. 4to. Lond. 1644.

Meibomius, De Fabrica Triremium. 4to. Amst. 1671.
> The internal arrangement of this author has been adopted by Witsen, and by Potter in the illustrations of his Grecian Antiquities. He has shown that by placing the rowers of the different tiers alternately nearer and farther from the ship's side, the vertical distance between them need not exceed eighteen inches. He places the upper rank next the side; but it would be impossible to pull oars as he has represented them, from the necessary disproportion between the length of oar outside and inside of the vessels. See page 225.

Melville (General), On the Rowers in Ancient Gallies, in the Appendix to "Pownall on the Study of Antiquities." 8vo. Lond. 1782.
> See remarks on p. 213.

Monson (Sir William), Naval Tracts, in Churchill's Collection of voyages. Vol. iii.

Montfaucon (Bernard de), L'Antiquité expliquée. Fol. Par. 1719, tom. iv. pt. 1.
> Compiled from Scheffer, Fabretti, and Potter. He, however, gives an original engraving of the Seville marble, representing a naval combat, pl. 228

Morisoto, Orbis Maritimus. Fol. Div. 1643.

Neuman's Marine Dictionary. 12mo. Lond. 1800.

Nortumbrio (Dudley, Duca di), Arcano del Mare. Firenze, 1661.
> Good figures of ships of the period.

Opelius, De Fabrica Triremium, ap. Græv. Thes. tom. xii.

Palmerius, Exercitationes in Auctores Græcos. 8vo. Lug. Bat. 1669.
> Contains good remarks on the arrangement of the rowers.

Pantero Pantera, L'Armata Navale. 4to. Rome, 1614.
> Contains a vocabulary of Italian nautical terms of the period. The word Artimone does not occur in it. The author's remarks on the trireme are not very intelligible: he says it was "cosi chiamata delle tre remi con che si vogava ad ogni banco."

Pitture Antiche di Ercolano. Fol. Nap. 1763.

Plinii Historia Naturalis. 8vo. Lond. 1829.

Pollux (Julius), Onomasticon ex Recensione Bekkeri. 8vo. Ber. 1846.

————— Lederlini et Hemsterhuisii. Fol. Amst. 1706.

Rennell (Major), On the Geography of Herodotus. 4to. Lond. 1800.
> Contains remarks on the rate of sailing of ancient ships, p. 678. See page 208.

Le Roy (D.), Mémoires sur la Marine des Anciens, Hist. de l'Acad. des Sciences, t. xxxviii. p. 542.

————— La Marine des anciens Peuples expliquée. 8vo. Par. 1777.

————— Les Navires des Anciens considerés par Rapport à leurs Voiles. 8vo. Par. 1783.

————— Nouveaux Recherches sur les Navires des Anciens, Mém. del Institut, an vii. p. 478.
> See remarks on this author in note to p. 176.

Saverien, Dizionario di Marina. 4to. Ven. 1769.
> See page 190.

Savile (Sir Henry), Translation of Tacitus. Fol. Lond. 1604.
> Appended to it is "A View of certain military Matters for the better understanding of the ancient Roman Stories," which contains an account of the different classes of ships.

Schefferus, De Militia navali Veterum. 4to. Upsal. 1654.
——— De Varietate Navium, Gronovii Thes. xi. 770.

> See remarks on this author, p. 186. His work "De Varietate Navium" is confined to the rowing galleys.

Sovereign of the Seas (Account of). Lond. 1673.

> For the title of this curious work, see p. 181. note.

Stewechius, Commentarius ad Vegetii Libros de Re Militari. 8vo. Ves. 1670.

> The author supposes, with Bayfius and other authors, that the rowers were on the same level, in groups of seven each. His descriptions are not very intelligible, and his figures in illustration unsupported by any authority.

Strutt (Joseph), View of the Manners and Customs of the English, &c., till the time of Henry VIII. 4to. Lond. 1774-6.

> Gives good figures of mediæval ships from the drawings which illustrate MSS. The paddle rudders appear as late as the reign of Stephen.

Vegetius, De Re Militari, ap. Veteres de Re Militari Scriptores. 8vo. Vesal. 1670.

> Treats of naval warfare. The largest galleys in his time had five ranks; but his descriptions afford no clue to the mode in which the rowers were arranged.

Virgilii Opera, Lat. Ital. Fol. Rome, 1761. Illustrated with vignettes from the antique.

> See page 200.

Vitruvius. Poleni, 4to, Utini, 1829.

Vossius (Isaac), Observationes variæ, de Triremium Constructione, &c. 4to. Lond. 1693.
——— Idem, Grævii Thes. tom. xii.

> See page 185.

Us et Coutumes de la Mer. 4to. Rouen, 1672.

> See page 111.

Willet (Ralph), On British Naval Architecture, Archæologia, xi. 154.

Winkelmann, Monumenti antiche inedite. Fol. Rom. 1783.

Witsen (Nicolaes), Aeloude en Hædendaegsche Scheepsbow, &c. Fol. Amst. 1671.

> That is, "Ancient and modern Ship-building." This work gives a good account of the state of naval architecture, and the mode in which ships were rigged, when the work was written. The author, however, cannot have had any practical knowledge of his subject, otherwise he would not have given such absurd restorations of ancient ships as he has done. Amongst others, he has given a restoration of the great galley of Ptolemy Philopator. It is said by Athenæus to have been 280 cubits (420 feet) long. Taking this as a scale, Witsen's representation is that of a ship 100 feet high above the water, with a palace on her deck nearly 100 feet more, or 200 feet in all. All his other restorations (for he has given several) are equally absurd. In the appendix he gives the figures of Meibomius, published at Amsterdam the same year as Witsen. Baron Zach, in his correspondence, speaks of this work as follows :—" M. Le Roy, qui a beaucoup travaillé et écrit sur la marine, et sur l'architecture navale des anciens, n'a point connu l'ouvrage de Witsen, apparemment parcequ'il est écrit en Hollandois, langue connue encore moins que l'Allemande. Mais sur tout parceque ce livre est devenu si excessivement rare qu'on ne le trouve pas même en Hollande à aucun prix ; il y en a cependant un exemplaire à la bibliothèque du Roi a Paris. Tout ce qui regarde la marine des anciens y est traité avec une exactitude et une érudition égale."—*Zach*, ix. 97. There are copies of this work in the British Museum and in the library of the Royal Society.

DISSERTATION IV.

ON THE GEOLOGICAL CHANGES IN ST. PAUL'S BAY.

In attempting to identify places on the sea coast with the descriptions or notices in ancient authors, we must always take into account the geological changes which may or must have taken place in the interval.* Such changes must be owing to one or other of the following causes: —

First, Violent disturbances, such as would affect the configuration of the land.

Second, Movements of elevation or depression.

Third, The wasting action of the sea.

Fourth, The siltage of the disintegrated matter.

With regard to the first of these causes, there is no reason to suppose that any change has been produced by these since the island has been inhabited by man.

---

* Major Rennel is, if I mistake not, the first author who pointed out the necessity of this in his paper " On the Place where Julius Cæsar landed in Britain." (*Archæologia*, p. 499.)

Captain Copeland, R. N., who states that he is not a geologist, speaking of the sea coast of Megara, says, " The localities described by Thucydides do not agree in any one particular with the present features of the coast." (*Arnold's Thucydides*, ii. 396.) My friend, Captain Spratt, R. N., who is a geologist, has proved, that if we allow for the necessary changes, the notices of Thucydides agree perfectly with the localities. See *Journal of Geographical Society*, viii. 205.

Nor is there any reason to suppose that any movement of elevation has taken place within the same period. There has, however, been a slight movement of depression within the human period, but it belongs to a remote antiquity, anterior, in all probability, to the time of the shipwreck. That such a movement has taken place is proved by the tracks of wheels, not connected with existing roads, which are deeply impressed on the upper surface of the rocks, and are seen at different points of the island to pass under the sea.*

There is, however, a geological proof that the extent of this change of level has been very small, and not sufficient to have produced any perceptible change on the relative positions of the soundings, and of the headlands and shores of the bay.

The proof is this: In the narrow channel which separates the sea, on the outside of Selmoon Island, from St. Paul's Bay (a place where two seas meet), there is to be seen under water a vertical escarpment, running across from the island to the mainland (see dotted line on chart), which is evidently an ancient sea cliff, and which must have been scooped out by the action of the sea, during the period of stationary level which preceded the present. From the transparency of the water, it can easily be observed. I estimate the change of level which this appearance indicates at ten feet. In Captain Smyth's chart the difference in the soundings on each side of the escarpment is two fathoms, which agrees very well with my estimate. If we

---

* See a paper by the Author on Recent Depressions in the Land, *Journal of the Geological Society*, Aug. 1847, p. 235.

assume that the depression has taken place since the shipwreck, it would make only a slight change in the absolute position of the soundings, and of the two headlands of the bay; but none at all in their relative positions. The point of Koura, before the last depression, must have extended farther to the north, but so must the line of twenty fathoms. The point of Salmonetta, or Selmoon Island, must have extended farther to the east; but the line of fifteen fathoms must have been just so much farther to the east; hence the reasoning in both cases would be the same. It is only necessary to look at the dotted line parallel to the coast, which marks the depth of three fathoms, to show that a much greater change of level than what has actually taken place would make but a trifling alteration in the contour of the shores of the bay. If, then, the depression did take place since the shipwreck, the conclusions to be drawn from the comparison of the locality with the narrative would be the same.

The only effect which the wasting action of the sea could have, would be that of rendering it impossible to ascertain the exact point of appulse of the ship when she was run ashore; but this I have not attempted to do. In every other respect, an allowance for the changes arising from this cause strengthens the conclusions we draw from the present state of the coast.

The shore from Salmonetta Island to Mestara Valley is now girt with mural cliffs, where a ship could not be stranded with safety; but there is a creek in this line of cliff, now without a beach, but which we know, from the form of the land, must at one time have had a beach which has been worn away in the course of ages, by the wasting action of the sea. The degradation of the land actually taking place at this point is proceeding with more than usual rapidity, owing to the inclination of the beds, and the tendency which large fragments of the rock have to fall over when undermined by the sea.* I therefore think it not improbable that the beach existed at the time of the shipwreck. If so, this creek, which, as may be seen on the chart, is immediately to the south of the place which Captain Smyth has marked as the traditional place of the wreck, agrees perfectly with the spot where a ship from the eastward anchored in the entrance of the bay would be driven in a gale from the E. N. E. (Euro-aquilo), and is close to a place where two seas meet.

The rate of siltage at the bottom of the sea must, from the structure and size of the island, be extremely slow. The rocks disintegrate into minute particles, which are of course carried by the action of the waves and the currents to a great distance, before they are finally deposited on the bottom of the sea. There is but little alluvium washed down by streams from any part of the island; and at St. Paul's Bay there is scarcely any. The surface of the island, which is very flat, is composed of a series of beds of tertiary rock, which overlies a thick stratum of clay. The superincumbent rock is much fissured. The rain, which falls on the surface, passes through the fissures, is

* Abela, who wrote in 1642, states, on the authority of an ancient manuscript, that the ruins of the residence of Publius, the chief man of the island, stood here. He says: "Villam hospitalem S. Publii, vicinam rupibus dithalassis quibus (Act. 27.) navis Pauli quassata maris tempestate stetit impacta donec solveretur a fluctibus, fuisse in clivo ad orientem ac septentriones adversum," &c.—p. 230.

absorbed by the clay, and finally reappears in springs. No stream flows into St. Paul's Bay, except one which issues from a translucent spring, which the natives term " Ayn tal Razzul," or " The Apostle's Fountain," a name which proves the great antiquity of the tradition; for the signification of the Phœnician word Razzul (Apostle) is unknown to the Maltese.*

During the excavation of the dry docks at Valetta, my friend, Mr. John Anderson, of the engineer department, paid particular attention to the phenomena, from which the amount of siltage during the human period could be deduced. According to his report, in that branch of the harbour of Valetta, works of art are not found more than six or eight feet below the present bottom of the sea. But the deposit there must be much more rapid than in any part of St. Paul's Bay.

The dock is situated in a deep inlet, at the mouth of an extensive valley, and its shores have been from the earliest times the site of a town. In such a situation, the rate of siltage must have been much quicker than in the comparatively shallow inlet of St. Paul's Bay, where none

---

* "Fons Paulinianus ex arenti solo in mare profluit cui nomen Ayn tal Razzul . . . ignota nunc indigenis significatione nominis; at Tyris et Phœnicibus fontem Apostoli sonat."—Quoted from an ancient MS. by Bres, a Maltese: *Malta Antica Illustrata*, p. 395.

On a stone near this fountain there are inscribed, or rather were, for I was unable to discover them, the following lines, which I give from Bryant (p. 67.).—

"Hac sub rupe cava, quam cernis ad æquoris undas,
 Exiguus trepidat fons salientis aquæ,
 Religione sacra latices venerare, viator;
 Naufragus has dederit cum tibi Paulus aquas."

of those causes of rapid deposition operate. The events of the shipwreck, moreover, did not take place in the bay, but in the open sea, at its mouth, where the action of the waves and currents would tend to prevent deposition. From these considerations, I am satisfied that no change in the depth of the sea, caused by siltage, could in any part, which a ship driven in to this part of the coast from Crete, must have passed over, have been perceptible in so rough a measurement as that where the smallest quantity is a fathom.

The rocky point of Koura must anciently have extended farther to the north than it does at present; hence a ship driving into St. Paul's Bay, eighteen centuries ago, must have been nearer the breakers than one at the present day, under the same circumstances, would be. Hence the possibility of passing them unobserved was less then than it is at present; and consequently the agreement between the locality and the narrative even more perfect.

APPENDIX.

No. I.

David Urquhart, Esq., M. P., to James Smith, Esq.

Invertropach, near Callander,
Dec. 4. 1848.

MY DEAR SIR,

I should be consulting my own inclination to delay writing to you until I had finished your book, but having arrived at page 51. (89. of this edition), I am compelled to send you what I think you will find to be a confirmation of your exposition. Loutro is an admirable harbour. You open it like a box;—unexpectedly the rocks stand apart, and the town appears within. I have spent a month between Gozo and the main, every day standing off and on. In fact my interest in the East, in navigation, &c., were all connected with the incident to which I refer. I was by accident on board the brig "Sauveur," whose first cruise was on that spot, to intercept a Turkish corvette. We were constantly blown off our cruising ground, and although she was a splendid vessel, all we could do was to hold our own. Excepting Loutro, all the other harbours looking to the southward are exposed to the south or east. My acquaintance with Loutro was made in chasing a pirate schooner. We thought that we had cut him off, and that we were driving him right upon the rocks. Suddenly he disappeared, and, rounding in after him, like a change of scenery, the little basin, its shipping, and the town, all lined and crested with that picturesque people, glittering with arms, revealed themselves. We had instantly to put about, and just escaped. Five minutes more and our decks would have been swept by the long rifles in their dexterous hands. . . . .

I think it was at Loutro, that the Isis frigate had the desperate affair in which she lost fifteen men. At all events Loutro was, next to Grabouza the most important piratical station.

Believe me, &c.

No. II.

Capt. Spratt, R. N., to James Smith, Esq.

Constantinople, Feb. 13. 1855.

HAVING in 1853 examined generally the south coast of Crete, I was fully convinced that Lutro was the Phenice of St. Paul. For it is the only bay to the westward of Fair Havens in which a vessel of any size could find any shelter during the winter months; and you will see, by the enclosed tracing from Capt. Graves's survey, or rather by Lieutenant Mansell's, when under Capt. Graves in Volage, that by hauling inside of the island, and securing to the south shore of the bay, a vessel is nearly land-locked: S. E. and E. only could endanger her; but with the former, where the fetch is greatest, the wind would not blow home against such a mountain as the White Mountain so immediately over the bay, rising to an elevation of 9000 feet.

For a ship circumstanced as St. Paul's ship was, and in those days of navigation, Lutro Bay would been a desirable place to reach, and I have no doubt, with four anchors, would have been secure there. . . . .

Lasea was discovered by me on the coast about two miles

east of Fair Havens. There is a small island, with an ancient causeway nearly reaching it, lying off the site of Lasea. This island served as its port.* Thalassea seems to have been its proper name in ancient authors. The sketch of Schranz is not half a mile from the site, through which Pashley and he must have passed, but did not observe the ruins. . . . .

From the Same to the Same.

London, Feb. 28. 1856.

In respect to the gale of wind I met with after starting from Fair Havens for Messara Bay; we left with a light southerly wind and clear sky; every indication of a fine day, until we rounded the cape (Matala), to haul up for the head of the bay. There we saw Mount Ida covered in a dense cloud, and met a strong northerly breeze, — one of the summer gales in fact so frequent in the Levant, but which in general are accompanied by terrific gusts and squalls from those high mountains, the wind blowing direct from Mount Ida, as it usually does at this point with all northerly gales, winter and summer; and some such a gale with its accompanying squalls I have no doubt was experienced by St. Paul in the attempt to reach the Port of Phenice; and this I believe to be the explanation of the Euroclydon.

* Messrs. Tennent and Brown discovered in 1856 the ruins of an antient city, which still bear the name of Lasea, about five miles to the east of Fair Havens. We can scarcely suppose that any of the cities of Crete, even in its palmiest days, could have extended from it to the ruins discovered by Captain Spratt. The explanation probably is, that the port of Lasea was situated here. There is in fact no shelter nearer. The island mentioned by Captain Spratt is named Trapho by Mr. Brown; the causeway having been observed by Mr. Tennent's party between it and the shore. See p. 262.

No. III.

Extract from the Journal of the Yacht St. Ursula, Hugh Tennent, Esq., of Wellpark, Glasgow, dated Calolimounias, 16th January, 1856, by the Rev. George Brown.

The St. Ursula left Malta for Alexandria on Thursday, 10th January, 1856, and, being favoured with fair winds and fine weather, by Sunday afternoon she sighted the west end of the island of Candia, whose snowy mountains stretched for many miles along the horizon. By 10 P.M. we were abreast of the island, and it was resolved by Mr. Tennent to take the opportunity presented of visiting, if possible, the two places mentioned in the narrative of the voyage of St. Paul, in the 27th chapter of the Acts. These places are, the Fair Havens and Phenice; the one being the harbour which the Apostle's ship left on the eve of the storm in which she was wrecked, and the other the harbour where she was to have spent the winter, but which the gale in question prevented her from reaching. The latter, being furthest to the westward, claimed attention first.

The position of Phenice, as we learned from Mr. Smith's Essay on Paul's Voyage, has been a point considerably disputed among commentators. He says, page 48., "Phenice no longer retains its name. Ptolemy mentions both a city and a port of Phenice, or rather Phœnix. Lutro, Sphakia, and Franko Castello, places on the south coast of Crete, have each been supposed to be Port Phenice. For our present purpose of ascertaining the ship's course, it is not very material which of these is meant. I am, however, satisfied that it is the harbour of Lutro." Mr. Smith supports his decision by very satisfactory evidence, in a dissertation of several pages; but as he had not visited the spot, and as he says he could find no hydrographical description of the harbour in question, in any sailing directions, ancient or modern, we resolved to touch at Lutro, examine the place, and find out if possible, its ancient name, from the inhabitants.

At daybreak on Monday, we ran along the south coast of the island, before a freshening western breeze. The coast for many miles is magnificent. Lofty precipices overhang the sea, and between them the slopes of *debris* are so steep as almost to preclude vegetation. Immediately behind rise the White Mountains (Λευκα 'Ορη), their Alpine sides dotted with trees, and their brows and summits covered with snow. Lutro is put down in the charts as about thirty-two miles east of Cape St. John, and as almost due north of the island of Gozzo: and these accordingly were our directions for reaching it. Owing, however, to a slight error in the chart which we followed, and to the circumstance that the port in question makes no appearance from the sea, we ran past it for a point further to the eastward. (9 A. M. wind suddenly fell; succeeded by puffs and light airs from south and south-east; becalmed till midday.) After lying for some time off a village, we resolved to land, and examine a bay two miles beyond it. Mr. Tennent, Mr. Paul, and myself, with four seamen, got into the jolly boat, and pulled towards the bay, leaving the vessel becalmed. Before, however, we could reach the bay, we saw a heavy squall from the north blowing out of it; and, to avoid a wetting, pulled right ashore for a creek with a gravelly beach, half-way between the village and the bay. There we landed, and hauled up our boat; the St. Ursula, meanwhile, shortening sail as fast as possible.

All agreed that it would be a risk to attempt to reach her till the squall should blow over, for it was now spreading rapidly over the sea, and opposite to every glen was raising clouds and vortices of spray. The place where we landed was surrounded by steep conglomerate rocks; and one or two of the natives appeared, peeping at us over them. At last we brought them to a parley; but found that they could speak nothing but Greek, and that, of course, in dialect and accent, very different from the Greek we had learned at the schools. They let us know, however, that the village hard by was Sphakia; that we had passed Lutro by several miles; and that there was a Turkish governor in the neighbourhood. We then gave a boy a shilling to go for the governor: but, thinking such a proceeding disrespectful, one of the men and myself followed the boy. Mr. Tennent and Mr. Paul sat down under shelter of a rock, and two of the men remained close to the boat (in which were two muskets). The Greeks then all disappeared; but Dan and I had not gone very far, when we met a large party of them, some with knives in their girdles, and others with yataghans. It occurred to us that it was imprudent to separate from the rest, in so unknown and remote a place; and so we slowly retraced our steps, joined Mr. Tennent and Mr. Paul, and returned to the boat. The Greeks hallooed to us, and came skipping over the rocks like goats. One of the men, whose acquaintance with the inhabitants had rendered him suspicious, urged us not to trust them, but to attempt to regain the vessel, and pulled the boat's head round; but the prospect to leeward seemed hopeless. The vessel was two miles off, or at least a mile and a half, labouring heavily under a three-reefed mainsail and fore-stay-sail. Sometimes her hull disappeared behind the seas; and sometimes we lost sight of more than her hull, in the whirlwinds of spindrift. We felt extremely anxious, of course, about her management; still our boat was small, and had seven persons (more than her complement) on board; and in a sea broken by the current, it seemed next to impossible that she should live. We were about a hundred yards or so from the shore of the creek by this time; and now that we were convinced we must hug the land, it was no easy matter to regain it. It cost us three quarters of an hour hard pulling, and a good wetting, to reach a creek to the west of the one we had left.

This creek was a semicircle; almost surrounded by precipices sixty or seventy feet in height; and these were hollowed out into caves of considerable depth. At one point it was possible to land on some pointed rocks; but nowhere could the boat be hauled up. Soon the Greeks appeared in great numbers, nestling on the ledges of rock, like gulls and scarts on the Craig of Ailsa, and holding on with their hands, to keep themselves from being blown over. The creek looked like a pot of potatoes beginning to boil,—the squalls falling from above upon its centre, and radiating all round in hissing foam. Occasionally it was calm; but sometimes the oars were blown out of the row-locks. Sometimes men appeared with gayer dresses than the rest, and armed with silver-mounted firelocks. Poor Dan and Tom felt certain they were going to fire upon us; though we assured them that if the men's intentions were hostile, they would conceal rather than display their arms. At last a very handsome young man, with richly mounted pistols, came down towards the point, accompanied by a person who hailed us in Italian, asking who we were, and what we wanted. We told him we had a clean bill of health from Malta, and a passport visé'd by the consul of the Sublime Porte. As we could hardly hear each other speak for the wind, I leaped ashore, and went up to the young man (who proved to be a Turkish commandant), to show him the passport. He would not touch it, or me, and told me, through the interpreter, that there was no health officer nearer than Lutro, and that nobody else could examine our papers. He said, however, that we might land, and report ourselves to the Turkish governor at Sphakia; or else row round to that village. Now Sphakia was at the bottom of the bay to the west, and it was questionable whether we could face the tempest which raged on the other side of the point. The men were clear for passing the night in the creek; but we told them that, cold and wet as we were, and hungry besides, we would, for our part, "box Harry" at the governor's, or at any body else's who would take us in. I stepped on board again to deliberate, and the commandant proceeded to strike a light.

Tom became terrified that it was for his matchlock; but when, to our great amusement, the gentleman simply lighted his pipe, Tom felt wonderfully re-assured; and, finding his own creature cravings awakened by what he saw, exclaimed, "Well he don't look such a bad feller after all: I think I'll just step ashore, and ask him for a light." A man then came down with a bottle of rum, put it on the edge of the rock, and desired us to put the money into a hole. We did so. They stirred about the money well with a stick in the puddle, and at last took it. We were shivering with cold, and found the rum a most seasonable cordial. But how silly we must have looked, paddling about in the creek overlooked by fifty or sixty men, many of them armed! Our deliberations were cut short by the appearance of a caique, or fishing boat, which came round the point, manned by stout rowers, and steered by an aged Greek with a long white beard. The old man of the sea hailed us in Italian, and said that the governor had sent him round to give us a tow. Our men, however, felt revived by the rum, and declared themselves able for the pull without assistance: so, telling the Greek to lead the way, we bent to our oars; and then came the tug of war.

Mr. Tennent steered right in the wake of the caique, through the blinding spray and spindrift, and amidst the cheers of the crowd on the rocks. We struggled gradually onwards, now driven back for a moment by a squall, and then making progress in the succeeding lull. In less than an hour, we gained the beach of Sphakia; a gun was fired, I suppose in honour of our arrival, and most of the inhabitants seemed gathered about the governor, who stood on a breastwork, with his pipe, his sabre, and his beads. The St. Ursula in the meanwhile had been obliged to lower her mainsail, in order to get the fourth reef down, and had made three tacks; but, being sadly baffled by varying squalls, had been driven further and further from shore, and was now standing far to the westward.

We asked the governor, through the interpreter, if he would

give us rooms, or man a large caique to send us off to the vessel. He said the caique would never get back again, and so he would give us a house, if we promised to touch nobody; for, till the health officer came, we must remain in quarantine. I was amused at his way of keeping order. When the crowd became too curious, and a man approached too near us, he lifted a little stone, and pelted the intruder.

The old Greek was appointed our guardian, and led us to our lazaretto. It was a house overhanging the sea-shore, consisting of one apartment, which somewhat resembled the lower story of the Little Cumbrae Castle. There was no furniture, and the floor was made of clay. Two unglazed windows were closed with wooden shutters, and a wide chimney in one corner showed the possibility of a fire. A man soon came round to say that he had orders from the governor to get us whatever we wanted. We replied, everything he could possibly think of: a fire, beds, chairs, coffee, bread and butter, milk and eggs, and some beef steaks. He said, beds were out of the question, for we were "sporci" (unclean), being in quarantine. It made one indignant to hear him say that to our faces; as if we would not suffer much more than the beds, by coming to close quarters. Then, as for eggs, the Sphakia hens don't lay in winter; and beef was quite unknown. However, things began to drop in: a barrel with a chauffer of charcoal in it, as big as a washing tub; a good supply of firewood for the chimney; a bag of bread as hard and dry as Bath brick; several coffee pots; a paralytic table, with cups; and seven chairs. Three eggs and three fishes were also procured. It was now sunset, 5. 30. P.M.: and after having given thanks, we made a tolerable meal. In fact, between cooking and eating, and drying ourselves at a blazing fire, we spent nearly two hours. The inhabitants were very inquisitive about us; and although, owing to the Turkish manners of the place, the more curious sex could not make their appearance, yet the men showed curiosity enough to serve for all.

Mr. Tennent, who was dressed in a Yacht Club coat with gilt buttons, and had a gold band about his cap, was an object of great respect. I overheard one Greek say to another, while looking at Mr. Tennent, ΣΤΡΑΤΗΓΟΣ ΜΕΓΑΛΟΣ! (a great commander); Μαλιστα (undoubtedly), was the reply. Our Greek guardian, when we had supped, asked leave to partake of our provisions. I said to him, "Remember they are compromised." " Ohe in verità," said he, " a poor man must not lose such a supper for quarantine laws: " and a hearty meal he made. He then suggested a glass of wine, for, said he, I am seventy years old! We ordered it for him, and Mr. Tennent desired him to drink to the Inglesi, Francesi, Turci, and Greci. He gave a roguish laugh and exclaimed, " Viva I Muscoviti ! " and drank it off.

The Sphakian mountains are inhabited by Greeks, who, having suffered dreadfully in the War of Independence (1821–30), and having groaned ever since under the Turkish yoke, naturally look to Russia as their ally. The town of Sphakia seemed to contain between one and two hundred houses; but at least half of them are in ruins. Many of the inhabitants of the mountains winter there. There seems to be little communication between the southern and northern parts of the island, especially in winter, when the passes must be encumbered with snow.

At eight o'clock, the half-dozen Greeks who had intruded into our apartment suddenly disappeared, and the governor was announced. He came, attended by two Turkish soldiers, and made us a graceful salaam at the door; placing his right hand on his left breast, and bending slowly forwards. He then sat down between us and the door; and as the latter would not remain shut, he made a soldier sit down on the threshold, and put his back to it. He introduced himself as Zaïr Bey, governor of the πολιτεία or province of Sphakia; and we had a long interview through means of the old Greek. Joannes Nicephorus (for such was our interpreter's name), had but a small stock of Italian; but when people are anxious to understand each other, a few words go a great way. The scene was picturesque enough: the flickering light of our fire now blinked on one group, and now on another, revealing capriciously their varied forms and features. Our crooked appearance, as we crouched over the fire, was a fine foil to the graceful picture presented by the Turk, who, smoking his long tchibouque, and wrapped in his elegant mantle, seemed the very image of repose. And then the sailors, who had all come to anchor under the lee of the charcoal stove, in the best berths they could find, were quite as strong a contrast to the pale effeminate Roumelian guards. Nicephorus was the Nestor of the party; the faint rays of our cruse, falling on his weathered face and silvery beard, made him look truly venerable. After an hour's conference, the governor took his leave, promising to see us in the morning.

Not forgetful of our object, we asked Nicephorus (the old Greek already mentioned) what was the ancient name of Lutro? He replied, without hèsitation, "Phœniki," but that the old city exists no longer. This, of course, proved at once the correctness of Mr. Smith's conclusion. We were told further that the anchorage is excellent, and that our schooner could enter the harbour without difficulty. We next inquired the ancient name of the island of Gozzo, and he said at once, Chlavda, or Chlavda nesa (Χλανδα or Κλανδα Νησος) a reply equally satisfactory. He told us also that there was a tradition in these parts that ἉΓΙΟΣ ΠΑΥΛΟΣ ΑΠΟΣΤΟΛΟΣ, had visited Calolimounias (the Fair Havens), and had baptized many people there.

Instead of beds, we had the floor strewn with withered bushes of thyme, for neither straw nor hay was to be had. Before retiring to rest, we cleared the room once more of the Turks and Greeks who had dropped in, by telling them we were going to worship. Nicephorus and one other man remained, and seemed pleased at our proceeding. We sung the twenty-third

Psalm, which sounded very sweet in my ears; and then, thanking our Father in Heaven for our protection from the storm, we committed ourselves, and our friends aboard the vessel, to his gracious care. I had a parcel of modern Greek tracts, which Mrs. Paul had given me; and as I sat spelling out one of them by the fire, an intelligent young Greek begged it from me, saying he could read. I gave him the packet; he hid it in his bosom, thanked me, and disappeared with his treasure.

The Euroclydon blew a gale all night, which made the sailors observe, that no wonder St. Paul was blown off the coast in such weather. Towards daylight it moderated, and at six we saw the yacht's white sails appearing on the south-western horizon. She was evidently making for Sphakia, where they had concluded we had passed the night. The shopkeeper, who had served us the evening before, brought up some coffee and fresh bread for our breakfast; and we were setting the table, when a new misfortune took place. One of the men put two or three bunches of dried thyme on the fire at once, as our wood was exhausted. It blazed up the chimney and set fire to the roof. When I saw the flames glowing in the ceiling, I thought the whole would fall a prey to them in a few minutes, for just above the rafters there was a wattling of sticks. The roof, however, was flat, and covered with lime, which prevented a draught. One of our men soon climbed to the top of the house, and let down a sash, to which we fixed our solitary pitcher of water. By pouring it down and around the chimney, the fire in the rafters was extinguished, though the wattling still spread the flames. The Greeks assembled at some distance, but would not bring us any more pitchers, and indeed seemed rather entertained at the misfortune; I suppose, because the house belonged to the governor, who was a Turk; or at least to the government. Our pitcher, however, was often replenished from the sea; and Tom, filling a bason repeatedly, dashed buckets-full of water upon the ceiling from below. This he did with such skill, that in half an hour the fire was quite put out. The governor, with true Turkish indifference, came sailing round the corner at his usual pace, and stood calmly smoking his long pipe, without saying a word.

After breakfast and prayers, we saw the St. Ursula off Lutro, three miles to the westward. She had been boarded by the health officer there, in his caïque, who had received a message from our friend the Bey, ordering him to let them know that we were well. The captain did not rightly understand him, but stood on for Sphakia. The governor, when we proposed to go on board, seemed uneasy, but at length allowed us, on our promising to send him a certificate that we had been sheltered and protected. He said he was responsible for our treatment to Vely Pacha, the chief man of the island. When the vessel came near, we pulled off, and found all well; though the men, of course, were fatigued with their labours. They said no boat could have boarded them in such a sea as they had the previous day: so had we gone off, our only chance would have been to run for Gozzo (Clauda), fully fifteen miles to leeward.

Soon after we reached the vessel, it fell calm; and we were all day trying to work up to Lutro. At last, about 2 o'clock, we took the boat once more (Mr. Tennent not being disposed to give up his point), and row to the harbour. The captain's instructions were to follow us with the vessel. After an hour's pull along the shore, we reached the port, and took the soundings; we found the shores steep, and perfectly clean. There are fifteen fathoms in the middle of the harbour, diminishing gradually to two, close to the village. The lead brought up stiff white clay. As the beach is extremely narrow, and the hills immediately behind steep and rocky, the harbour cannot have altered its form materially since the days of the Apostle. Mr. Smith, following an old French chart, supposes that the island lies opposite the harbour mouth, affording two entrances, one to the N. E. (Βλέποντα κατὰ Λίϐα), the other to the S.W. (Βλέποντα κατὰ χῶρον). We found, however, that the island is merely a continuation of the rocky point which defends the harbour on the south, and that there is only 3 to 6 feet of water between it and the land. Again, the land cannot have

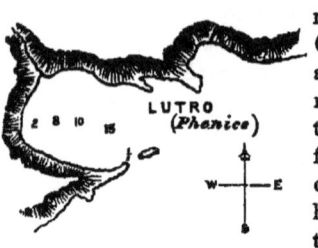

risen materially since the Christian era, for we found an ancient tomb or Columbarium, with its entrance close to the water's edge (not 8 feet above it), in the inside of the point; and if the land has sunk since ancient times, then the island and point must have formed one. The health officer told me, that though the harbour is open to the east, yet the easterly gales never blow home, being *lifted* by the high land behind, and that even in storms the sea rolls in gently ("piano, piano"). He says *it is the only secure harbour, in all winds, on the south coast of Crete;* and that during the wars between the Venetians and the Turks (the latter took the island in 1688, I think) as many as twenty or twenty-five war galleys had found shelter in its waters. He further showed us an inscription on a large slab which he says was found among some ruins on the point, and took us up the hill to see the traces of the site of the ancient Phœniki. The outline of its ramparts is clearly discernible, and some cisterns hollowed in the rock; but the ploughshare has been driven over its site, and it displays "the line of confusion and the stones of emptiness." I hastened back to decipher the inscription; but it was growing dark; and before our boat left the shore, all I had made out was the following :—

JOVI O. M. OPTIMO MAXIMO
IMPERATORE CÆSARE NERVA
ALEXANDRIÆ GUBERNATOR
HOC MAGNUM OPUS DIC.

(Nerva, who succeeded Domitian about the end of the first century, was of Cretan extraction). Looking east from the

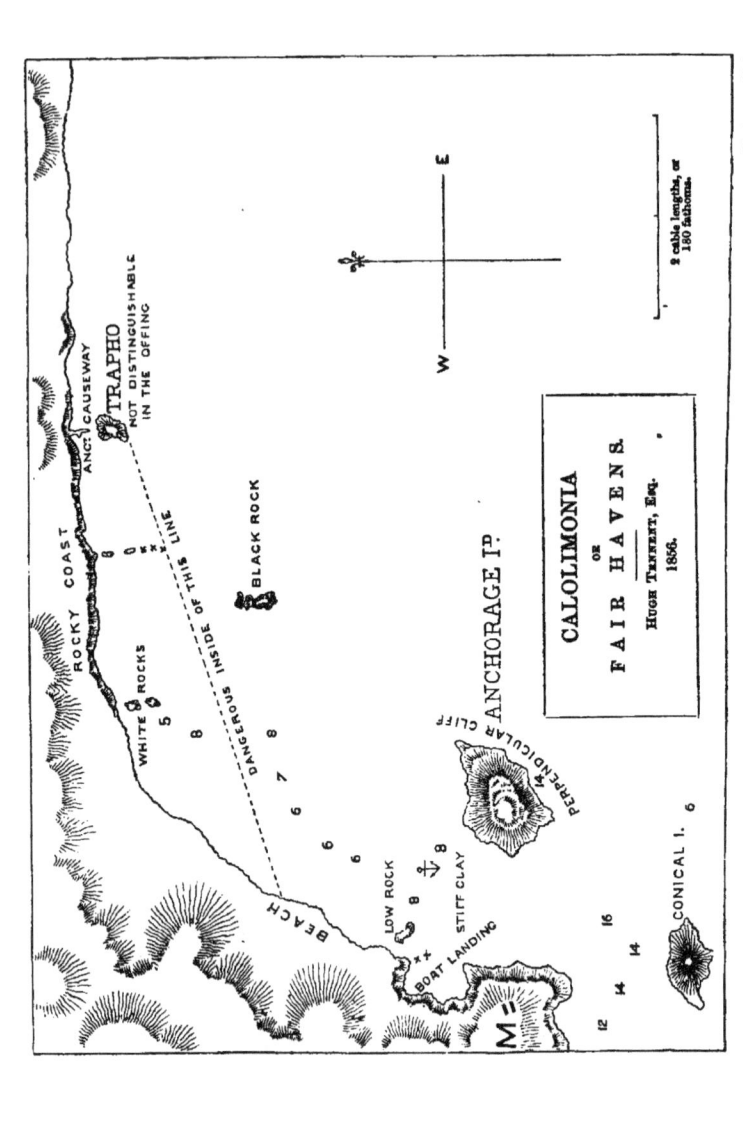

APPENDIX NO. III.

harbour of Lutro, the grand pyramid Mount Ida is in full view 40 miles off. We then got on board, the vessel being now at hand, and set sail for the Fair Havens. They lie 40 miles to the eastward, just beyond Cape Matala. The wind blowing pretty fresh, we were opposite to them at day-break, and easily recognised the spot from the drawing in Mr. Smith's work.

Wednesday, 16th January. No soundings being given in any of our charts, Mr. Tennent, the captain, and myself, with two men, pulled in among the islands, in the boat, to survey the harbour. We found good anchorage inside with 8 or 10 fathoms. The charts are very incorrect. An island marked "Anchorage Island," and lying to the eastward, has a bad reef of rocks behind and around it, and is called by the natives Trapho; while the true anchorage island lies due south of the bay. We brought in the vessel, and came to at the spot indicated by an anchor in the chart. The captain subsequently made a survey of the place with the bearings, which we shall preserve.

Early in the afternoon some natives appeared on the beach, and hailed us. We landed, but found that they were Greeks, and could speak only their native tongue. One said he was Guardiano of the place, and pointed out to us his house two miles off. The country round the harbour is a sad wilderness, the land high and rocky, with here and there stunted trees and thorny shrubs. The Guardiano took us to see the ruins of a monastery (marked M.), which he called ἉΓΙΟΣ ΠΑΥΛΟΣ, and which, he said with great indignation, had been destroyed by the Turks. Two or three broken columns of white marble lie among the rubbish, and on one of them are the remains of an inscription, but all that is legible is a K, two Omicrons, and a Π which has lost a leg. Fit puzzle for an antiquary!

The Greek spoke much of a monastery in the mountains, ΜΟΝΑΣΤΗΡΙΟΣ ΑΠΕΣΑΝΕΣ ἉΓΙΟΣ ΑΝΤΟΝΙΟΣ, which he said was great and beautiful; had twenty fathers, and many

METOIKOI, or dependencies; and that it was only three hours distant. Now it occurred to me that surely there somebody could speak Italian or French, and that we might get interesting information about that part of Crete from the Fathers, and perhaps procure some old manuscripts or records. Mr. Tennent felt quite inclined to go. The Guardiano, whose name is Joannes, promised to bring his mule the next day, and to be our guide; and, in short, the expedition was agreed upon. I suspect we were "out of order" in going up the country, as our bill of health had not been visé'd or approved. The health officer at Lutro would not examine it, as we did not come to anchor; and besides, he kept us at arms' length, and said something about performing quarantine. But then, on the other hand, the Guardiano asked no questions, and the nearest Bey lived three hours off, quite in another direction from the monastery: so the Campbells' proverb, "It's a far cry to Loch Awe," was our comfort.

On Thursday morning Mr. Tennent and I left the vessel at ten o'clock, and landed opposite Trapho, taking two men with us in their white blowses and blue collars, the club uniform. The men had each a musket, and we had six-barrel'd revolvers; so we looked very respectable indeed. I believe that in Candia the Greeks have been kept quite down by the Turks since 1830; but we hear that in these countries it is always the custom for travellers to carry arms. There was something peculiarly interesting in exploring this part of Candia. It is not described in *Murray*, and it has seldom been visited by our countrymen: the monastery perhaps never. A range of mountains, called the Mountains of Messara, runs parallel with the coast. They are from two to three thousand feet high, except one of them, Mount Kophinos, which lies to the east, and must be five thousand. Beyond this chain, on the north, lies the great plain of Messara, and from its northern side again, springs the magnificent Mount Ida (Psilority), Psiloriti. Well, under the guidance of Joannes, we walked along near the coast for two miles, by a steep and difficult path, among ravines, till we reached the Platē Pyrămata, a valley with a dry river course, and high, steep hills on either side. The loneliness of the country struck me exceedingly. Nobody was to be seen in the three miles we travelled up the vale; and yet its level bed, level like the vale of Lucerna*, might bear good crops; and its sides, if cultivated with care, might overflow with wine and oil. An olive tree here and there showed us what might be produced. It was the first time I had seen the blighting effects of the Turkish yoke; and as I wandered on, I fell into a long train of musings on the subject. "Lord, what shall the end of these things be?" Why should the countries where the gospel was first preached be a prey to the spoiler? Here is Crete, where Titus was busy in 62 or 64, ordaining elders in all its hundred cities; and now a wilderness!

After walking to the end of the level part (northwards), we came upon two peasants; and soon after, turning to the right, saw, high above us, the little village of Adheschāri. The day was hot; and we sat down to rest and bait, in sight, at least, of human habitations. After much climbing, we approached the pass that leads to the plains on the north; and on gaining it, found a plateau to the right, on which the monastery was situated. It is like a great farm-yard, with low buildings round it, flat-roofed. The church stands attached to one side. As we approached, I could have fancied it was the times of the Crusades; so quaint and old-fashioned did everything seem. Stiff pre-Raphaelite-like trees stood waiting patiently here and there; it did not clearly appear for what purpose. The houses positively had the uneasy look of a drawing that is all out of perspective; and the whole scene would have made a copy to illuminate a manuscript. We entered the outer gate, and found three aged πατηρες, sitting with long staves in their hands on a stone settle, stroking their beards and looking before them.

---

* In Piedmont.

They slowly rose and did obeisance to us, and we took off our hats to them. Then they led us into the court, which might be 160 feet square, and knocked at the door of the ἡγούμενος or abbot, whose name was Julius. He came out, and led us into his apartment; but we found, to our great disappointment, that no one in the place could speak anything but Romaïc Greek. It was but a few words that I could understand or speak, and of course anything like conversation was impossible. The ἡγούμενος was a most pleasing person: middle-aged, with a mild and intellectual, or at least thoughtful face. I requested a sight of the library; but he said, with a sigh, that all the books and manuscripts had been burnt by the Turks. However, a Father brought me an old Lucretius (1640), and made one of the boys read a passage, which he did with a Greek accent, disregarding all the quantities of the syllables. They showed us a Gospel of John, printed at Venice in 1811, and richly bound. It was in the ancient Greek; but when I read a verse or two aloud, they smiled at my disregard of accents, &c. All their books seem to come from Venice; which is natural, as the island of Candia belonged to Venice down to the end of the 17th century. There are ten Διδάσκαλοι, or youths under training, in the monastery. The Fathers teach them,—cultivate the land, look after the flocks and herds, perform the daily services in the church, and occasional services in the METOIKOI, or out-stations. The boys were playful and healthy; and the Fathers had not the sinister or dronish look with which one is disgusted in the monks of Italy. The abbot wore a Greek dress and turban, but had a monastic habit to put on over it. We had been four hours and a half on our journey, owing to the badness of the track, and the heat; and it was now three o'clock. As they pressed us to stay all night, we agreed to do so rather than be obliged to go over the difficult ground by moonlight. The tablecloth was then spread; and bread, cheese, wine, honey, and coffee were set before us. Our men looked very *blate* when bidden take their dinner with an abbot.

After dinner we climbed a hill in the neighbourhood, a few hundred feet above the pass; it commanded a grand and extensive view of the interior of the island. The plains of Messara lay at our feet to the north; and Mount Ida, the birthplace of Jupiter, rose beyond the plain, towering to a great height. Κωφινος, a very remarkable hill, like an exaggerated Scuir of Eigg, was the prominent feature to the east. We must have been 2000 feet, at least, above the sea. In the southern and western horizons, the sea was the boundary, and Clauda (Gozzo) and its Chicken were distinctly visible. This view well repaid our toil.

Two coarse swaggering Turkish soldiers, and a subaltern officer, had arrived at the monastery, and, though evidently unwelcome guests, were taking up their quarters for the night with the air of lords of the soil. I read them our passport (not a word of which they understood), and their commander bowed most graciously. The Hegoumenos seemed to dislike their company extremely, and came and sat beside Mr. Tennent and me at the kitchen fire. Supper, however, was set for the Turks and our party in his own apartment, though he did not appear. Halil Aga, the officer, sat next Tennente Effendi (for so they called him), on the sofa; only the Aga sat cross-legged, and Mr. Tennent as a European. After supper we went to the kitchen; and one or two of the Fathers, and several of their pupils, gathered around us. The boys seemed to be on excellent terms with their teacher. One of them made me understand that the latter was the ποιμὴν (shepherd), and that they were τὰ πρόϐατα (the sheep). Finer boys I never saw: we were both delighted with their intelligence and good manners. I drew out a packet of Greek tracts (not of a controversial nature) from my pocket, and they read one aloud, in turn, with great spirit and animation. I then divided the packet among them and the Fathers, who all seemed pleased with the little gift. A little fresh literature in those parts must be a great acquisition; but who knows whether true love to Christ may not burn in such a retreat? Perhaps something our tracts contained may have refreshed some thirsty soul.

We slept, with our men, in an upper chamber. At evening worship, we prayed that peace might rest on the house. At daybreak we rose, and found many peasants, men and women, assembling in the church for morning prayers. The service, alas! was unmeaning enough. They wanted us to wait and breakfast; but being anxious to enjoy the cool of the morning, we started at 6.30; and had a charming walk down the glen. Between eight and nine o'clock, we took some biscuit and beer, sitting under the shadow of a great rock, and after a hot march from our resting-place, reached the vessel at half past ten.

Friday, 18th. Nothing now remained to be done but to ascertain the exact position of Lasea, a city which Luke says was nigh to the Fair Havens. Mr. Smith notes that it is mentioned by no other writer, and that its ruins have not been observed. I asked our friend the Guardiano, που εστι Λασεα (Λασαια)? He said at once, that it was two hours' walk to the eastward, close to Cape Leonda; but that it is now a desert place (τοπω ερημω). Mr. Tennent was eager to examine it; so getting under weigh, we ran along the coast before a S. W. wind. Cape Leonda is called by the Greeks Λεωνα, evidently from its resemblance to a lion couchant, which nobody could fail to observe either from the west or the east. Its face is to the sea, forming a promontory 350 or 400 feet high. Just after we passed it, Miss Tennent's quick eye discovered two white pillars standing on an eminence near the shore. Down went the helm; and putting the vessel round, we stood in close, wore, and hove to. Mr. H. Tennent and I landed immediately, just inside the Cape, to the eastward, and found the beach lined with masses of masonry. These were formed of small stones, cemented together with mortar so firmly that even where the sea had undermined them, huge fragments lay on the sand. This sea wall extended a quarter of a mile

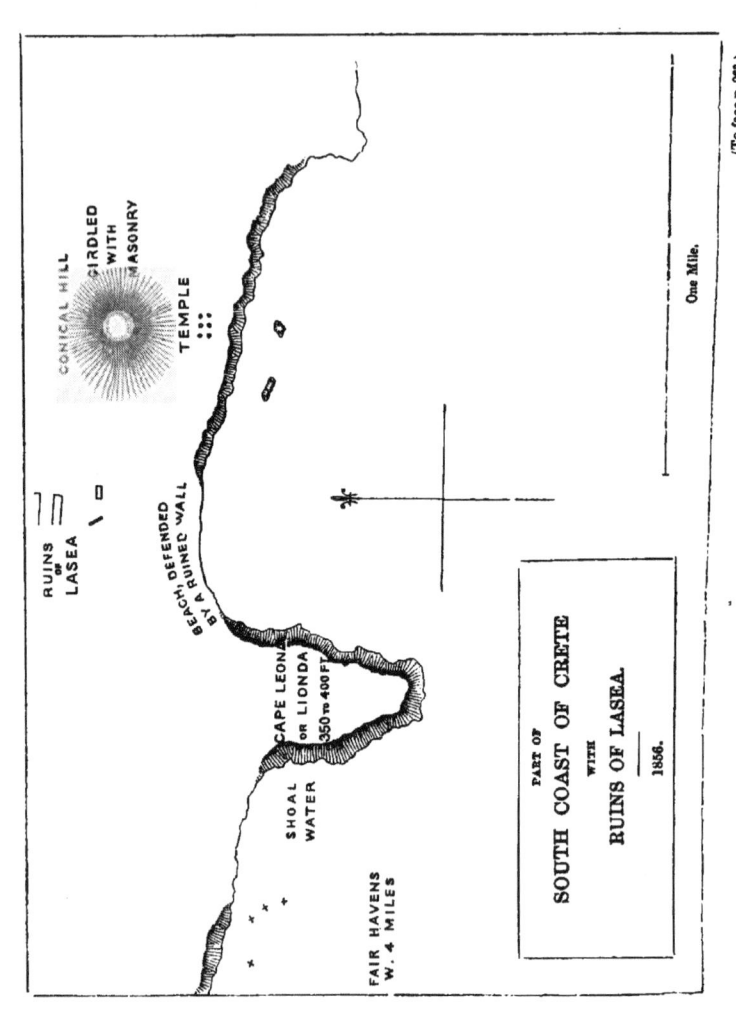

along the beach, from one rocky face to another, and was evidently intended for the defence of the city. Above we found the ruins of two temples. The steps which led up to the one remain, though in a shattered state; and the two white marble columns noticed by Miss Tennent belonged to the other. Many shafts, and a few capitals of Grecian pillars, all of marble, lie scattered about, and a gully worn by a torrent lays bare the substructions down to the rock. To the east a conical rocky hill is girdled by the foundations of a wall; and on a platform between this hill and the sea, the pillars of another edifice lie level with the ground. Some peasants came down to see us from the hills above, and I asked them the name of the place. They said at once, "Lasea;" so there could be no doubt. Cape Leonda lies five miles east of the Fair Havens; but there are no roads whatever in that part of Candia. We took away some specimens of marble, and boarded our vessel; at 4 P.M. sailed for Alexandria.

Alexandria, 22nd January. We have plans of Lutro and Fair Havens *in retentis*, which I dare say will interest Mr. Smith. The gale we had at Candia has been severely felt here, three vessels having been wrecked.

No. IV.

ON EURO-AQUILO.

(*From* Dr. BENTLEY'S "*Remarks on a late Discourse on Freethinking,*" p. 97.)

" STEPHENS followed what he found in the *King of France*'s copies, Acts xxvii. 14., ανεμος τυφωνικος ὁ καλουμενος Ευροκλυδων, and he is followed by your translators, 'There arose against it a tempestuous wind called *Euroclydon;* . . . if the printer had the use of your *Alexandrian* MS., which exhibits here Ευρακυλων, it's very likely he would have given it the preference in his text; and then the Doctor, upon his own principles, must have stickled for this.

"The wind *Euroclydon* was never heard of but here; it's compounded of Ευρος and κλυδων, the *wind* and the *waves,* and it seems plain, *à priori,* from the disparity of these two ideas, that they could not be joined in one compound; nor is there any other example of the like composition.

"But *Eurakulon,* or, as the Vulgate *Latin* here has it, *Euro-aquilo,* approved by *Grotius* and others, is so apposite to the context, and to all the circumstances of the place, that it may fairly challenge admittance as the word of *St. Luke.*

"'Tis true, according to *Vitruvius, Seneca,* and *Pliny,* who make *Eurus* to blow from the winter solstice, and *Aquilo* between the summer solstice and the north point, there can be no such wind or word as *Euro-aquilo,* because the *Solanus,* or *Apeliotes* from the cardinal point of east comes between them. But *Eurus* is here taken, as *Gellius,* ii. 22., and the *Latin* poets use it, for the middle equinoctial east, the same as *Solanus;* and then in the table of the XII. winds, according to the ancients, between the two cardinal winds, *Septentrio* and *Eurus,* there are two at stated distances, *Aquilo* and Καικιας. The *Latins* had no name for Καικιας, 'Quem ab oriente solstitiali excitatum Græci Καικιαν vocant, apud nos sine nomine est,' says Seneca, *Nat. Quæst.* v. 16.

"Καικιας, therefore, blowing between *Aquilo* and *Eurus,* the Roman seamen (for want of a specific word) might express the same wind by the compound *Euro-aquilo,* in the same analogy as the *Greeks* call Ευρονοτος the middle wind between *Eurus* and *Notus*, and as you say now *North-east* and *South-east*. Since, therefore, we have now found that *Euro-aquilo* was the *Roman* mariner's word for the Greek Καικιας, there will soon appear a just reason why *St. Luke* calls it ανεμος τυφωνικος, a tempestuous wind, *Vorticosus*, a whirling wind, for that is the peculiar character of Καικιας in those climates, as appears from several authors, and from that known proverbial verse—

Ἑλκων εφ' αὑτον ὡς ὁ Καικιας νεφη.

So, with submission, I think our *Luther's* and the *Danish* version have done more right than the *English* to your sacred text, by translating it *Nord-est*, *North-east;* though according to the present compass, divided into xxxii, *Euro-aquilo* answers nearest to *East-north-east*, which is the very wind which would directly drive the ship from Crete to the African *Syrtis*, according to the pilot's fears in the 17th verse."

No. V.

NOTE ON THE READING "EURO-AQUILO."

(*From* GRANVILLE PENN'S *translation of the "New Covenant"* (*Testament*).)

"OF the two readings, Ευρακυλων and Ευροκλυδων, the former has the testimony of the highest antiquity. Bishop Marsh, with Shaw, and all his other learned predecessors, thought it peculiar to the *Alex.* MS. (Michaelis, *Introd.* vol. ii. p. 110. 620.), but it is the reading also of the far more ancient *Vatican* MS., and is witnessed also by *Jerome*, and the *first* or Latin translation. The difficulties experienced by commentators in endeavouring to settle the reading of this word have been owing to a pre-assumption that it is to be interpreted from *the Greek;* and if any one should attempt to explain σπεκουλατωρ, φραγελλοω, or κνησος, by *the Greek*, he would find himself in a similar dilemma. Dr. Shaw, objecting to the reading *Euraquilo* in his *Travels,* &c. (p. 360. fol.), observes: 'As the ship was of Alexandria, sailing to Italy, we *may suppose* the mariners to have been *Grecian*, and too well acquainted with the received and vernacular *terms* of their occupation to admit of this *Græco-Latin* or *barbarous* appellation, as they may think it;' but it would be full as reasonable to suppose that the mariners might have been *Egyptian*, or even *Italian*, as the ship was freighted for Italy, to supply that country with corn. Dr. Bloomfield enforces Shaw's objection, by observing that *Euro-aquilo* would be *heterogeneously compounded of Greek and Latin.* Now this objection would extend equally to prove that *no wind* was denominated by the Latins ' *Euro-auster,*' for Aulus Gellius (lib. ii. c. 22.) expressly declares *Auster* to be a *Latin* term; and yet we know that the S.E. wind was actually so denominated by the Latins. Besides, every reader of Virgil and Horace knows that the name Eurus had become so thoroughly naturalised in Rome, as no longer to be regarded as a foreign name. The latter of those learned writers observes, ' Ακυλων could not represent *Aquilo;*' yet, if he had referred to the relative orthographies *Aquila* and Ακυλας, in Acts xviii. 2., Rom. xvi. 3., &c., and had recollected the relative dialectic terminations *o* and ων of the two languages (Plato, Πλατων), he would have perceived that *Aquilo* must have been represented in Greek orthography by Ακυλων. We cannot reason positively and accurately of winds from the employment of their names by the poets, because they used them with licence, according to the demands of their metre. In Aulus Gellius we have a minute enumeration of them, with their names and quarters, as follows:

APPENDIX NO. V. 267

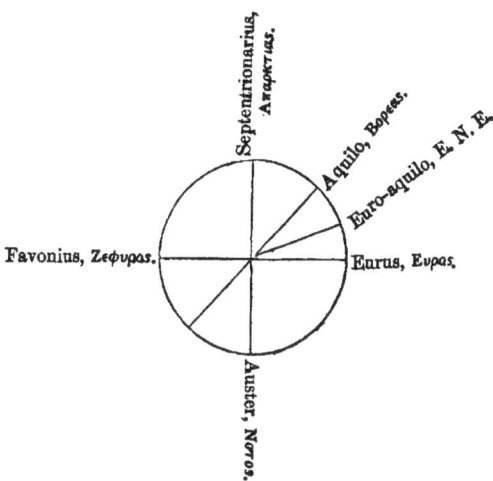

"Pliny places *Aquilo* 'inter septentrionem et exortum solstitialem' (*N. H.* ii. 47.), *Euro-aquilo* will be still more eastward, or *East-north-east*. The *Eth.* version paraphrases *ventus Aquilonarius*, a N. E. *wind*. Ευροκλυδων of the *jun*. Greek texts, as also Ευρυκλυδων, Ευτρακηλων *Copt.*, Ευρακλυδων *Syra post.*, Ευρακυκλων *Arm.*, Ευρακηλων *Sahid.*, will all, therefore, have been transcriptural *errata*. Dr. Bloomfield thinks it clear, that both external and internal evidence unite in requiring the common reading, Ευροκλυδων, to be retained, and that it was sometimes used as an adjective, as appears from the adjective ερικλυδων, which is used by a later Greek writer *ap. Steph. Thes.* We are much obliged to the learned annotator for drawing our attention to this solitary word, which might otherwise have remained for ever unnoticed. This word is employed in a metrical chronicle of one of the

Byzantine historians, Constantine Manasses, who lived in the middle of the twelfth century.

'Ο Καισαρ γαρ εφυσησε, βορρας ως βαρυβοας,
ως ερικλυδων αγριος, ως δυσπνους απαρκτιας.—p. 104.

Which lines are thus interpreted by Leunclavius:—*Cæsar autem adflabat, tanquam graviter spirans Aquilo, vel sævus ille tempestatesque ciens Subsolanus.*

"Leunclavius has certainly assumed ερικλυδων here to be an *adjective,* but a little closer inspection will reveal to us that the poet used it, not as an adjective, but as a *substantive,* as the proper name of one of three north and east winds, which he specifies, and, in fact, the very wind mentioned by St. Luke: which, in the *junior* or Constantinopolitan copies of the Scriptures best known to the poet, had been changed to ευροκλυδων, and in the printed copy of this poem to ερικλυδων.

'For Cæsar raged like the deep-roaring Boreas;
'Like the fierce Ericlydon; and like the hard-blowing Aparctias.'

"But we have specially to consider that St. Luke heard the name of the wind on board an Alexandrian ship, that the two oldest documents which record the name are Alexandrian, and that both record the name Ευρακυλων, *Euraquilo*; and farther, that the technical language of the conquering nation was extensively adopted in the countries enclosing the Mediterranean, particularly in those maritime cities that were in most frequent and active intercourse with Rome, as was eminently *Alexandria*. The whole context is wanting in the *Cod. Ephr.* from c. xxvi. 20. to xxvii. 16., and in the *Cod. Bezæ* from c. xxii. to the end of the book."

No. VI.

REMARKS ON THE MELITA OF ACTS, XXVIII.

(*From* BOCHART's "*Chanaan*," lib. i. cap. xxvi.)

" SED altera hic sese offert majoris momenti quæstio ad utram appulerat Paulus. Sunt enim quibus videtur de Illyrica egisse Lucas. In his Constantinus Porphyrogenneta, a quo ponitur in censu insularum Illyrici littoris : Νησος ετερα μεγαλη τα Με-λετα, ητοι το Μαλοξεαται, ην εν ταις Πραξεσι των Αποστολων ὁ ἁγιος Λουκας μεμνηται, Μελιτην ταυτην προσαγορευων. *Alia magna insula quæ Meleta ceu Malozeatæ vocatur, cujus in Actis Apostolorum meminit Sanctus Lucas, Melitam eam nominans.*

"Cui sententiæ favere volunt:—1. Quod in Adria jactatur Paulus antequam in Meliten appellat (Actor. 27. 27.), unde colligunt agi de insula sinus Adriatici. 2. Quod barbaros habuit incolas (Actor. 28. 2. 4.), cum Africanam Meliten Græci pridem incoluerant. 3. Quod in insula Melite nullius oppidi meminit Lucas, cum Africana urbem habuerit insulæ cognominem quæ superstes hodieque est.

"Sed hæ objectiunculæ tanti non sunt, ut quemquam dimovere debeant a vulgari sententia quam firmissimæ rationes adstruunt. Primo, enim (Actor. 27. 13. 14.), circa Cretam quum navigaret Paulus, excitatur ανεμος τυφωνικος ὁ καλουμενος Ευροκλυδων,—*ventus turbulentus* quæ vocatur *Euroclydon*, vel, ut legit Vulgatus Interpres, Ευρο-ακυλων, *Euro-aquilo*, quem lectionem si sequaris, res est confecta ; neque enim *Euro-aquilo*, potuit navem in Illyricam impellere. Præstitisset id *Euronotus*, non subcontrarius *Euro-aquilo*, ut docet situs locorum. Sed quocunque modo legas, ventum illum Euroclydonem in Austrum inclinasse potius quam in Septentrionem inde palam est, quod illo flante nautæ metuunt ne in Africæ Syrtim incidant. (Actor.

27. 17.) Nihil tale formidaturi si ventus navem Illyricam impulisset, quæ ora est Syrti et Africæ obversa.

"2. Actor. 27. 41.: Πριπεσοντες εις τοπον διθαλασσον επωκειλαν την ναυν, *cum incidissent in locum bimarem illæserunt navem.* In locum bimarem, id est in isthmum. Horat. *Od.* 7. lib. i.:

> 'Aut Ephesum bimarisve Corinthi
> Mœnia.'

Ovid. eleg. 12. lib. i. *Trist.*:

> 'Aut postquam bimarem cursu superavimus Isthmum.'

Hic Isthmus ad insulæ ortum æstivum hodieque ostenditur, et vocatur ab incolis, *La Cala di S. Paolo*, S. Pauli adpulsus.

"3. Actor. 28. 7.: *Circa locum illum erant* χωρια τῳ πρωτῳ του νησου ονοματι Ποπλιῳ, *prædia primo insulæ nomine Publio.* Eum intelligo quem insulæ Romani præfecerant. Nam hujus insulæ præfectos ita nominari solitos et ex hoc loco colligere est, et ex veteri epitaphio quod in marmore Græcis literis se Melitæ vidisse refert Quintinus: Λ. ΚΑ. ΥΙΟΣ. ΚΥΡ. ΙΠΠΕΥΣ. ΡΩΜΑΙΩΝ. ΠΡΩΤΟΣ. ΜΕΛΙΤΑΙΩΝ. *L. Ca. filius Cyr. eques Romanorum*, PRIMUS *Melitensium.* Nempe idem antea nominis fuerat præfectis Carthaginiensibus, qui Punica phrasi dicebantur הראשונים, *primi*. Sic Dan. 10. 13.: Michael est unus principum, הראשונים, *primorum.* Proinde ראש, *caput, dux, princeps*, et ראשון, *primus*, sunt conjugata. Atque hoc ipso loco pro primo Syrus habet ריש et Arabs רוים, *caput*. Eodem fecit quod Arabice, ut ארל *primus*, ita אאל est præficere, sed et provinciam regere, quasi πρωτευειν dicas.

"4. Tres menses continuos in illa insula hæsit Paulus cum centurione et aliis (Act. 28. 11.), qui numerus hominum fuit cclxxvi (Act. 27. 37.). Quod vix quisquam crediderit de Illyrica Melite; quia cum nonnisi quatuor passuum millibus a continenti distet, et Epidaurum in conspectu habeat, portum celeberrimum et hospitibus commodissimum, centurio Romanus maluisset eo trajicere, quam totam hyemem in misera insula degere, in qua tam multas advenas sine gravibus incommodis diversari fuisset nefas.

"5. Jam quod iidem dicuntur Puteolos vecti fuisse in Alexandrina nave quæ in eadem insula hyemaverat (Act. 28. 11.), quis de Illyrica Melita intellexerit? Cum ab Ægypto Puteolos contendentibus, Africana Melite pene invitis sese offerat. At quisquis Alexandria Puteolos iturus Illyricam Melitem petit merito dici queat, sin minus toto cœlo, saltem toto salo, aberrasse.

"6. Hoc potissimum quod Lucas e Melite profectos addit primo Syracusas deinde Rhegium appulisse (Act. 28. 12, 13.); quæ via, quam est recta si profectio fuit ex Africana Melita, tam flexuosa fuerit et præpostera, si ex Illyrica discesserunt, e qua potius per Rhegium, quia Rhegium est vicinius.

"7. Jam si authoritate certatur Constantino Porphyrogenneta, longe antiquior est Arator Sub-Diaconus, qui sic habet, lib. ii. *Historiæ Apostolicæ*:—

'Sicanio lateri remis vicina Melite.'

"Nec difficile est solvere quicquid contra objiciunt. Nam in Adria quidem jactari dicitur navis appulsura Melitem (Act. 27. 27.); non tamen in Adriatico sinu, quo multo latius patet Adria, seu quod Idem est Adriaticum Mare. Sinus enim Adriaticus cum Illyrico desinit. At Mare Adriaticum idem est cum Ionio: Hesychius—$Ιονιον\ πελαγος\ ὁ\ νυν\ Αδριας$, *Ionium Mare quod nunc Adria*. Juvenalis, vetus scholiastes—*Diu navigaturus de Tyrrheno mari ad Adriacum;* Adriacum pro Ionio dixit. Ita cum Juvenalis:—

'Tyrrhenos igitur fluctus, lateque sonantem
Pertulit Ionium.'

"Hinc Ptolomæus Siciliam ab ortu, Epirum et Achaiam a meridie, et Peloponnesum adeoque Cretam ab occasu definit Adriatico pelago. Et in Ovidio non semel Adriam ab Ægæo dividit Isthmus Corinthiacus. Sic lib. iv. *Fastorum:*—

'Adriacumque patens late bimaremque Corinthum.'

et in lib. i. *Trist.* eleg. 12. : —

    ' Aut hæc me gelido tremerem cum mense Decembri
      Scribentem mediis Adria vidit aquis,
    Aut postquam bimarem cursu superavimus Isthmum,
      Alteraque est nostræ sumpta carina fugæ.'

"Proinde Philostratus, lib. ii. *Imaginum*, in Palæmone, eum isthmum scribit, Αιγαιου και Αδριου μεσον κεισθαι, *medium esse inter mare Ægæum et Adriaticum*. Et in *Apollonio* suo, lib. iv. cap. 8., Neronem idem tradit de hoc isthmo scindendo cogitasse ut Adriaticum Ægæo mari misceret. Eodem fecit quod Alpheus apud Suidam in Αλφειος et rursus in Αρεθουσα, e Peloponneso in Siciliæ Arethusam influere legitur δυομενος δια της Αδριαδος θαλασσης, *pelagus subiens per mare Adriaticum*. Hinc de Alpheo Pausanias in *Arcadicis* Εμελλε δε αρα μηδε Αδριας επισχησειν αυτον του προσω, *neque illius cursum Adria cohibitura erat*. Cætera ibi vide.

"Quid quod Adriaticum mare ad Africam usque extensum est, si Ethicum sequimur et Orosium, apud quos Tripolitana provincia, ubi Arzuges et Leptis Magno, habet a septentrione mare Adriaticum, et a meridie Creta finitur *mari Lybico, quod et Adriaticum vocant*.

"Nec aliter sensit Hieronymus in *Vita Hilarionis*, ubi medium Adrium pertranseunt ab Ægypti Parætonio ad Siciliæ Pachynum appulsuri. Sed ad rem id maxime est quod in Procopii *Vandalicis*, lib. i., insulæ Gaulus et Melita Αδριατικον και Τυρσηνικον πελαγος διοριζουσιν, *Adriaticum et Tuscum pelagus disterminant*. Scite, igitur, sacer scriptor et ex geographicorum usu e Creta Melitam delatos, vi ventorum ingruentium jactari dicit in Adria. Porro in eadem insula barbarorum nomine Pœnos ab illo designari docuimus quorum reliquiæ in agros hæserant. Oppidi denique non meminit, quia nihil erat necesse. Ita, Actor. 21. 1., Paulus appulisse narratur in insulas Coum et Rhodum, absque mentione urbium quas tamen utraque habuit insulæ cognomines."

No. VII.

ON THE ACCOUNT OF THE NIGHT MARCH OF THE PELOPONNESIANS.

(*Thucydides*, lib. ii. cap. 93.)

THE discovery of the inventories of the Attic navy clears up in a great measure the difficulties in the account given by Thucydides of the night march of the Peloponnesians across the isthmus of Corinth. They show, in the first place that it was necessary that they should carry their oars, with all their appurtenances, along with them; because those belonging to the galleys were always taken out of them, and kept in separate storehouses when the ships were laid up; and, as the space between Megara and the port at Minoa was walled in, the storehouses in this case were probably inaccessible.

The tables show, in the next place, that the oars of a trireme were of such dimensions as not to be too heavy to be carried by one man each.

Dr. Bishop, in a note on the oars of ancient triremes, appended to Arnold's edition of Thucydides, offers some explanatory conjectures which require to be noticed, because they have been to a certain degree admitted by subsequent writers. (*Thirlwall's Greece*, iii. 125.) He supposes that the tropoter (προπωτηρ), instead of being a thong of hide to keep the oar to the peg or thole, was a coil of rope which "was used, certainly not as a fulcrum, but probably for the triple purpose of a counterpoise, a nut, and a loop;" and has given a figure of an oar of the same thickness throughout, with the rope coiled round it at the upper end, to act as a counterpoise to the extra weight of the oar outside of the ship. He assigns the following reasons for concluding with certainty that the tropoter could not be used as a fulcrum:— "The use of pegs

T

at all is only a consequence of the rowlocks being constructed on the upper edge or gunwale." This is by no means so clear: unless the oar-ports were very small, a peg, and consequently a thong, would be as necessary in the under tiers as in the upper one. But even if the thongs were not required as fulcrums, they might be required to prevent the oar from being pulled away by the enemy; and, at all events, we cannot suppose that the upper tier oars were left behind; but, if they were not, the thongs or grummets must have been taken also. Thucydides, in his enumeration, evidently meant no more than that everything was taken which was necessary to enable them to pull the galleys from Minoa to the Piræus. Without oars and thongs they could not have done so: and the thong could make no sensible addition to the weight. It is not quite so clear why they took the hyperesia, or seat-covers. I agree with Dr. Bishop and Mitford, that it could not be that they might sit softer; but I cannot agree with the former, that it was to prevent their sliding upon their seats: their object was not to run a race, and that extreme nicety required where a few feet may be of consequence could be of none in a surprise. The hyperesium was a sheepskin with the fleece (ὑπηρεσιον εστι κωας, κ.τ.λ. Scholiast on passage). By rolling it up it became a cushion or pillow; and I suspect this was all that was allowed to the rowers for sleeping on. Hesychius and Julius Pollux inform us that it was synonymous with προσκεφαλαιον (Hesych. ad verb. Jul. Poll. lib. x. c. 40.); and it was resting upon this that our Lord slept in the storm on the Lake of Tiberias. (Mark iv. 38.) But we can as little suppose that on such an occasion as that related by Thucydides they would make preparation for sleeping as for sitting soft. Mitford supposes it may have been for the purpose of making oar-coats or bags to keep out the water (note to cap. xv. s. 11.), and refers to a marble in the Vatican, which is evidently the same as that described by Winkelmann, where the oars are represented with such an appendage, which was, no doubt, necessary in a heavy

APPENDIX NO. VII. 275

sea, but could scarcely be required between Minoa and the Piræus. But although a cushion or fleece would not be required in any of the supposed cases, there is one case where it would be of obvious utility, namely, placed between the oars and the shoulders of those who carried them: men who had to carry oars for five or six miles could scarcely dispense with a cushion; or they may have been required to muffle the oars, a common precaution in a surprise.

Dr. Bishop's conjecture respecting the tropoter is quite at variance with the evidence of ancient authors. Thus Julius Pollux tells us that "the tropoter is that by which the oars are bound to the scalmus or thole (lib. i. 87.), ὅθεν μεν αἱ κωπαι εκδεδενται σκαλμος, ᾧ δε εκδεδενται τροπωτηρ; and Hesychius tells us they are bands made of hide, by which oars are kept in their places when they row : η οἱ κατεχοντες τας κωπας δεσμοι δερματινοι ὁταν ελαυνωσιν, οἱ τροπωτηρες.

Dr. Bishop observes that "There are two things to be particularly remarked in gunwale oars of a good construction: first, that the loom or part within board is very much thicker than the neck or part adjacent to the blade. Now it is a law in mechanics that the strength of a machine is to be measured by that of its weakest part. The increased size of the loom cannot add to the strength of the oar as a whole, but is, in fact, merely supplied as a dead weight." But it is only where the strain is equal that this law applies. The mechanical principle is, not that every part of a machine should be equally strong, but that every part should bear the same proportion to the strain which it is intended to bear.

The maximum of strain in an oar, so far as the strain arises from the force of the rower, is at the fulcrum; and in going towards either end of the oar, diminishes in proportion to the distance from the fulcrum till it becomes zero at either end. The strain, so far as it arises from the weight of the oar, is also a maximum at the fulcrum, and diminishes in going towards either end of the oar, till it becomes zero. This diminution is not, however, proportional to the distance from the fulcrum; and the strain at any point in the upper part of the oar is greater than the strain at the corresponding point in the lower part.

The increased thickness of an oar at its upper end is therefore requisite for strength, still more than it is for weight. A cylindrical oar, like Dr. Bishop's figure, would either be too weak or too heavy; it would break at the fulcrum long before there was any tendency to break at any other point.

If we consider the necessary thickness of a ship's side it is not easy to imagine that the oar-ports were small enough to serve as rowlocks; and the evidence points altogether the other way. We hear of spears being darted through the oar-ports. Herodotus tells us that the captain of a galley was pilloried for remissness in duty, by having his head pushed through the lower ports, διa Θαλαμιης (lib. v. cap. 33.); and the ports of the "Navicella" at Rome, which has all the appearance of being formed to a scale, are quite large enough for that purpose.

The weight of a *fir* oar of the dimensions mentioned in the Attic tables, I found to be between twelve and thirteen pounds; hence it could easily be carried on the shoulder.

THE END.

A CATALOGUE
OF
NEW WORKS IN GENERAL LITERATURE
PUBLISHED BY
LONGMAN, GREEN, LONGMAN, AND ROBERTS
39 PATERNOSTER ROW, LONDON.

CLASSIFIED INDEX

Agriculture and Rural Affairs.

Bayldon on Valuing Rents, &c.	5
Cecil's Stud Farm	8
Hoskyns's Talpa	11
Loudon's Agriculture	14
Morton on Landed Estates	17
" (J. C.) Handbook of Dairy Husbandry	17

Arts, Manufactures, and Architecture.

Brande's Dictionary of Science, &c.	6
" Organic Chemistry	6
Cresy's Civil Engineering	8
Fairbairn's Information for Engineers	9
" on Mills and Millwork	9
Falkener's Dædalus	9
" Museum of Classical Antiquities	9
Goodeve's Elements of Mechanism	9
Gwilt's Encyclopædia of Architecture	10
Harford's Plates from M. Angelo	10
Humphreys's *Parables* Illuminated	12
Jameson's Sacred and Legendary Art	12
" Commonplace-Book	12
König's Pictorial Life of Luther	10
Loudon's Rural Architecture	14
Love's Art of Dyeing	14
Lowndes's Engineers' Handbook	15
MacDougall's Campaigns of Hannibal	15
" Theory of War	15
Moseley's Engineering	17
Piesse's Art of Perfumery	18
" Laboratory of Chemical Wonders	18
Richardson's Art of Horsemanship	19
Scoffern on Projectiles, &c.	20
Steam Engine, by the Artisan Club	6
Ure's Dictionary of Arts, &c.	23

Biography.

Arago's Lives of Scientific Men	5
Baillie's Memoir of Bate	5
Brialmont's Wellington	6
Bunsen's Hippolytus	7
Bunting's (Dr.) Life	7
Crosse's (Andrew) Memorials	8
Green's Princesses of England	10
Harford's Life of Michael Angelo	10
Lardner's Cabinet Cyclopædia	13
Marshman's Life of Carey, Marshman, and Ward	15
" Life of Havelock	15
Maunder's Biographical Treasury	15
Mountain's (Col.) Memoirs	17
Palleske's Life of Schiller	18
Parry's (Admiral) Memoirs	18
Peel's Sketch of Sir R. Peel's Life and Character	18
Piozzi's Autobiography and Letters	18
Russell's Memoirs of Moore	16
" (Dr.) Life of Mezzofanti	20
SchimmelPenninck's (Mrs.) Life	20
Shee's Life of Sir M. A. Shee	21
Southey's Life of Wesley	21
Stephen's Ecclesiastical Biography	22
Strickland's Queens of England	22
Sydney Smith's Memoirs	21
Waterton's Autobiography and Essays	24

Books of General Utility.

Acton's Cookery-Book	5
Black's Treatise on Brewing	6
Cabinet Gazetteer	7
" Lawyer	7
Cust's Invalid's Own Book	8
Hensman's Handbook of the Constitution	11
Hints on Etiquette	11
Hudson's Executor's Guide	12
" on Making Wills	12
Hunter's Art of Writing Précis	12
Kesteven's Domestic Medicine	13
Lardner's Cabinet Cyclopædia	13
Loudon's Lady's Country Companion	14
Maunder's Treasury of Knowledge	15
" Biographical Treasury	15
" Geographical Treasury	16
" Scientific Treasury	15
" Treasury of History	16
" Natural History	15
Piesse's Art of Perfumery	18
Pitt's How to Brew Good Beer	18
Pocket and the Stud	10
Pycroft's English Reading	19
Richardson's Art of Horsemanship	19
Riddle's Latin Dictionaries	19
Roget's English Thesaurus	19
Rowton's Debater	20
Short Whist	21
Simpson's Handbook of Dining	21
Sleigh's Personal Wrongs and Legal Remedies	21
Thomson's Interest Tables	22
Walford's Handybook of the Civil Service	23
Webster's Domestic Economy	23
West's How to Nurse Sick Children	24
Willich's Popular Tables	24
Wilmot's Blackstone	24

A

Botany and Gardening.

Hassall's British Freshwater Algæ	10
Hooker's British Flora	11
" Guide to Kew Gardens	11
Lindley's Introduction to Botany	13
" Synopsis of the British Flora	13
" Theory of Horticulture	13
Loudon's Hortus Britannicus	14
" Amateur Gardener	14
" Trees and Shrubs	13
" Gardening	13
" Plants	14
Pereira's Materia Medica	18
Rivers's Rose Amateur's Guide	19
Wilson's British Mosses	24

Chronology.

Brewer's Historical Atlas	6
Bunsen's Ancient Egypt	7
Haydn's Beatson's Index	10
Jaquemet's Abridged Chronology	12

Commerce and Mercantile Affairs.

Gilbart's Logic of Banking	9
Lorimer's Young Master Mariner	13
M'Culloch's Commerce and Navigation	15
Thomson's Interest Tables	22
Tooke's History of Prices	22

Criticism, History, and Memoirs.

Brewer's Historical Atlas	6
Bunsen's Ancient Egypt	7
" Hippolytus	7
Burke's Vicissitudes of Families	7
Chapman's Gustavus Adolphus	8
Clough's Greek History from Plutarch	8
Conolly's Sappers and Miners	8
Conybeare and Howson's St. Paul	8
Crowe's History of France	8
Fraser's Letters during the Peninsular and Waterloo Campaigns	9
Gurney's Historical Sketches	10
Hayward's Essays	11
Hensman's Handbook of the Constitution	11
Herschel's Essays and Addresses	11
Jeffrey's (Lord) Contributions	12
Kemble's Anglo-Saxons	13
Lardner's Cabinet Cyclopædia	13
Latham's Works on the English Language	13
Lowe's Campaigns in Central India	14
Macaulay's Critical and Hist. Essays	14
" History of England	14
" Miscellaneous Writings	14
" Speeches	14
Mackintosh's Miscellaneous Works	15
" History of England	15
M'Culloch's Geographical Dictionary	15
Maunder's Treasury of History	16
Merivale's History of Rome	16
" Roman Republic	16
Moore's (Thomas) Memoirs, &c.	17
Mure's Greek Literature	18
Pulleske's Life and Works of Schiller	18
Piozzi's Autobiography and Letters	18
Porter's Knights of Malta	18
Raikes's Journal	19
Rich's Roman and Greek Antiquities	19
Riddle's Latin Dictionaries	19
Rogers's Essays from Edinb. Review	19
" (Sam.) Recollections	19
Roget's English Thesaurus	19

SchimmelPenninck's Memoirs of Port-Royal	20
" Principles of Beauty	20
Schmitz's History of Greece	20
Southey's Doctor	21
Stephen's Ecclesiastical Biography	22
" Lectures on French History	22
Sydney Smith's Works	21
" Lectures	21
" Memoirs	21
Thirlwall's History of Greece	22
Turner's Anglo-Saxons	23
White and Riddle's Latin Dictionary	24
Whiteside's Italy	24
Wilkins's Political Ballads	24
Wilmot's Brougham's Law Reforms	24

Geography and Atlases.

Brewer's Historical Atlas	6
Butler's Geography and Atlases	7
Cabinet Gazetteer	7
Johnston's General Gazetteer	13
M'Culloch's Geographical Dictionary	15
Maunder's Treasury of Geography	16
Murray's Encyclopædia of Geography	17
Sharp's British Gazetteer	20

Juvenile Books.

Amy Herbert	20
Cleve Hall	20
Earl's Daughter (The)	20
Experience of Life	20
Gertrude	20
Howitt's Boy's Country Book	12
" (Mary) Children's Year	11
Ivors	20
Katharine Ashton	20
Laneton Parsonage	20
Margaret Percival	20
Piesse's Chymical, Natural, and Physical Magic	18
" Laboratory of Chymical Wonders	18
Pycroft's Collegian's Guide	19

Medicine, Surgery, &c.

Brodie's Psychological Inquiries	6
Bull's Hints to Mothers	6
" Management of Children	6
Copland's Dictionary of Medicine	8
Cust's Invalid's Own Book	8
Holland's Mental Physiology	11
" Medical Notes and Reflections	11
Kesteven's Domestic Medicine	13
Pereira's Materia Medica	18
Spencer's Principles of Psychology	21
Todd's Cyclopædia of Anatomy and Physiology	22
West on Children's Diseases	24
" Nursing Sick Children	24

Miscellaneous Literature.

Bacon's (Lord) Works	6
Boase's Philosophy of Nature	6
Bray on Education of the Feelings	6
Defence of Eclipse of Faith	9
Eclipse of Faith	9
Greyson's Select Correspondence	10
Gurney's Evening Recreations	10
Hassall's Adulterations Detected, &c.	10
Haydn's Book of Dignities	10
Holland's Mental Physiology	11

CLASSIFIED INDEX TO CATALOGUE. 3

Hooker's Kew Guide	11
Howard's Gymnastic Exercises	11
Howitt's Rural Life of England	12
" Visits to Remarkable Places	12
Jameson's Commonplace-Book	12
Jeffrey's (Lord) Essays	12
Macaulay's Critical and Hist. Essays	14
" Speeches	14
Mackintosh's Miscellaneous Works	15
Martineau's Miscellanies	15
Newman on University Education	17
" Office & Work of Universities	17
" 's Lectures and Essays	17
Pycroft's English Reading	19
Rich's Dictionary of Antiquities	19
Riddle's Latin Dictionaries	19
Rowton's Debater	20
Sir Roger De Coverley	21
Smith's (Rev. Sydney) Works	21
Southey's Doctor, &c.	21
Spencer's Essays	21
Stephen's Essays	22
Stow's Training System	22
Thomson's Laws of Thought	22
Trevelyan on the Native Languages of India	22
White & Riddle's Latin Dictionary	24
Wit and Wisdom of Sydney Smith	21
Yonge's English-Greek Lexicon	24
" Latin Gradus	24
Zumpt's Latin Grammar	24

Natural History in general.

Agassiz on Classification	5
Catlow's Popular Conchology	8
Ephemera's Book of the Salmon	9
Garratt's Marvels of Instinct	9
Gosse's Natural History of Jamaica	10
Hartwig's Sea and its Living Wonders	10
Kirby and Spence's Entomology	13
Lee's Elements of Natural History	13
Maunder's Natural History	15
Quatrefages' Rambles of a Naturalist	19
Stonehenge on the Dog	22
Turton's Shells of the British Islands	23
Waterton's Essays on Natural History	23
Youatt's The Dog	24
" The Horse	24

One-Volume Encyclopædias and Dictionaries.

Blaine's Rural Sports	6
Brande's Science, Literature, and Art	6
Copland's Dictionary of Medicine	8
Cresy's Civil Engineering	8
Gwilt's Architecture	10
Johnston's Geographical Dictionary	13
Loudon's Agriculture	14
" Rural Architecture	14
" Gardening	14
" Plants	14
" Trees and Shrubs	14
M'Culloch's Geographical Dictionary	15
" Dictionary of Commerce	15
Murray's Encyclopædia of Geography	17
Sharp's British Gazetteer	20
Ure's Dictionary of Arts, &c.	23
Webster's Domestic Economy	23

Religious and Moral Works.

Afternoon of Life	5
Amy Herbert	20
Bloomfield's Greek Testament	6
Bloomfield's Supplementary Annotations on the Greek Testament	6
Bray on Education of the Feelings	6
Bunyan's Pilgrim's Progress	7
Calvert's Wife's Manual	7
Catz and Farlie's Moral Emblems	8
Cleve Hall	20
Conybeare and Howson's St. Paul	8
Cotton's Instructions in Christianity	8
Dale's Domestic Liturgy	9
Defence of Eclipse of Faith	9
Earl's Daughter (The)	20
Eclipse of Faith	9
Experience (The) of Life	20
Gertrude	20
Hoare on the Veracity of Genesis	11
Horne's Introduction to Scriptures	11
" Abridgment of ditto	11
Humphreys's Parables Illuminated	12
Ivors, by the Author of Amy Herbert	20
Jameson's Saints and Martyrs	12
" Monastic Legends	12
" Legends of the Madonna	12
" on Female Employment	12
Jeremy Taylor's Works	13
Katharine Ashton	20
König's Pictorial Life of Luther	10
Laneton Parsonage	20
Lyra Germanica	7
Maguire's Rome	15
Margaret Percival	15
Marshman's Serampore Mission	15
Martineau's Christian Life	15
" Hymns	15
" Studies of Christianity	15
Merivale's Christian Records	16
Moore on the Use of the Body	17
" " Soul and Body	17
" 's Man and his Motives	17
Morning Clouds	17
Moseley's Astro-Theology	17
Neale's Closing Scene	17
Powell's Christianity without Judaism	18
" Order of Nature	19
Readings for Lent	20
" Confirmation	20
Riddle's Household Prayers	19
Robinson's Lexicon to the Greek Testament	19
Schimmel Penninck's Sacred Musings	20
Self-Examination for Confirmation	20
Sewell's History of the Early Church	20
" Passing Thoughts on Religion	20
Smith's (Sydney) Moral Philosophy	21
" (G.) Wesleyan Methodism	21
" (J.) Shipwreck of St. Paul	21
Southey's Life of Wesley	21
Spitta's Lyra Domestica	22
Stephen's Ecclesiastical Biography	22
Theologia Germanica	7
Thumb Bible (The)	22

Poetry and the Drama.

Aikin's (Dr.) British Poets	5
Arnold's Merope	5
" Poems	5
Calvert's Wife's Manual	7
Goldsmith's Poems, illustrated	9
L. E. L.'s Poetical Works	13
Linwood's Anthologia Oxoniensis	13
Lyra Germanica	7
Macaulay's Lays of Ancient Rome	14
MacDonald's Within and Without	14
" Poems	14
Montgomery's Poetical Works	17

Moore's Poetical Works	16
" Selections (illustrated)	16
" Lalla Rookh	16
" Irish Melodies	16
" National Melodies	16
" Sacred Songs (*with Music*)	16
" Songs and Ballads	16
Power's Virginia's Hand	19
Shakspeare, by Bowdler	20
Southey's Poetical Works	21
Spitta's Lyra Domestica	22
Thomson's Seasons, illustrated	22
Warburton's Hunting Songs	23
Wilkins's Political Ballads	24

The Sciences in general and Mathematics.

Arago's Meteorological Essays	5
" Popular Astronomy	5
Boase's Philosophy of Nature	6
Bourne on the Steam Engine	6
" 's Catechism of Steam-Engine	6
Boyd's Naval Cadet's Manual	6
Brande's Dictionary of Science, &c.	6
" Lectures on Organic Chemistry	6
Conington's Chemical Analysis	8
Cresy's Civil Engineering	8
De la Rive's Electricity	9
Grove's Correlation of Physical Forces	10
Herschel's Outlines of Astronomy	11
Holland's Mental Physiology	11
Humboldt's Aspects of Nature	12
" Cosmos	12
Hunt on Light	12
Lardner's Cabinet Cyclopædia	13
Marcet's (Mrs.) Conversations	15
Morell's Elements of Psychology	17
Moseley's Astro-Theology	17
" Engineering and Architecture	17
Ogilvie's Master-Builder's Plan	17
Owen's Lectures on Comp. Anatomy	17 & 18
Pereira on Polarised Light	18
Peschel's Elements of Physics	18
Phillips's Mineralogy	18
" Guide to Geology	18
Piesse's Laboratory of Chymical Wonders	18
Powell's Unity of Worlds	18
" Christianity without Judaism	19
" Order of Nature	19
Ramsay's Glaciers of North Wales and Switzerland	19
Smee's Electro-Metallurgy	21
Steam-Engine, by the Artisan Club	6
Tate on Strength of Materials	22
Twisden's Examples in Mechanics	23
Webb's Celestial Objects for Common Telescopes	23

Rural Sports.

Baker's Rifle and Hound in Ceylon	5
Blaine's Dictionary of Sports	6
Cecil's Stable Practice	8
" Stud Farm	8
Dead Shot (The)	9
Ephemera on Angling	9
" Book of the Salmon	9
Freeman and Salvin's Falconry	9
Hamilton's Reminiscences of an Old Sportsman	10
Hawker's Young Sportsman	10
Howard's Athletic Exercises	11
The Hunting-Field	10
Idle's Hints on Shooting	12
Pocket and the Stud	10
Practical Horsemanship	10
Pycroft's Cricket-Field	19
Richardson's Horsemanship	19
Ronalds's Fly-Fisher's Entomology	19
Salmon Fishing in Canada	5
Stable Talk and Table Talk	10
Stonehenge on the Dog	22
" " Greyhound	22
The Stud, for Practical Purposes	10

Veterinary Medicine, &c.

Cecil's Stable Practice	8
" Stud Farm	8
Hunting-Field (The)	10
Miles's Horse-Shoeing	16
" on the Horse's Foot	16
Pocket and the Stud	10
Practical Horsemanship	10
Richardson's Horsemanship	19
Stable Talk and Table Talk	10
Stonehenge on the Dog	22
Stud (The)	10
Youatt's The Dog	24
" The Horse	24

Voyages and Travels.

Baker's Wanderings in Ceylon	5
Barth's African Travels	5
Burton's East Africa	7
" Lake Regions of Central Africa	7
" Medina and Mecca	7
Domenech's Deserts of North America	9
" Texas and Mexico	9
Forester's Sardinia and Corsica	9
Hill's Peru and Mexico	11
Hinchliff's Travels in the Alps	11
Hind's North American Exploring Expeditions	11
Howitt's Victoria	11
Huc's Chinese Empire	12
Hudson and Kennedy's Mont Blanc	12
Humboldt's Aspects of Nature	12
Hutchinson's Western Africa	12
Kane's Wanderings of an Artist	13
Lady's Tour round Monte Rosa	13
Lowe's Central India in 1857 and 1858	14
M'Clure's North-West Passage	17
Minturn's New York to Delhi	16
Möllhausen's Journey to the Pacific	17
Peaks, Passes, and Glaciers	18
Ramsay's Glaciers of North Wales and Switzerland	19
Senior's Journal in Turkey and Greece	20
Snow's Tierra del Fuego	21
Tennent's Ceylon	22
Weld's Vacations in Ireland	24
" Two Months in the Highlands	24
" Pyrenees, West and East	24
" United States and Canada	24
Whiteside's Italy	24
Wills's "Eagle's Nest"	24

Works of Fiction.

Cruikshank's Falstaff	8
Howitt's Tallangetta	11
Moore's Epicurean	16
Sewell's Ursula	20
Simpkinson's Washingtons	21
Sir Roger De Coverley	21
Sketches (The), Three Tales	21
Southey's Doctor, &c.	21
Trollope's Barchester Towers	23
" Warden	23

ALPHABETICAL CATALOGUE
of
NEW WORKS and NEW EDITIONS
PUBLISHED BY
LONGMAN, GREEN, LONGMAN, AND ROBERTS,
PATERNOSTER ROW, LONDON.

Miss Acton's Modern Cookery for Private Families, reduced to a System of Easy Practice in a Series of carefully-tested Receipts, in which the Principles of Baron Liebig and other eminent writers have been as much as possible applied and explained. Newly-revised and enlarged Edition; with 8 Plates, comprising 27 Figures, and 150 Woodcuts. Fcp. 8vo. 7s. 6d.

The Afternoon of Life. By the Author of *Morning Clouds*. New and cheaper Edition. Fcp. 8vo. 5s.

Agassiz.—An Essay on Classification [the Mutual Relation of Organised Beings]. By LOUIS AGASSIZ. 8vo. 12s.

Aikin's Select Works of the British Poets from Ben Jonson to Beattie; with Biographical and Critical Prefaces. New Edition, comprising Selections from more recent Poets. 8vo. 18s.

Alexander.—Salmon-Fishing in Canada. By a RESIDENT. Edited by Colonel Sir JAMES EDWARD ALEXANDER, K.C.L.S. Map and Woodcuts. Post 8vo. 10s. 6d.

Arago (F.)—Biographies of Distinguished Scientific Men. Translated by Admiral W. H. SMYTH, D.C.L., F.R.S., &c.; the Rev. BADEN POWELL, M.A.; and ROBERT GRANT, M.A., F.R.A.S. 8vo. 18s.

Arago's Meteorological Essays. With an Introduction by BARON HUMBOLDT. Translated under the superintendence of Lieut.-Col. E. SABINE, R.A., Treasurer and V.P.R.S. 8vo. 18s.

Arago's Popular Astronomy. Translated and edited by Admiral W. H. SMYTH, D.C.L., F.R.S.; and ROBERT GRANT, M.A., F.R.A.S. With 25 Plates and 358 Woodcuts. 2 vols. 8vo. price £2. 5s.

Arnold.—Merope, a Tragedy. By MATTHEW ARNOLD. With a Preface and an Historical Introduction. Fcp. 8vo. 5s.

Arnold.—Poems. By Matthew ARNOLD. FIRST SERIES. Third Edition. Fcp. 8vo. 5s. 6d. SECOND SERIES, price 5s.

Lord Bacon's Works. A New Edition, collected and edited by R. L. ELLIS, M.A., JAMES SPEDDING, M.A., and D. D. HEATH, Esq., Barrister-at-Law. VOLS. I. to V. comprising the Division of *Philosophical Works*; with a copious INDEX. 5 vols. 8vo. price £4. 6s. VOLS. VI. and VII. comprising the Division of *Literary and Professional Works*, with a full INDEX. 2 vols. 8vo. price £1. 16s.

Baker.—The Rifle and the Hound in Ceylon. By S. W. BAKER, Esq. New Edition, with 13 Illustrations engraved on Wood. Fcp. 8vo. 4s. 6d.

Baker. — Eight Years' Wanderings in Ceylon. By S. W. BAKER, Esq. With 6 coloured Plates. 8vo. 15s.

Barth.—Travels and Discoveries in North and Central Africa: Being the Journal of an Expedition undertaken under the auspices of Her Britannic Majesty's Government in the Years 1849—1855. By HENRY BARTH, Ph.D., D.C.L. With numerous Maps and Illustrations. 5 vols. 8vo. £5. 5s. cloth.

Bate. — Memoir of Captain W. Thornton Bate, R.N. By the Rev. JOHN BAILLIE. *New Edition*; with Portrait and 4 Illustrations. Fcp. 8vo. 5s.

Bayldon's Art of Valuing Rents and Tillages, and Claims of Tenants upon Quitting Farms, at both Michaelmas and Lady-day; as revised by Mr. DONALDSON. *Seventh Edition*, enlarged and adapted to the Present Time. By ROBERT BAKER, Land-Agent and Valuer. 8vo. price 10s. 6d.

Black's Practical Treatise on Brewing, based on Chemical and Economical Principles: With Formulæ for Public Brewers, and Instructions for Private Families. 8vo. 10s. 6d.

Blaine's Encyclopædia of Rural Sports; or, a complete Account, Historical, Practical, and Descriptive, of Hunting, Shooting, Fishing, Racing, &c. *New Edition*, revised and corrected; with above 600 Woodcut Illustrations, including 20 Subjects from Designs by JOHN LEECH. 8vo. price 42s.

Bloomfield.—The Greek Testament: with copious English Notes, Critical, Philological, and Explanatory. Especially adapted to the use of Theological Students and Ministers. By the Rev. S. T. BLOOMFIELD, D.D., F.S.A. Ninth Edition, revised. 2 vols. 8vo. with Map, £2. 8s.

Dr. Bloomfield's Critical Annotations on the New Testament, being a Supplemental Volume to the Ninth Edition. 8vo. 14s.

Dr. Bloomfield's College & School Edition of the Greek Testament: With brief English Notes, chiefly Philological and Explanatory. Seventh Edition; with Map and Index. Fcp. 8vo. 7s. 6d.

Dr. Bloomfield's College & School Lexicon to the Greek Testament. New Edition, revised. Fcp. 8vo. price 7s. 6d.

Boase.—The Philosophy of Nature: A Systematic Treatise on the Causes and Laws of Natural Phenomena. By HENRY S. BOASE, M.D., F.R.S., and G.S. 8vo. 12s.

Boyd.—A Manual for Naval Cadets. Published with the sanction and approval of the Lords Commissioners of the Admiralty. By JOHN M'NEILL BOYD, Captain, R.N. Second Edition; with 253 Illustrations (13 coloured). Fcp. 8vo. 12s. 6d.

Bourne.—A Treatise on the Steam Engine, in its Application to Mines, Mills, Steam Navigation, and Railways. By the Artisan Club. Edited by JOHN BOURNE, C.E. New and greatly improved Edition; with many Plates and Wood Engravings. 4to. *[Nearly ready.*

Bourne's Catechism of the Steam Engine in its various Applications to Mines, Mills, Steam Navigation, Railways, and Agriculture: With Practical Instructions for the Manufacture and Management of Engines of every class. With 89 Woodcuts. Fcp. 8vo. 6s.

Brande's Dictionary of Science, Literature, and Art; comprising the History, Description, and Scientific Principles of every Branch of Human Knowledge; with the Derivation and Definition of all the Terms in general use. Third Edition, revised and corrected; with numerous Woodcuts. 8vo. 60s.

Professor Brande's Lectures on Organic Chemistry, as applied to Manufactures, including Dyeing, Bleaching, Calico Printing, Sugar Manufacture, the Preservation of Wood, Tanning, &c. Edited by J. SCOFFERN, M.B. Fcp. Woodcuts, 7s. 6d.

Bray.—The Education of the Feelings. By CHARLES BRAY. Third Edition. 8vo. 5s.

Brewer.—An Atlas of History and Geography, from the Commencement of the Christian Era to the Present Time: Comprising a Series of Sixteen Coloured Maps, arranged in Chronological Order, with Illustrative Memoirs. By the Rev. J. S. BREWER, M.A. *Second Edition*, revised and corrected. Royal 8vo. 12s. 6d. half-bound.

Brialmont and Gleig's Life of Wellington.—History of the Life of Arthur Duke of Wellington: The Military Memoirs from the French of Captain BRIALMONT, with Additions and Emendations; the Political and Social Life by the Rev. G. R. GLEIG, M.A. With Maps, Plans of Battles, and Portraits. 4 vols. 8vo. £2. 14s.

Brodie.—Psychological Inquiries, in a Series of Essays intended to illustrate the Influence of the Physical Organisation on the Mental Faculties. By Sir BENJAMIN C. BRODIE, Bart. Third Edition, Fcp. 8vo. 5s.

Dr. Bull on the Maternal Management of Children in Health and Disease. New Edition. Fcp. 8vo. 5s.

Dr. Bull's Hints to Mothers on the Management of their Health during the Period of Pregnancy and in the Lying-in Room: With an Exposure of Popular Errors in connexion with those subjects, &c.; and Hints upon Nursing. New Edition. Fcp. 8vo. 5s.

Bunsen.—Christianity and Mankind, their Beginnings and Prospects. By Baron C. C. J. BUNSEN, D.D., D.C.L., D.Ph. Being a New Edition, corrected, re-modelled, and extended, of *Hippolytus and his Age.* 7 vols. 8vo. £5. 5s.—Or,

1. Hippolytus and his Age; or, the Beginnings and Prospects of Christianity. 2 vols. 8vo. £1. 10s.

2. Outline of the Philosophy of Universal History applied to Language and Religion; containing an Account of the Alphabetical Conferences. 2 vols. 32s.

3. Analecta Ante-Nicæna. 3 vols. 8vo. £2. 2s.

Bunsen. — Lyra Germanica. Translated from the German by CATHERINE WINKWORTH. FIRST SERIES, Hymns for the Sundays and Festivals of the Christian Year. SECOND SERIES, the Christian Life. Fcp. 8vo. 5s. each Series.

An Edition of the FIRST SERIES of *Lyra Germanica,* with Illustrations from Original Designs by JOHN LEIGHTON, F.S.A., engraved on Wood under his superintendence. Fcp. 4to. price 21s.

HYMNS from *Lyra Germanica,* 18mo. 1s.

*** These selections of German Hymns have been made from collections published in Germany by Baron BUNSEN; and form companion volumes to

Theologia Germanica. Translated by SUSANNA WINKWORTH. With a Preface by the Rev. CHARLES KINGSLEY; and a Letter by Baron BUNSEN. Fcp. 8vo. 5s.

Bunsen.—Egypt's Place in Universal History: An Historical Investigation, in Five Books. By Baron C. C. J. BUNSEN, D.C.L., D.Ph. Translated from the German by C. H. COTTRELL, Esq., M.A. With many Illustrations. 4 vols. 8vo. £5. 8s.

Bunting. — The Life of Jabez Bunting, D.D.: With Notices of contemporary Persons and Events. By his Son, THOMAS PERCIVAL BUNTING. VOL. I. with 2 Portraits and Vignette. Third Thousand, post 8vo. 7s. 6d.: or *(large paper and Proof Engravings)* square crown 8vo. 10s. 6d.

Bunyan's Pilgrim's Progress: With 126 Illustrations engraved on Steel and on Wood from Original Designs by CHARLES BENNETT; and a Preface by the Rev. CHARLES KINGSLEY, Rector of Eversley. Fcp. 4to. price 21s. cloth.

Burke.—Vicissitudes of Families. By Sir BERNARD BURKE, Ulster King of Arms. FIRST and SECOND SERIES, crown 8vo. 12s. 6d. each.

Burton.—The Lake Regions of Central Africa: A Picture of Exploration. By RICHARD F. BURTON, Captain H.M. Indian Army; Fellow and Gold Medallist of the Royal Geographical Society. With Map and numerous Illustrations. 2 vols. 8vo. 31s. 6d.

Captain Burton's First Footsteps in East Africa; or, an Exploration of Harar. With Maps and coloured Plates. 8vo. 18s.

Captain Burton's Personal Narrative of a Pilgrimage to El Medinah and Meccah. *Second Edition,* revised; with coloured Plates and Woodcuts. 2 vols. crown 8vo. 24s.

Bishop Butler's Sketch of Modern and Ancient Geography. New Edition, thoroughly revised, with such Alterations introduced as continually progressive Discoveries and the latest information have rendered necessary. Post 8vo. 7s. 6d.

Bishop Butler's General Atlas of Modern and Ancient Geography; comprising Fifty-four full-coloured Maps; with complete Indices. New Edition, enlarged, and greatly improved. Edited by the Author's Son. Royal 4to. 24s.

The Cabinet Lawyer: A Popular Digest of the Laws of England, Civil and Criminal; with a Dictionary of Law Terms, Maxims, Statutes, and Judicial Antiquities; Correct Tables of Assessed Taxes, Stamp Duties, Excise Licenses, and Post-Horse Duties; Post-Office Regulations; and Prison Discipline. 18th Edition, comprising the Public Acts of the Session 1860. Fcp. 8vo. 10s. 6d.

The Cabinet Gazetteer: A Popular Exposition of All the Countries of the World. By the Author of *The Cabinet Lawyer.* Fcp. 8vo. 10s. 6d.

Calvert. — The Wife's Manual; or, Prayers, Thoughts, and Songs on Several Occasions of a Matron's Life. By the Rev. W. CALVERT, M.A. Ornamented from Designs by the Author in the style of *Queen Elizabeth's Prayer-Book.* Crown 8vo. 10s. 6d.

Catlow's Popular Conchology; or, the Shell Cabinet arranged according to the Modern System: With a detailed Account of the Animals, and a complete Descriptive List of the Families and Genera of Recent and Fossil Shells. With 405 Woodcuts. Post 8vo. 14s.

Cats and Farlie's Book of Emblems.—Moral Emblems, with Aphorisms, Adages, and Proverbs of all Nations, from J. CATZ and R. FARLIE: comprising 60 circular Vignettes, 60 Tail-Pieces, and a Frontispiece composed from their works by J. LEIGHTON, F.S.A., and engraved on Wood. The Text translated, &c., by R. PIGOT. Imperial 8vo. 31s. 6d. cloth; or 52s. 6d. bound in morocco.

Cecil.—The Stud Farm; or, Hints on Breeding Horses for the Turf, the Chase, and the Road. Addressed to Breeders of Race-Horses and Hunters, Landed Proprietors, and Tenant Farmers. By CECIL. Fcp. 8vo. 5s.

Cecil's Stable Practice; or, Hints on Training for the Turf, the Chase, and the Road; with Observations on Racing and Hunting, Wasting, Race-Riding, and Handicapping : Addressed to all who are concerned in Racing, Steeple-Chasing, and Fox-Hunting. Second Edition. Fcp. 8vo. with Plate, 5s.

Chapman.—History of Gustavus Adolphus, and of the Thirty Years' War up to the King's Death: With some Account of its Conclusion by the Peace of Westphalia, in 1648. By B. CHAPMAN, M.A. 8vo. Plans, 12s. 6d.

Clough.—Greek History from Themistocles to Alexander, in a Series of Lives from Plutarch. Revised and arranged by A. H. CLOUGH, sometime Fellow of Oriel College, Oxford. Fcp. 8vo. with 44 Woodcuts, 6s.

Conington.—Handbook of Chemical Analysis, adapted to the Unitary System of Notation. By F. T. CONINGTON, M.A., F.C.S. Post 8vo. 7s. 6d. Also, *Tables of Qualitative Analysis,* designed as a Companion. Price 2s. 6d.

Connolly's History of the Royal Sappers and Miners: Including the Services of the Corps in the Crimea and at the Siege of Sebastopol. *Second Edition;* with 17 coloured Plates. 2 vols. 8vo. 30s.

Conybeare and Howson's Life and Epistles of Saint Paul: Comprising a complete Biography of the Apostle, and a Translation of his Epistles inserted in Chronological Order. *Third Edition,* revised and corrected; with several Maps and Woodcuts, and 4 Plates. 2 vols. square crown 8vo. 31s. 6d.
*** The Original Edition, with more numerous Illustrations, in 2 vols. 4to. price 48s. may also be had.

Dr. Copland's Dictionary of Practical Medicine : Comprising General Pathology, the Nature and Treatment of Diseases, Morbid Structures, and the Disorders especially incidental to Climates, to Sex, and to the different Epochs of Life; with numerous approved Formulæ of the Medicines recommended. Now complete in 3 vols. 8vo. price £5. 11s. cloth.

Bishop Cotton's Instructions in the Doctrine and Practice of Christianity. Intended as an Introduction to Confirmation. 4th Edition. 18mo. 2s. 6d.

Cresy's Encyclopædia of Civil Engineering, Historical, Theoretical, and Practical. Illustrated by upwards of 3,000 Woodcuts. *Second Edition,* revised and extended. 8vo. 63s.

Crosse.—Memorials, Scientific and Literary, of Andrew Crosse, the Electrician. Edited by Mrs. CROSSE. Post 8vo. 9s. 6d.

Crowe.—The History of France. By EYRE EVANS CROWE. In Five Volumes. VOL. I. 8vo. 14s.; VOL. II. 15s.

Cruikshank.—The Life of Sir John Falstaff, illustrated in a Series of Twenty-four original Etchings by George Cruikshank. Accompanied by an imaginary Biography, by ROBERT B. BROUGH. Royal 8vo. 12s. 6d. cloth.

Lady Cust's Invalid's Own Book : A Collection of Recipes from various Books and various Countries. Fcp. 8vo. 2s. 6d.

The Rev. Canon Dale's Domestic Liturgy and Family Chaplain, in Two Parts: PART I. Church Services adapted for Domestic Use, with Prayers for Every Day of the Week, selected from the Book of Common Prayer ; PART II. an appropriate Sermon for Every Sunday in the Year. Post 4to. 21s. cloth ; 31s. 6d. calf ; or 50s. morocco.
Separately { THE FAMILY CHAPLAIN, 12s.
THE DOMESTIC LITURGY, 10s. 6d.

The Dead Shot; or, Sportsman's Complete Guide; being a Treatise on the Use of the Gun, with Rudimentary and Finishing Lessons in the Art of Shooting Game of all kinds; Dog-breaking, Pigeon-shooting, &c. By MARKSMAN. Fcp. 8vo. with 6 Illustrations, 5s.

De la Rive's Treatise on Electricity in Theory and Practice. Translated for the Author by C. V. WALKER, F.R.S. 3 vols. 8vo. Woodcuts, £3. 13s.

Domenech.—Seven Years' Residence in the Great Deserts of North America. By the ABBÉ DOMENECH. With a Map, and about Sixty Illustrations. 2 vols. 8vo. £1. 16s.

Abbé Domenech's Missionary Adventures in Texas and Mexico: A Personal Narrative of Six Years' Sojourn in those Regions. 8vo. 10s. 6d.

The Eclipse of Faith; or, a Visit to a Religious Sceptic. 10th Edition. Fcp. 8vo. 5s.

Defence of The Eclipse of Faith, by its Author. 3d Edition, revised. Fcp. 8vo. 3s. 6d.

Ephemera's Handbook of Angling; teaching Fly-fishing, Trolling, Bottom-Fishing, Salmon-Fishing: With the Natural History of River-Fish, and the best Modes of Catching them. With Woodcuts. Fcp. 8vo. 5s.

Ephemera's Book of the Salmon: The Theory, Principles, and Practice of Fly-Fishing for Salmon; Lists of good Salmon Flies for every good River in the Empire; the Natural History of the Salmon, its Habits described, and the best way of artificially Breeding it. Fcp. 8vo. with coloured Plates, 14s.

Fairbairn.—A Treatise on Mills and Millwork. By WILLIAM FAIRBAIRN, F.R.S., F.G.S. With numerous Illustrations. 2 vols. 8vo. [In the press.

Fairbairn.—Useful Information for Engineers: A First Series of Lectures delivered to the Working Engineers of Yorkshire and Lancashire. By WILLIAM FAIRBAIRN, F.R.S., F.G.S. Third Edition; with Plates and Woodcuts. Crown 8vo. 10s. 6d.

SECOND SERIES OF FAIRBAIRN's Useful Information for Engineers, uniform with the above, nearly ready.

Falkener.—Dædalus; or, the Causes and Principles of the Excellence of Greek Sculpture. By EDWARD FALKENER, Member of the Archæological Institutes of Rome and Berlin. With numerous Illustrations and 2 Medallions from the Antique. Royal 8vo. 42s.

Falkener.—Museum of Classical Antiquities: A Series of Thirty-five Essays on Ancient Art, by various Writers, edited by EDWARD FALKENER. With 25 Plates and many Woodcuts. Imperial 8vo. 42s.

Forester's Rambles in the Islands of Corsica and Sardinia: With Notices of their History, Antiquities, and present Condition. With coloured Map; and numerous Illustrations from Drawings by Lieut.-Col. M. A. Biddulph, R.A. Imperial 8vo. 28s.

Letters of Sir A. S. Fraser, K.C.B. Commanding the Royal Horse Artillery under the Duke of Wellington: Written during the Peninsular and Waterloo Campaigns. Edited by MAJOR-GENERAL SABINE, R.A. With Portrait, 2 Maps, and Plans. 8vo. 18s.

Freeman and Salvin.—Falconry: Its Claims, History, and Practice. By the Rev. G. E. FREEMAN, M.A. ("Peregrine" of the *Field*); and Captain F. H. SALVIN. Post 8vo. with Woodcut Illustrations from Drawings by Wolf, price 10s. 6d. cloth.

Garratt.—Marvels and Mysteries of Instinct; or, Curiosities of Animal Life. By GEORGE GARRATT. Second Edition, improved. Fcp. 8vo. 4s. 6d.

Gilbart's Logic of Banking: A Familiar Exposition of the Principles of Reasoning, and their Application to the Art and the Science of Banking. 12mo. with Portrait, 12s. 6d.

The Poetical Works of Oliver Goldsmith. Edited by BOLTON CORNEY, Esq. Illustrated by Wood Engravings, from Designs by Members of the Etching Club. Square crown 8vo. cloth, 21s.; morocco, £1. 16s.

Goodeve. — The Elements of Mechanism, designed for Students of Applied Mechanics. By T. M. GOODEVE, M.A., Professor of Natural Philosophy in King's College. Post 8vo. with 206 Figures, 6s. 6d.

Gosse.—A Naturalist's Sojourn in Jamaica. By P. H. GOSSE, Esq. With Plates. Post 8vo. 14s.

Green.—Lives of the Princesses of England. By Mrs. MARY ANNE EVERETT GREEN, Editor of the *Letters of Royal and Illustrious Ladies*. With numerous Portraits. Complete in 6 vols. post 8vo. 10s. 6d. each.

Greyson.—Selections from the Correspondence of R. E. GREYSON, Esq. Edited by the Author of *The Eclipse of Faith*. New Edition. Crown 8vo. 7s. 6d.

Grove.—The Correlation of Physical Forces. By W. R. GROVE, Q.C., M.A. *Third Edition*. 8vo. 7s.

Gurney.—St. Louis and Henri IV.: Being a Second Series of Historical Sketches. By the Rev. JOHN H. GURNEY, M.A. Fcp. 8vo. 6s.

EveningRecreations; or, Samples from the Lecture-Room. Edited by Rev. J. H. GURNEY. Crown 8vo. 5s.

Gwilt's Encyclopædia of Architecture, Historical, Theoretical, and Practical. By JOSEPH GWILT. With more than 1,000 Wood Engravings, from Designs by J. S. GWILT. 8vo. 42s.

Hamilton.—Reminiscences of an Old Sportsman. By Colonel J. M. HAMILTON, K.H., Author of *Travels in the Interior of Columbia*. 2 vols. post 8vo. with 6 Illustrations, 18s.

Hare (Archdeacon).—The Life of Luther, in Forty-eight Historical Engravings. By GUSTAV KÖNIG. With Explanations by Archdeacon HARE and SUSANNAH WINKWORTH. Fcp. 4to. 28s.

Harford.—Life of MichaelAngelo Buonarroti: With Translations of many of his Poems and Letters; also Memoirs of Savonarola, Raphael, and Vittoria Colonna. By JOHN S. HARFORD, Esq., D.C.L., F.R.S. Second Edition, revised; with 20 Plates. 2 vols. 8vo. 25s.

Illustrations, Architectural and Pictorial, of the Genius of Michael Angelo Buonarroti. With Descriptions of the Plates, by the Commendatore CANINA; C. R. COCKERELL, Esq., R.A.; and J. S. HARFORD, Esq., D.C.L., F.R.S. Folio, 73s. 6d. half-bound.

Harry Hieover's Stable Talk and Table Talk; or, Spectacles for Young Sportsmen. New Edition, 2 vols. 8vo. Portrait, 24s.

Harry Hieover.—The Hunting-Field. By HARRY HIEOVER. 2d Edition; with 2 Plates. Fcp. 8vo. 5s.

Harry Hieover. — Practical Horsemanship. *Second Edition*; with 2 Plates. Fcp. 8vo. 5s. half-bound.

Harry Hieover.—The Pocket and the Stud; or, Practical Hints on the Management of the Stable. 3d Edition. Fcp. 8vo. with Portrait, 5s.

Harry Hieover.—The Stud, for Practical Purposes and Practical Men: Being a Guide to the Choice of a Horse. 2d Edition, with 2 Plates. Fcp. 5s.

Hartwig. — The Sea and its Living Wonders. By Dr. GEORGE HARTWIG. With numerous Wood Engravings, and a new series of Illustrations in Chromo-xylography from original designs by Henry Noel Humphreys. 8vo. 18s.

Hassall.—Adulterations Detected; or, Plain Instructions for the Discovery of Frauds in Food and Medicine. By ARTHUR HILL HASSALL, M.D. Lond., Analyst of *The Lancet Sanitary Commission*, and Author of the Reports of that Commission published under the title of *Food and its Adulterations* (which may also be had, in 8vo. price 28s.). With 225 Illustrations, engraved on Wood. Crown 8vo. 17s. 6d.

Dr. Hassall's History of the British Freshwater Algæ: Including Descriptions of the Desmideæ and Diatomaceæ. 2 vols. 8vo. with 103 Plates, £1. 15s.

Col. Hawker's Instructions to Young Sportsmen in all that relates to Guns and Shooting. 11th Edition, revised by the Author's Son, Major P. W. L. HAWKER. With Portrait, Plates, and Woodcuts. Sq. crown 8vo. 18s.

Haydn's Book of Dignities: Containing Rolls of the Official Personages of the British Empire, Civil, Ecclesiastical, Judicial, Military, Naval, and Municipal, from the Earliest Periods to the Present Time. Together with the Sovereigns of Europe, from the Foundation of their respective States; the Peerage and Nobility of Great Britain, &c. 8vo. 25s.

Hayward.—Biographical and Critical Essays, reprinted from Reviews, with Additions and Corrections. By A. HAYWARD, Esq., Q.C. 2 vols. 8vo. 24s.

Hensman.—Handbook of the Constitution: Being a short account of the Rise, Progress, and Present State of the Laws of England. By ALFRED P. HENSMAN, Barrister-at-Law. Fcp. 8vo. 4s.

Sir John Herschel's Outlines of Astronomy. Fifth Edition, revised and corrected to the existing state of astronomical knowledge; with Plates and Woodcuts. 8vo. 18s.

Sir John Herschel's Essays from the *Edinburgh* and *Quarterly Reviews*, with Addresses and other Pieces. 8vo. 18s.

Hill.—Travels in Peru and Mexico. By S. S. HILL, Esq., Author of *Travels in Siberia*, &c. 2 vols. post 8vo. 21s.

Hinchliff.—Summer Months among the Alps: With the Ascent of Monte Rosa. By THOS. W. HINCHLIFF, Barrister-at-Law. Post 8vo. 10s. 6d.

Hind.—Narrative of the Canadian Red River and Assinniboine and Saskatchewan Exploring Expeditions: With a Description of the Physical Geography, Geology, and Climate of the Country traversed. By HENRY YOULE HIND, M.A., F.R.G.S., Professor of Chemistry and Geology in Trinity College, Toronto; in Charge of the Assinniboine and Saskatchewan Exploring Expedition. With Maps and numerous Illustrations. 2 vols. 8vo. [*Just ready.*

Hints on Etiquette and the Usages of Society: With a Glance at Bad Habits. New Edition, revised (with Additions) by a Lady of Rank. Fcp. 8vo. 2s. 6d.

Hoare.—The Veracity of the Book of Genesis: With the Life and Character of the Inspired Historian. By the Rev. WILLIAM H. HOARE, M.A., late Fellow of St. John's College, Cambridge. 8vo. 9s. 6d.

Holland.—Medical Notes and Reflections. By Sir HENRY HOLLAND, M.D., F.R.S., &c., Physician in Ordinary to the Queen and Prince-Consort. Third Edition. 8vo. 18s.

Sir H. Holland's Chapters on Mental Physiology, founded chiefly on Chapters contained in *Medical Notes and Reflections*. Post 8vo. 8s. 6d.

Hooker's (Sir W. J.) Popular Guide to the Royal Botanic Gardens of Kew. With many Woodcuts. 16mo. 6d.

Hooker and Arnott's British Flora; comprising the Phænogamous or Flowering Plants, and the Ferns. Seventh Edition, with numerous Figures illustrative of the Umbelliferous Plants, the Composite Plants, the Grasses, and the Ferns. 12mo. with 12 Plates, 14s.; with the Plates coloured, price 21s.

Horne's Introduction to the Critical Study and Knowledge of the Holy Scriptures. *Tenth Edition*, revised, corrected, and brought down to the present time. Edited by the Rev. T. HARTWELL HORNE, B.D. (the Author); the Rev. JOHN AYRE; and S. PRIDEAUX TREGELLES, LL.D. With 4 Maps and 22 Vignettes and Facsimiles. 4 vols. 8vo. £3. 13s. 6d.

Horne.—A Compendious Introduction to the Study of the Bible. By the Rev. T. HARTWELL HORNE, B.D. New Edition, with Maps, &c. 12mo. 9s.

Hoskyns.—Talpa; or, the Chronicles of a Clay Farm: An Agricultural Fragment. By CHANDOS WREN HOSKYNS, Esq. Fourth Edition. With 24 Woodcuts from Designs by GEORGE CRUIKSHANK. 16mo. 5s. 6d.

Howard.—Athletic and Gymnastic Exercises. With 64 Illustrations, and a Description of the requisite Apparatus. By JOHN H. HOWARD. 16mo. 7s. 6d.

Howitt.—The Children's Year. By MARY HOWITT. With Four Illustrations. Square 16mo. 5s.

Howitt.—Tallangetta, the Squatter's Home: A Story of Australian Life. By WILLIAM HOWITT. 2 vols. post 8vo. 18s.

Howitt.—Land, Labour, and Gold; or, Two Years in Victoria: With Visit to Sydney and Van Diemen's Land. By WILLIAM HOWITT. Second Edition, Two Volumes in One. Crown 8vo. 6s.

W. Howitt's Visits to Remarkable Places: Old Halls, Battle-Fields, and Scenes illustrative of Striking Passages in English History and Poetry. With about 80 Wood Engravings. *New Edition.* 2 vols. square crown 8vo. 25s.

William Howitt's Boy's Country Book: Being the Real Life of a Country Boy, written by himself; exhibiting all the Amusements, Pleasures, and Pursuits of Children in the Country. With 40 Woodcuts. Fcp. 8vo. 6s.

William Howitt's Rural Life of England. With Woodcuts by Bewick and Williams. Medium 8vo. 21s.

The Abbé Huc's Work on the Chinese Empire, founded on Fourteen Years' Travel and Residence in China. People's Edition, with 2 Woodcut Illustrations. Crown 8vo. 5s.

Hudson's Executor's Guide. New and improved Edition; with the Statutes enacted, and the Judicial Decisions pronounced since the last Edition, incorporated. Fcp. 8vo. 6s.

Hudson's Plain Directions for Making Wills in conformity with the Law. New Edition, corrected and revised by the Author; and practically illustrated by Specimens of Wills containing many varieties of Bequests, also Notes of Cases judicially decided since the Wills Act came into operation. Fcp. 8vo. 2s. 6d.

Hudson and Kennedy's Ascent of Mont Blanc by a New Route and Without Guides. *Second Edition*, with Plate and Map. Post 8vo. 5s. 6d.

Humboldt's Cosmos. Translated, with the Author's authority, by Mrs. SABINE. VOLS. I. and II. 16mo. Half-a-Crown each, sewed; 3s. 6d. each, cloth; or in post 8vo. 12s. each, cloth. VOL. III. post 8vo. 12s. 6d. cloth; or in 16mo. Part I. 2s. 6d. sewed, 3s. 6d. cloth; and PART II. 3s. sewed, 4s. cloth. VOL. IV. PART I. post 8vo. 15s. cloth; 16mo. 7s. 6d. cloth.

Humboldt's Aspects of Nature. Translated, with the Author's authority, by Mrs. SABINE. 16mo. price 6s.; or in 2 vols. 3s. 6d. each, cloth; 2s. 6d. each, sewed.

Humphreys.— Parables of Our Lord, illuminated and ornamented in the style of the Missals of the Renaissance by H. N. HUMPHREYS. Square fcp. 8vo. 21s. in massive carved covers; or 30s. bound in morocco, by Hayday.

Hunt's Researches on Light in its Chemical Relations; embracing a Consideration of all the Photographic Processes. 8vo. 10s. 6d.

Hunter.— Introduction to the *Writing of Précis or Digests*, as applicable to Narratives of Facts or Historical Events, Correspondence, Evidence, Official Documents, and General Composition: With numerous Examples and Exercises. By the Rev. JOHN HUNTER, M.A. 12mo. 2s.

KEY, 12mo. *just ready.*

Hutchinson's Impressions of Western Africa: With a Report on the Peculiarities of Trade up the Rivers in the Bight of Biafra. Post 8vo. 8s. 6d.

Idle's Hints on Shooting, Fishing, &c., both on Sea and Land, and in the Fresh-Water Lochs of Scotland. Fcp. 8vo. 5s.

Mrs. Jameson's Two Lectures on the Social Employments of Women, *Sisters of Charity* and the *Communion of Labour.* New Edition. Fcp. 2s.

Mrs. Jameson's Legends of the Saints and Martyrs, as represented in Christian Art. Third Edition; with 17 Etchings and upwards of 180 Woodcuts. 2 vols. square crown 8vo. 31s. 6d.

Mrs. Jameson's Legends of the Monastic Orders, as represented in Christian Art. Second Edition, enlarged; with 11 Etchings by the Author and 88 Woodcuts. Sq. crown 8vo. 28s.

Mrs. Jameson's Legends of the Madonna, as represented in Christian Art. Second Edition, corrected and enlarged; with 27 Etchings and 165 Wood Engravings. Square crown 8vo. 28s.

Mrs. Jameson's Commonplace-Book of Thoughts, Memories, and Fancies, Original and Selected. *Second Edition*; with Etchings and Woodcuts. Crown 8vo. price 18s.

Jaquemet's Chronology for Schools: Containing the most important Dates of General History, Political, Ecclesiastical, and Literary, from the Creation of the World to the end of the Year 1857. Fcp. 8vo. 3s. 6d.

Lord Jeffrey's Contributions to The Edinburgh Review. A New Edition, complete in One Volume, with Portrait and Vignette. Square crown 8vo. 21s. cloth; or 30s. calf.— Or in 3 vols. 8vo. price 42s.

Bishop Jeremy Taylor's Entire Works: With Life by Bishop HEBER. Revised and corrected by the Rev. C. P. EDEN. Now complete in 10 vols. 8vo. price 10s. 6d. each.

Kane's Wanderings of an Artist among the Indians of North America; from Canada to Vancouver's Island and Oregon, through the Hudson's Bay Company's Territory, and back again. With Map, Illustrations in Colours, and Wood Engravings. 8vo. 21s.

Kemble. — The Saxons in England: A History of the English Commonwealth till the Conquest. By J. M. KEMBLE, M.A. 2 vols. 8vo. 28s.

Keith Johnston's Dictionary of Geography, Descriptive, Physical, Statistical, and Historical: Forming a complete General Gazetteer of the World. *Third Edition*, revised to April 1860. In 1 vol. of 1,360 pages, comprising about 56,600 Names of Places, 8vo. 30s. cloth; or half-bound in russia, 35s.

Kesteven. — A Manual of the Domestic Practice of Medicine. By W. B. KESTEVEN, F.R.C.S.E., &c. Square post 8vo. 7s. 6d.

Kirby and Spence's Introduction to Entomology; or, Elements of the Natural History of Insects: Comprising an Account of Noxious and Useful Insects, of their Metamorphoses, Food, Stratagems, Habitations, Societies, Motions, Noises, Hybernation, Instinct, &c. *Seventh Edition*, with an Appendix relative to the Origin and Progress of the work. Crown 8vo. 5s.

A Lady's Tour round Monte Rosa; with Visits to the Italian Valleys of Anzasca, Mastalone, Camasco, Sesia, Lys, Challant, Aosta, and Cogne. With Map, 4 Illustrations from Sketches by Mr. G. Barnard, and 8 Woodcuts. Post 8vo. 14s.

Lardner's Cabinet Cyclopædia of History, Biography, Literature, the Arts and Sciences, Natural History, and Manufactures. A Series of Original Works by EMINENT WRITERS. Complete in 132 vols. fcp. 8vo. with Vignette Titles, price £19. 19s. cloth lettered.

The Works *separately*, in single Volumes or Sets, price 3s. 6d. each Volume, cloth lettered.

Latham. — The English Language. By R. G. LATHAM, M.A., M.D., F.R.S., late Professor of the English Language in University College, London. Fourth Edition. 2 vols. 8vo. 28s.

Dr. Latham's Handbook of the English Language for the Use of Students of the Universities and Higher Classes of Schools. *Third Edition.* Post 8vo, 7s. 6d.

Mrs. R. Lee's Elements of Natural History; or, First Principles of Zoology: Comprising the Principles of Classification, interspersed with amusing and instructive Accounts of the most remarkable Animals. New Edition; Woodcuts. Fcp. 8vo. 7s. 6d.

L.E.L. — The Poetical Works of Letitia Elizabeth Landon; comprising the *Improvisatrice*, the *Venetian Bracelet*, the *Golden Violet*, the *Troubadour*, and Poetical Remains. 2 vols. 16mo. 10s. cloth; morocco, 21s.

Dr. John Lindley's Theory and Practice of Horticulture; or, an Attempt to explain the principal Operations of Gardening upon Physiological Grounds. With 98 Woodcuts. 8vo. 21s.

Dr. John Lindley's Introduction to Botany. New Edition, with corrections and copious Additions. 2 vols. 8vo. with Plates and Woodcuts, 24s.

Dr. Lindley's Synopsis of the British Flora arranged according to the Natural Orders (containing Vasculares or Flowering Plants. Fcp. 8vo. 6s.

Linwood's Anthologia Oxoniensis, sive Florilegium e Lusibus poeticis diversorum Oxoniensium Græcis et Latinis decerptum. 8vo. 14s.

Lorimer's Letters to a Young Master Mariner on some Subjects connected with his Calling. Fcp. 8vo. price 5s. 6d.

Loudon's Encyclopædia of Gardening: Comprising the Theory and Practice of Horticulture, Floriculture, Arboriculture, and Landscape-Gardening. With 1,000 Woodcuts. 8vo. 31s. 6d.

Loudon's Encyclopædia of Trees and Shrubs, or *Arboretum et Fruticetum Britannicum* abridged: Containing the Hardy Trees and Shrubs of Great Britain, Native and Foreign, Scientifically and Popularly Described. With about 2,000 Woodcuts. 8vo. 50s.

Loudon's Encyclopædia of Agriculture: Comprising the Theory and Practice of the Valuation, Transfer, Laying-out, Improvement, and Management of Landed Property, and of the Cultivation and Economy of the Animal and Vegetable Productions of Agriculture. With 1,100 Woodcuts. 8vo. 31s. 6d.

Loudon's Encyclopædia of Plants: Comprising the Specific Character, Description, Culture, History, Application in the Arts, and every other desirable Particular respecting Plants found in Great Britain. With above 12,000 Woodcuts. 8vo. 73s. 6d.

Loudon's Encyclopædia of Cottage, Farm, and Villa Architecture and Furniture. New Edition, edited by Mrs. LOUDON; with more than 2,000 Woodcuts. 8vo. 63s.

Loudon's Hortus Britannicus; or, Catalogue of all the Plants found in Great Britain. New Edition, corrected by Mrs. LOUDON. 8vo. 31s. 6d.

Mrs. Loudon's Lady's Country Companion; or, How to Enjoy a Country Life Rationally. Fcp. 8vo. 5s.

Mrs. Loudon's Amateur Gardener's Calendar, or Monthly Guide to what should be avoided and done in a Garden. Crown 8vo. Woodcuts, 7s. 6d.

Love's Art of Cleaning, Dyeing, Scouring, and Finishing on the most approved English and French Methods: Being Practical Instructions in Dyeing *Silks, Woollens,* and *Cottons, Feathers, Chip, Straw,* &c.; Scouring and Cleaning *Bed* and *Window Curtains, Carpets, Rugs,* &c.; French and English Cleaning any Colour or Fabric of *Silk, Satin,* or *Damask.* Post 8vo. 7s. 6d.

Lowe. — Central India during the Rebellion of 1857 and 1858: A Narrative of Operations of the British Forces from the Suppression of Mutiny in Aurungabad to the Capture of Gwalior under Major-General Sir HUGH ROSE, G.C.B., &c., and Brigadier Sir C. STUART, K.C.B. By THOMAS LOWE, M.R.C.S.E. Post 8vo. with Map, price 9s. 6d.

Lowndes's Engineer's Handbook; explaining the Principles which should guide the young Engineer in the Construction of Machinery, with the necessary Rules, Proportions, and Tables. Post 8vo. 5s.

Lord Macaulay's Miscellaneous Writings; comprising his Contributions to *Knight's Quarterly Magazine,* Articles contributed to the Edinburgh Review not included in his *Critical and Historical Essays,* Biographies written for the *Encyclopædia Britannica,* Miscellaneous Poems and Inscriptions. 2 vols. 8vo. with Portrait, 21s.

Macaulay. — The History of England from the Accession of James II. By the Right Hon. Lord MACAULAY. New Edition. VOLS. I. and II. 8vo. 32s.; VOLS. III. and IV. 36s.

Lord Macaulay's History of England from the Accession of James II. New Edition of the first Four Volumes of the Octavo Edition, revised and corrected. 7 vols. post 8vo. 6s. each.

Lord Macaulay's Critical and Historical Essays contributed to The Edinburgh Review. Four Editions:—

1. A LIBRARY EDITION (the *Eighth*), in 3 vols. 8vo. price 36s.
2. Complete in ONE VOLUME, with Portrait and Vignette. Square crown 8vo. price 21s. cloth; or 30s. calf.
3. Another NEW EDITION, in 3 vols. fcp. 8vo. price 21s. cloth.
4. The PEOPLE'S EDITION, in 2 vols. crown 8vo. price 8s. cloth.

Lord Macaulay's Lays of Ancient Rome, with *Ivry* and the *Armada.* 16mo. price 4s. 6d. cloth; or 10s. 6d. bound in morocco.

Lord Macaulay's Lays of Ancient Rome. With Illustrations, Original and from the Antique, drawn on Wood by G. Scharf, jun. Fcp. 4to. 21s. boards; or 42s. bound in morocco.

Macaulay. — Speeches of the Right Hon. Lord MACAULAY. Corrected by HIMSELF. 8vo. 12s.

Mac Donald.—Poems. By George MAC DONALD, Author of *Within and Without.* Fcp. 8vo. 7s.

Mac Donald. — Within and Without: A Dramatic Poem. By GEORGE MAC DONALD. Fcp. 8vo. 4s. 6d.

Mac Dougall. — The Theory of War illustrated by numerous Examples from History. By Lieutenant-Colonel P. L. MAC DOUGALL, Commandant of the Staff College. *Second Edition,* revised. Post 8vo. with Plans, 10s. 6d.

Mac Dougall.—The Campaigns of Hannibal, arranged and critically considered, expressly for the use of Students of Military History. By Lt.-Col. P. L. MacDougall. Post 8vo. 7s. 6d.

Sir James Mackintosh's Miscellaneous Works: Including his Contributions to the Edinburgh Review. Square crown 8vo. 21s. cloth; or 30s. bound in calf: or in 3 vols. fcp. 8vo. 21s.

Sir James Mackintosh's History of England from the Earliest Times to the final Establishment of the Reformation. 2 vols. 8vo. 21s.

M'Culloch's Dictionary, Practical, Theoretical, and Historical, of Commerce, and Commercial Navigation. Illustrated with Maps and Plans. New Edition. 8vo. price 50s. cloth; or 55s. half-russia. SUPPLEMENT to the Edition published in 1859, containing the late Commercial Treaty with France, the New Indian Tariff, &c. price 2s. 6d.

M'Culloch's Dictionary, Geographical, Statistical, and Historical, of the various Countries, Places, and principal Natural Objects in the World. With 6 Maps. 2 vols. 8vo. 63s.

Maguire. — Rome; its Ruler and its Institutions. By JOHN FRANCIS MAGUIRE, M.P. *Second Edition*, enlarged. Post 8vo. 10s. 6d.

Mrs. Marcet's Conversations on Natural Philosophy, in which the Elements of that Science are familiarly explained. With 34 Plates. Fcp. 8vo. price 10s. 6d.

Mrs. Marcet's Conversations on Chemistry, in which the Elements of that Science are familiarly explained and illustrated. 2 vols. fcp. 8vo. 14s.

Marshman's Life of General Havelock.—Memoirs of Major-General Sir Henry Havelock, K.C.B. By JOHN CLARK MARSHMAN. With Portrait, Map, and 2 Plans. 8vo. 12s. 6d.

Marshman.—The Life and Times of Carey, Marshman, and Ward: Embracing the History of the Serampore Mission. By JOHN CLARK MARSHMAN. 2 vols. 8vo. 25s.

Martineau. — Studies of Christianity: A Series of Original Papers, now first collected, or New. By JAMES MARTINEAU. Crown 8vo. 7s. 6d.

Martineau. — Endeavours after the Christian Life: Discourses. By JAMES MARTINEAU. 2 vols. post 8vo. price 7s. 6d. each.

Martineau. — Hymns for the Christian Church and Home. Collected and edited by JAMES MARTINEAU. *Eleventh Edition*, 12mo. 3s. 6d. cloth, or 5s. calf; *Fifth Edition*, 32mo. 1s. 4d. cloth, or 1s. 8d. roan; an Edition in 18mo. price 2s. 10d. cloth.

Martineau.—Miscellanies: Comprising Essays chiefly religious and controversial. By JAMES MARTINEAU. Crown 8vo. 9s.

Maunder's Scientific and Literary Treasury: A new and popular Encyclopædia of Science and the Belles-Lettres; including all Branches of Science, and every subject connected with Literature and Art. Thoroughly revised Edition, with Corrections and Additions. Fcp. 8vo. 10s.

Maunder's Biographical Treasury; consisting of Memoirs, Sketches, and brief Notices of above 12,000 Eminent Persons of All Ages and Nations, from the Earliest Period of History: Forming a complete Dictionary of Universal Biography. *Eleventh Edition*, corrected and extended. Fcp. 8vo. 10s.

Maunder's Treasury of Knowledge and Library of Reference: Comprising an English Dictionary and Grammar, a Universal Gazetteer, a Classical Dictionary, a Chronology, a Law Dictionary, a Synopsis of the Peerage, numerous useful Tables, &c. New Edition, reconstructed by B. B. WOODWARD, B.A.; assisted by J. MORRIS, Solicitor, and W. HUGHES, F.R.G.S. Fcp. 8vo. 10s.

Maunder's Treasury of Natural History; or, a Popular Dictionary of Animated Nature: In which the Zoological Characteristics that distinguish the different Classes, Genera, and Species, are combined with a variety of interesting Information illustrative of the Habits, Instincts, and General Economy of the Animal Kingdom. With 900 Woodcuts. Fcp. 10s.

Maunder's Historical Treasury; comprising a General Introductory Outline of Universal History, Ancient and Modern, and a Series of Separate Histories of every principal Nation that exists; their Rise, Progress, and Present Condition, the Moral and Social Character of their respective Inhabitants, their Religion, Manners, and Customs, &c. New Edition, carefully revised throughout; with a new INDEX now first added. Fcp. 8vo. 10s.

Maunder's Treasury of Geography, Physical, Historical, Descriptive, and Political; containing a succinct Account of Every Country in the World: Preceded by an Introductory Outline of the History of Geography; a Familiar Inquiry into the Varieties of Race and Language exhibited by different Nations; and a View of the Relations of Geography to Astronomy and the Physical Sciences. New Edition, carefully revised throughout; with the Statistics throughout the volume brought, in every instance, up to the latest date of information. With 7 Maps and 16 Steel Plates. Fcp. 8vo. price 10s.

Merivale (Miss). — Christian Records: A Short History of Apostolic Age. By LOUISA A. MERIVALE. Fcp. 8vo. price 7s. 6d.

Merivale. — The Fall of the Roman Republic: A Short History of Last Century of the Commonwealth. By Rev. C. MERIVALE. 12mo. 7s. 6d.

Merivale. — A History of the Romans under the Empire. By the Rev. CHARLES MERIVALE, B.D., late Fellow of St. John's College, Cambridge. 8vo. with Maps :—

VOLS. I. and II. comprising the History to the Fall of *Julius Cæsar*. Second Edition, 28s.

VOL. III. to the Establishment of the Monarchy by *Augustus*. Second Edition......14s.

VOLS. IV. and V. from *Augustus* to *Claudius*, B.C. 27 to A.D. 54 ....32s.

VOL. VI. from the Reign of Nero, A.D. 54, to the Fall of Jerusalem, A.D. 70............16s.

Miles.—The Horse's Foot and How to Keep it Sound. *Eighth Edition*; with an Appendix on Shoeing in general, and Hunters in particular. 12 Plates and 12 Woodcuts. By W. MILES, Esq. Imperial 8vo. 12s. 6d.

Miles's Plain Treatise on Horse-Shoeing. With Plates and Woodcuts. Second Edition. Post 8vo. 2s.

Mintura.—From New York to Delhi by way of Rio de Janeiro, Australia, and China. By ROBERT B. MINTURN, Jun. With coloured Route-Map of India. Post 8vo. 7s. 6d.

Thomas Moore's Memoirs, Journal, and Correspondence. New Edition for the People, with 8 Portraits and 2 Vignettes on Steel. Edited and abridged from the First Edition by the Right Hon. LORD JOHN RUSSELL, M.P. Uniform with the *People's Edition of Moore's Poetical Works*. Square crown 8vo. 12s. 6d. cloth, gilt edges.

Thomas Moore's Poetical Works: Comprising the Author's Autobiographical Prefaces, latest Corrections, and Notes. Various Editions of the separate Poems and complete Poetical Works, as follows :—

	s.	d.
LALLA ROOKH, fcp. 4to. with Woodcut Illustrations by TENNIEL.........	21	0
LALLA ROOKH, 32mo. ruby type	1	0
LALLA ROOKH, 16mo. Vignette	2	6
LALLA ROOKH, square crown 8vo. Plates	15	0
IRISH MELODIES, 32mo. ruby type..	1	0
IRISH MELODIES, 16mo. Vignette ..	2	6
IRISH MELODIES, square crown 8vo. Plates	21	0
IRISH MELODIES, illustrated by MACLISE, super-royal 8vo..................	31	6
SONGS, BALLADS, and SACRED SONGS, 32mo. ruby type	2	6
SONGS, BALLADS, and SACRED SONGS, 16mo. Vignette	5	0
POETICAL WORKS, People's Edition, 10 PARTS, each..........................	1	0
POETICAL WORKS, Cabinet Edition, 10 VOLS. each............................	3	6
POETICAL WORKS, Traveller's Edition, crown 8vo...........................	12	6
POETICAL WORKS, Library Edition, medium 8vo.................................	21	0
SELECTIONS, "POETRY and PICTURES from THOMAS MOORE," fcp. 4to. Wood Engravings	21	0
MOORE'S EPICUREAN, 16mo. Vignette...	5	0

Editions printed with the Music.

IRISH MELODIES, People's Edition, small 4to.	12	0
IRISH MELODIES, imperial 8vo. small music size	31	6
HARMONISED AIRS from IRISH MELODIES, imperial 8vo...........	15	0
NATIONAL AIRS, People's Edition, small 4to.	12	0
NATIONAL AIRS, imperial 8vo. small music size	31	6
SACRED SONGS and SONGS from SCRIPTURE, imperial 8vo.	16	0

No Edition of Thomas Moore's Poetical Works can be published complete except by Messrs. LONGMAN and CO.

Mollhausen's Diary of a Journey from the Mississippi to the Coasts of the Pacific, with a United States Government Expedition. With an Introduction by Baron HUMBOLDT; Map and Illustrations. 2 vols. 8vo. 30s.

Moore.—The Power of the Soul over the Body, considered in relation to Health and Morals. By GEORGE MOORE, M.D. Fcp. 8vo. 6s.

Moore.—The Use of the Body in relation to the Mind. By G. MOORE, M.D. Fcp. 8vo. 6s.

Moore.—Man and his Motives. By GEORGE MOORE, M.D. Fcp. 8vo. 6s.

James Montgomery's Poetical Works: Collective Edition; with the Author's Autobiographical Prefaces, complete in One Volume; with Portrait and Vignette. Square crown 8vo. 10s. 6d. cloth; morocco, 21s.—Or, in 4 vols. fcp. 8vo. with Plates, 14s.

Morell. — Elements of Psychology: PART I., containing the Analysis of the Intellectual Powers. By J. D. MORELL, M.A., One of Her Majesty's Inspectors of Schools. Post 8vo. 7s. 6d.

Morning Clouds. By the Author of *The Afternoon of Life*. Second Edition, revised throughout. Fcp. 8vo. 5s.

Morton's Agricultural Handbooks. — Handbook of Dairy Husbandry: Comprising Dairy Statistics; Food of the Cow; Milk; Butter; Cheese; General Management; Calendar of Daily Dairy Operations; Appendix on Cheese-making; and Index. By JOHN CHALMERS MORTON. 16mo. 1s. 6d.

HANDBOOK of FARM LABOUR, Steam, Horse, and Water Power, *nearly ready.*

Morton.—The Resources of Estates: A Treatise on the Agricultural Improvement and General Management of Landed Property. By JOHN LOCKHART MORTON. With 25 Lithographic Illustrations. Royal 8vo. 31s.6d.

Moseley.—Astro-Theology. By the Rev. HENRY MOSELEY, M.A., F.R.S., Chaplain in Ordinary to the Queen, &c. Fcp. 8vo. 4s. 6d.

Moseley's Mechanical Principles of Engineering and Architecture. Second Edition, enlarged; with numerous Woodcuts. 8vo. 24s.

Memoirs and Letters of the late Colonel ARMINE MOUNTAIN, Adjutant-General of H. M. Forces in India. Edited by Mrs. MOUNTAIN. Second Edition, Portrait. Fcp. 8vo. 6s.

Mure.—A Critical History of the Language and Literature of Ancient Greece. By WILLIAM MURE, of Caldwell. VOLS. I. to III. 8vo. price 36s.; VOL. IV. 15s.; and VOL. V. 18s.

Murray's Encyclopædia of Geography, comprising a complete Description of the Earth: Exhibiting its Relation to the Heavenly Bodies, its Physical Structure, the Natural History of each Country, and the Industry, Commerce, Political Institutions, and Civil and Social State of All Nations. Second Edition; with 82 Maps, and upwards of 1,000 other Woodcuts. 8vo. 60s.

Neale.—The Closing Scene; or, Christianity and Infidelity contrasted in the Last Hours of Remarkable Persons. By the Rev. ERSKINE NEALE, M.A. 2 vols. fcp. 8vo. 6s. each.

Newman. — The Scope and Nature of University Education. By JOHN HENRY NEWMAN, D.D., of the Oratory. Second Edition. Fcp. 8vo. 6s.

By the same Author, fcp. 8vo. 6s. each,

LECTURES and ESSAYS on UNIVERSITY SUBJECTS.

The OFFICE and WORK of UNIVERSITIES.

Ogilvie.—The Master-Builder's Plan; or, the Principles of Organic Architecture as indicated in the Typical Forms of Animals. By GEORGE OGILVIE, M.D. Post 8vo. with 72 Woodcuts, price 6s. 6d.

Osborn.—The Discovery of the North-West Passage by H.M.S. *Investigator*, Captain R. M'CLURE, 1850-1854. Edited by Captain SHERARD OSBORN, C.B. Third Edition; with Portrait, Chart, and Illustrations. 8vo. 15s.

Professor Owen's Lectures on the Comparative Anatomy and Physiology of the Invertebrate Animals. Second Edition, with 235 Woodcuts. 8vo. 21s.

Professor Owen's Lectures on the Comparative Anatomy and Physiology of the Vertebrate Animals. Vol. I. 8vo. 14s.

Palleske's Life of Schiller. Translated by LADY WALLACE. Dedicated by permission to Her Majesty the Queen. 2 vols. post 8vo. with 2 Portraits, 21s.

Memoirs of Admiral Parry, the Arctic Navigator. By his Son, the Rev. E. PARRY, M.A. Seventh Edition; with a Portrait and coloured Chart of the North-West Passage. Fcp. 8vo. 5s.

Peaks, Passes, and Glaciers: a Series of Excursions by Members of the Alpine Club. Edited by JOHN BALL, M.R.I.A., F.L.S., President. Traveller's Edition (the *Fifth*), comprising all the Mountain Expeditions and the Maps, printed in a condensed form for the Pocket or Knapsack. 16mo. 5s. 6d.

The Fourth Edition of *Peaks, Passes, and Glaciers*, with 8 coloured Illustrations and many Woodcuts, may still be had, price 21s. Also the EIGHT SWISS MAPS, accompanied by a Table of the HEIGHTS of MOUNTAINS, 3s. 6d.

Peel.—Sketch of the Life and Character of Sir Robert Peel, Bart. By the Right Hon. Sir LAWRENCE PEEL. Post 8vo. 8s. 6d.

Dr. Pereira's Elements of Mate- ria Medica and Therapeutics. *Third Edition*, enlarged and improved from the Author's Materials by A. S. TAYLOR, M.D., and G. O. REES, M.D. Vol. I. 8vo. 28s.; Vol. II. Part I. 21s.; Vol. II. Part II. 26s.

Dr. Pereira's Lectures on Polar- ised Light, together with a Lecture on the Microscope. 2d Edition, enlarged from the Author's Materials by Rev. B. POWELL, M.A. Fcp. 8vo. Woodcuts, price 7s.

Peschel's Elements of Physics. Translated from the German, with Notes, by E. WEST. With Diagrams and Woodcuts. 3 vols. fcp. 8vo. 21s.

Phillips's Elementary Introduc- tion to Mineralogy. A New Edition, with extensive Alterations and Additions, by H. J. BROOKE, F.R.S., F.G.S.; and W. H. MILLER, M.A., F.G.S. With numerous Woodcuts. Post 8vo. 18s.

Phillips.—A Guide to Geology. By JOHN PHILLIPS, M.A., F.R.S., F.G.S., &c. Fourth Edition, corrected; with 4 Plates. Fcp. 8vo. 5s.

Piesse's Laboratory of Chymical Wonders: A Scientific Mélange intended for the Instruction and Entertainment of Young People. Fcp. 8vo. with Illustrations. [*Just ready*.

Piesse's Chymical, Natural, and Physical Magic, for the Instruction and Entertainment of Juveniles during the Holiday Vacation: with 30 Woodcuts and Portrait. Fcp. 8vo. 3s. 6d.

Piesse's Art of Perfumery, and Methods of Obtaining the Odours of Plants; with Instructions for the Manufacture of Perfumes for the Handkerchief, Scented Powders, Odorous Vinegars, Dentifrices, Pomatums, Cosmétiques, Perfumed Soap, &c.; and an Appendix on the Colours of Flowers, Artificial Fruit Essences, &c. *Second Edition*; Woodcuts. Crown 8vo. 8s. 6d.

Piozzi.—Autobiography, Letters, and Literary Remains of Mrs. Piozzi (Thrale), Author of *Anecdotes of Dr. Johnson*. Edited, with Notes and some account of her Life and Writings, by A. HAYWARD, Esq., Q.C. With a Portrait of Mrs. Piozzi, and an engraving from a Picture by Hogarth.

Pitt.—How to Brew Good Beer: A complete Guide to the Art of Brewing Ale, Bitter Ale, Table Ale, Brown Stout, Porter, and Table Beer. To which are added Practical Instructions for Making Malt. By JOHN PITT. Fcp. 8vo. 4s. 6d.

Porter.—History of the Knights of Malta, or the Order of the Hospital of St. John of Jerusalem. By Major WHITWORTH PORTER, R.E. With 5 Illustrations. 2 vols. 8vo. 24s.

Powell.—Essays on the Spirit of the Inductive Philosophy, the Unity of Worlds, and the Philosophy of Creation. By the Rev. BADEN POWELL, M.A., &c. Crown 8vo. Woodcuts, 12s. 6d.

Powell. — Christianity without Judaism: A Second Series of Essays on the Unity of Worlds and of Nature. By the Rev. BADEN POWELL, M.A., &c. Crown 8vo. 7s. 6d.

PUBLISHED BY LONGMAN, GREEN, AND CO.   19

Powell.—The Order of Nature considered in reference to the Claims of Revelation: A Third Series of Essays on the Unity of Worlds and of Nature. By the Rev. BADEN POWELL, M.A. Crown 8vo. 12s.

Power.—Virginia's Hand: a Poem. By MARGUERITE A. POWER. Fcp. 8vo. 5s.

Pycroft.—The Collegian's Guide; or, Recollections of College Days: Setting forth the Advantages and Temptations of a University Education. By the Rev. J. PYCROFT, B.A. Fcp. 8vo. 6s.

Pycroft's Course of English Reading; or, How and What to Read: Adapted to every taste and capacity. With Literary Anecdotes. Fcp. 8vo. 5s.

Pycroft's Cricket-Field; or, the Science and History of the Game of Cricket. Third Edition; Plates and Woodcuts. Fcp. 8vo. 5s.

Quatrefages' Rambles of a Naturalist on the Coasts of France, Spain, and Sicily. Translated by E. C. OTTÉ. 2 vols. post 8vo. 15s.

Thomas Raikes's Journal from 1831 to 1847: Comprising Reminiscences of Social and Political Life in London and Paris during that period. New Edition, complete in 2 vols. crown 8vo. price 12s.

Ramsay.—The Old Glaciers of North Wales and Switzerland. By A. C. RAMSAY, F.R.S. and G.S. With Map and 14 Woodcuts. Fcp. 8vo. price 4s. 6d.

Rich's Dictionary of Roman and Greek Antiquities, with nearly 2,000 Woodcuts representing Objects from the Antique. Forming an Illustrated Companion to the Latin Dictionary and Greek Lexicon. Second and cheaper Edition. Post 8vo. 12s. 6d.

Horsemanship; or, the Art of Riding and Managing a Horse, adapted to the Guidance of Ladies and Gentlemen on the Road and in the Field: With Instructions for Breaking-in Colts and Young Horses. By Captain RICHARDSON, late of the 4th Light Dragoons. With 5 Plates. Square crown 8vo. 14s.

Riddle's Household Prayers for Four Weeks: With additional Prayers for Special Occasions. To which is appended a Course of Scripture Reading for Every Day in the Year. Second Edition. Crown 8vo. 3s. 6d.

Riddle's Complete Latin-English and English-Latin Dictionary, for the use of Colleges and Schools. New Edition, revised and corrected. 8vo. 21s.

Riddle's Diamond Latin-English Dictionary. A Guide to the Meaning, Quality, and right Accentuation of Latin Classical Words. Royal 32mo. 4s.

Riddle's Copious and Critical Latin-English Lexicon, founded on the German-Latin Dictionaries of Dr. William Freund. Post 4to. 31s. 6d.

Rivers's Rose-Amateur's Guide; containing ample Descriptions of all the fine leading variety of Roses, regularly classed in their respective Families; their History and Mode of Culture. Sixth Edition. Fcp. 8vo. 3s. 6d.

Dr. E. Robinson's Greek and English Lexicon to the Greek Testament. A New Edition, revised and in great part re-written. 8vo. 18s.

Mr. Henry Rogers's Essays selected from Contributions to the *Edinburgh Review*. Second Edition, with Additions. 3 vols. fcp. 8vo. 21s.

Samuel Rogers's Recollections of Personal and Conversational Intercourse with Fox, Burke, Grattan, Porson, Horne Tooke, Talleyrand, Erskine, Scott, Lord Grenville, and the Duke of Wellington. *Second Edition.* Fcp. 8vo. 5s.

Dr. Roget's Thesaurus of English Words and Phrases classified and arranged so as to facilitate the Expression of Ideas and assist in Literary Composition. Ninth Edition, revised and improved. Crown 8vo. 10s. 6d.

Ronalds's Fly-Fisher's Entomology: With coloured Representation of the Natural and Artificial Insects, and a few Observations and Instructions on Trout and Grayling Fishing. *Fifth Edition*; with 20 new-coloured Plates. 8vo. 14s.

Rowton's Debater: A Series of complete Debates, Outlines of Debates, and Questions for Discussion; with ample References to the best Sources of Information. Fcp. 8vo. 6s.

Dr. C. W. Russell's Life of Cardinal Mezzofanti: With an Introductory Memoir of eminent Linguists, Ancient and Modern. With Portrait and Facsimiles. 8vo. 12s.

SchimmelPenninck (Mrs.) — Life of Mary Anne SchimmelPenninck. Edited by her relation, CHRISTIANA C. HANKIN. Fourth Edition, carefully revised throughout; with a few Additions and a Portrait of Mrs. SchimmelPenninck. Post 8vo. 10s. 6d.

SchimmelPenninck's (Mrs.) Select Memoirs of Port Royal. *Fifth Edition*, revised, &c. by C. C. HANKIN. 3 vols. post 8vo. 21s.

SchimmelPenninck's (Mrs.) Principles of Beauty; with an Essay on the Temperaments, and Thoughts on Grecian and Gothic Architecture. Edited by C. C. HANKIN. With 12 coloured Illustrations in Facsimile of Original Designs by Mrs. SchimmelPenninck. price 12s. 6d.

SchimmelPenninck's (Mrs.) Sacred Musings on Manifestations of God to the Soul of Man; with Thoughts on the Destiny of Woman, and other subjects. Edited by C. C. HANKIN; with Preface by the Rev. Dr. BAYLEE. Post 8vo. 10s. 6d.

Dr. L. Schmitz's History of Greece, mainly based upon Bishop Thirlwall's History. *Fifth Edition*, with Nine new Supplementary Chapters on the Civilisation, Religion, Literature, and Arts of the Ancient Greeks, contributed by C. H. WATSON, M.A. Trin. Coll. Camb.; also a Map of Athens and 137 Woodcuts designed by G. Scharf, jun., F.S.A. 12mo. 7s. 6d.

Scoffern (Dr.)—Projectile Weapons of War and Explosive Compounds. By J. SCOFFERN, M.B. Lond. *4th Edition*. Post 8vo. Woodcuts, 9s. 6d.

Senior.—Journal kept in Turkey and Greece in the Autumn of 1857 and the beginning of 1858. By NASSAU W. SENIOR, Esq. With 2 Maps and 2 Views. Post 8vo. 12s.

Sewell (Miss).—New Edition of the Tales and Stories of the Author of *Amy Herbert*, in 9 vols. crown 8vo. price £1. 10s. cloth; or each work complete in one volume, separately, as follows :—

AMY HERBERT............2s. 6d.
GERTRUDE................2s. 6d.
The EARL'S DAUGHTER..2s. 6d.
The EXPERIENCE of LIFE..2s. 6d.
CLEVE HALL..............3s. 6d.
IVORS, or the Two COUSINS 3s. 6d.
KATHARINE ASHTON....3s. 6d.
MARGARET PERCIVAL ..5s. 0d.
LANETON PARSONAGE ..4s. 6d.

Also by the Author of Amy Herbert.

Passing Thoughts on Religion. *New Edition.* Fcp. 8vo. 5s.

Ursula: A Tale of English Country Life. 2 vols. fcp. 8vo. 12s.

History of the Early Church: from the First Preaching of the Gospel to the Council of Nicea. 18mo. 4s. 6d.

Self-Examination before Confirmation: With Devotions and Directions for Confirmation-Day. 32mo.1s.6d.

Readings for a Month preparatory to Confirmation: Compiled from the Works of Writers of the Early and of the English Church. Fcp. 8vo. 4s.

Readings for every Day in Lent: Compiled from the Writings of Bishop JEREMY TAYLOR. Fcp. 8vo. 5s.

Bowdler's Family Shakspeare: In which nothing is *added* to the Original Text; but those words and expressions are *omitted* which cannot with propriety be read aloud. Illustrated with 36 Woodcut Vignettes. *Library Edition*, in One Volume, medium 8vo. price 21s.; *Pocket Edition*, in 6 vols. fcp. 8vo. price 5s. each; each *Play* separately, price 1s.

Sharp's New British Gazetteer, or Topographical Dictionary of the British Islands and narrow Seas: Comprising concise Descriptions of about 60,000 Places, Seats, Natural Features, and Objects of Note, founded on the best authorities. 2 vols. 8vo. £2. 16s.

Shee.—Life of Sir Martin Archer Shee, President of the Royal Academy, F.R.S., D.C.L. By his Son, MARTIN ARCHER SHEE, of the Middle Temple, Esq., Barrister-at-Law. 2 vols. 8vo. 21s.

Short Whist; its Rise, Progress, and Laws: With Observations to make any one a Whist-Player. Containing also the Laws of Piquet, Cassino, Ecarté, Cribbage, Backgammon. By Major A. New Edition; with Precepts for Tyros, by Mrs. B. Fcp. 8vo. 3s.

Simpkinson.—The Washingtons: a Tale of an English Country Parish in the Seventeenth Century. By the Rev. J. N. SIMPKINSON. Post 8vo. 10s. 6d.

Simpson.—Handbook of Dining; or, How to Dine, theoretically, philosophically, and historically considered: Based chiefly upon the *Physiologie du Goût* of Brillat-Savarin. By LEONARD FRANCIS SIMPSON, M.R.S.L. Fcp. 8vo. 5s.

Sir Roger De Coverley. From the Spectator. With Notes and Illustrations, by W. HENRY WILLS; and 12 Wood Engravings from Designs by F. TAYLER. Crown 8vo. 10s. 6d.; or 21s. in morocco by Hayday.

The Sketches: Three Tales. By the Authors of *Amy Herbert, The Old Man's Home,* and *Hawkstone.* Fcp. 8vo. price 4s. 6d.

Sleigh.—Personal Wrongs and Legal Remedies. By W. CAMPBELL SLEIGH, of the Middle Temple, Esq., Barrister-at-Law. Fcp. 8vo. 2s. 6d.

Smee's Elements of Electro-Metallurgy. Third Edition, revised; with Electrotypes and numerous Woodcuts. Post 8vo. 10s. 6d.

Smith (G.) — History of Wes-leyan Methodism. By GEORGE SMITH, F.A.S., Author of *Sacred Annals, &c.* VOL. I. *Wesley and his Times;* VOL. II. *The Middle Age of Methodism,* from 1791 to 1816. Crown 8vo. 10s. 6d. each.

Smith (J.) — The Voyage and Shipwreck of St. Paul: With Dissertations on the Life and Writings of St. Luke, and the Ships and Navigation of the Ancients. By JAMES SMITH, F.R.S. With Charts, Views, and Woodcuts. Crown 8vo. 8s. 6d.

The Wit and Wisdom of the Rev. Sydney Smith: a Selection of the most memorable Passages in his Writings and Conversation. 16mo. 7s. 6d.

A Memoir of the Rev. Sydney Smith. By his Daughter, LADY HOLLAND. With a Selection from his Letters, edited by Mrs. AUSTIN. *New Edition.* 2 vols. 8vo. 28s.

The Rev. Sydney Smith's Mis-cellaneous Works: Including his Contributions to The Edinburgh Review. Four Editions:—

1. A LIBRARY EDITION (the *Fourth*), in 3 vols. 8vo. with Portrait, 36s.
2. Complete in ONE VOLUME, with Portrait and Vignette. Square crown 8vo. 21s. cloth; or 30s. bound in calf.
3. Another NEW EDITION, in 3 vols. fcp. 8vo. 21s.
4. The People's Edition, in 2 vols. crown 8vo. price 8s. cloth.

The Rev. Sydney Smith's Ele-mentary Sketches of Moral Philosophy, delivered at the Royal Institution in the Years 1804 to 1806. Fcp. 8vo. 7s.

Snow.—Two Years' Cruise off Tierra del Fuego, the Falkland Islands, Patagonia, and in the River Plate: A Narrative of Life in the Southern Seas. By W. PARKER SNOW. With Charts and Illustrations. 2 vols. post 8vo. 24s.

Robert Southey's Complete Poet-ical Works; containing all the Author's last Introductions and Notes. Complete in One Volume, with Portrait and Vignette. Medium 8vo. 21s. cloth; 42s. bound in morocco. Or in 10 vols. fcp. 8vo. with Portrait and 19 Vignettes, 35s.

Southey's Doctor, complete in One Volume. Edited by the Rev. J. W. WARTER, B.D. With Portrait, Vignette, Bust, and coloured Plate. Square crown 8vo. 21s.

Southey's Life of Wesley; and Rise and Progress of Methodism. Fourth Edition, edited by Rev. C. C. SOUTHEY, M.A. 2 vols. crown 8vo. 12s.

Spencer.—Essays, Scientific, Po-litical, and Speculative. By HERBERT SPENCER, Author of *Social Statics.* Reprinted chiefly from Quarterly Reviews. 8vo. 12s. cloth.

Spencer. — The Principles of Psychology. By HERBERT SPENCER, Author of *Social Statics.* 8vo. 16s.

Spitta.—Lyra Domestica: Christian Songs for Domestic Edification. Translated from the *Psaltery and Harp* of C. J. P. SPITTA. By RICHARD MASSIE. Fcp. 8vo. with Portrait, price 4s. 6d.

Sir James Stephen's Essays in Ecclesiastical Biography. *4th Edition*, complete in One Volume; with Biographical Notice of the Author by his SON. 8vo. 14s.

Sir J. Stephen's Lectures on the History of France. Third Edition. 2 vols. 8vo. 24s.

Stonehenge.—The Dog in Health and Disease: Comprising the various Modes of Breaking and using him for Hunting, Coursing, Shooting, &c.; and including the Points or Characteristics of Toy Dogs. By STONEHENGE. With about 70 Illustrations engraved on Wood. Square crown 8vo. 15s.

Stonehenge's Work on the Greyhound: Being a Treatise on the Art of Breeding, Rearing, and Training Greyhounds for Public Running; their Diseases and Treatment: Containing also Rules for the Management of Coursing Meetings, and for the Decision of Courses. With Frontispiece and Woodcuts. Square crown 8vo. 21s.

Stow's Training System, Moral Training School, and Normal Seminary for preparing Schoolmasters and Governesses. Eleventh Edition; Plates and Woodcuts. Post 8vo. 6s. 6d.

Strickland.—Lives of the Queens of England. By AGNES STRICKLAND. Dedicated, by express permission, to Her Majesty. Embellished with Portraits of every Queen, engraved from the most authentic sources. Complete in 8 vols. post 8vo. 7s. 6d. each.

Tate on the Strength of Materials; containing various original and useful Formulæ, specially applied to Tubular Bridges, Wrought Iron and Cast Iron Beams, &c. 8vo. 5s. 6d.

Tennent.—Ceylon: An Account of the Island, Physical, Historical, and Topographical: with Copious Notices of its Natural History, Antiquities, and Productions. Illustrated by 9 Maps, 17 Plans and Charts, and 90 Engravings on Wood. By Sir J. EMERSON TENNENT, K.C.S., LL.D., &c. *Fifth Edition.* 2 vols. 8vo. price 50s.

Bishop Thirlwall's History of Greece. Library Edition; with Maps. 8 vols. 8vo. £3.—An Edition in 8 vols. fcp. 8vo. with Vignette Titles, 28s.

Thomson's Seasons. Edited by BOLTON CORNEY, Esq. Illustrated with 77 fine Wood Engravings from Designs by Members of the Etching Club. Square crown 8vo. 21s. cloth; or 36s. bound in morocco.

The Rev. Dr. Thomson's Outline of the Necessary Laws of Thought: A Treatise on Pure and Applied Logic. 4th Edition. Post 8vo. 5s. 6d.

Thomson's Tables of Interest, at Three, Four, Four-and-a-Half, and Five per Cent., from One Pound to Ten Thousand, and from 1 to 365 Days, in a regular progression of single Days; with Interest at all the above Rates, from One to Twelve Months, and from One to Ten Years. Also, numerous other Tables of Exchange, Time, and Discounts. 17th Edition, revised and stereotyped. 12mo. 3s. 6d.

The Thumb Bible; or, Verbum Sempiternum. By J. TAYLOR. Being an Epitome of the Old and New Testaments in English Verse. Reprinted from the Edition of 1693. 64mo. 1s. 6d.

Todd (Dr.)—The Cyclopædia of Anatomy and Physiology. Edited by ROBERT B. TODD, M.D., F.R.S., &c. Now complete in 5 vols. 8vo. pp. 5,350, with 2,853 Woodcuts, £6. 6s. cloth.

Tooke.—History of Prices, and of the State of the Circulation, during the Nine Years from 1848 to 1856 inclusive. Forming Vols. V. and VI. of Tooke's *History of Prices;* with full Index to the whole work. By THOMAS TOOKE, F.R.S. and WILLIAM NEWMARCH. 2 vols. 8vo. 52s. 6d.

Trevelyan (Sir C.) — Original Papers illustrating the History of the Application of the Roman Alphabet to the Languages of India. Edited by MONIER WILLIAMS, M.A. 8vo. 12s.

Trollope.—The Warden, a Novel. By ANTHONY TROLLOPE. New and cheaper Edition. Crown 8vo. 3s. 6d.

Trollope's Barchester Towers, a Sequel to *The Warden.* New and cheaper Edition, complete in One Volume. Crown 8vo. 5s.

The Traveller's Library: A Collection of original Works well adapted for *Travellers* and *Emigrants*, for School-room Libraries, the Libraries of *Mechanics' Institutions*, *Young Men's Libraries*, the *Libraries of Ships*, and similar purposes. The separate volumes are suited for *School Prizes*, *Presents to Young People*, and for general instruction and entertainment. The Series comprises fourteen of the most popular of Lord Macaulay's *Essays*, and his *Speeches* on Parliamentary Reform. The department of Travels contains some account of eight of the principal countries of Europe, as well as travels in four districts of Africa, in four of America, and in three of Asia. Madame Pfeiffer's *First Journey round the World* is included; and a general account of the *Australian Colonies*. In Biography and History will be found Lord Macaulay's Biographical Sketches of *Warren Hastings*, *Clive*, *Pitt*, *Walpole*, *Bacon*, and others; besides Memoirs of *Wellington*, *Turenne*, *F. Arago*, &c.; an Essay on the Life and Genius of *Thomas Fuller*, with Selections from his Writings, by Mr. Henry Rogers; and a history of the *Leipsic Campaign*, by Mr. Gleig, — which is the only separate account of this remarkable campaign. Works of Fiction did not come within the plan of the TRAVELLER'S LIBRARY; but the *Confessions of a Working Man*, by Souvestre, which is indeed a fiction founded on fact, has been included, and has been read with unusual interest by many of the working classes, for whose use it is especially recommended. Dumas's story of the *Maitre-d'Armes*, though in form a work of fiction, gives a striking picture of an episode in the history of Russia. Amongst the works on Science and Natural Philosophy, a general view of Creation is embodied in Dr. Kemp's *Natural History of Creation*; and in his *Indications of Instinct* remarkable facts in natural history are collected. Dr. Wilson has contributed a popular account of the *Electric Telegraph*. In the volumes on the *Coal-Fields*, and on the Tin and other Mining Districts of *Cornwall*, is given an account of the mineral wealth of England, the habits and manners of the miners, and the scenery of the surrounding country. It only remains to add, that among the Miscellaneous Works are a Selection of the best Writings of the Rev. Sydney Smith; Lord Carlisle's *Lectures and Addresses*; an account of *Mormonism*, by the Rev. W. J. Conybeare; an exposition of *Railway* management and mismanagement by Mr. Herbert Spencer; an account of the Origin and Practice of *Printing*, by Mr. Stark; and an account of *London*, by Mr. M'Culloch.—To be had, in *complete Sets only*, at £5. 5s. per Set, bound in cloth and lettered.

☞ *The Traveller's Library* may also be had as originally issued in 102 parts, 1s. each, forming 50 vols. 2s. 6d. each; or any separate parts or volumes.

Sharon Turner's History of the Anglo-Saxons, from the Earliest Period to the Norman Conquest. 3 vols. 36s.

Dr. Turton's Manual of the Land and Fresh-Water Shells of Great Britain: With Figures of each of the kinds. New Edition, with Additions by Dr. J. E. GRAY, F.R.S. Crown 8vo. with 12 coloured Plates, 15s.

Twisden. — Elementary Examples in Practical Mechanics, comprising copious Explanations and Proofs of the Fundamental Propositions. By the Rev. JOHN F. TWISDEN, M.A., Professor of Mathematics in the Staff College. Crown 8vo. 12s.

Dr. Ure's Dictionary of Arts, Manufactures, and Mines: Containing a clear Exposition of their Principles and Practice. New Edition, chiefly rewritten and greatly enlarged; with nearly 2,000 Woodcuts. Edited by ROBERT HUNT, F.R.S., F.S.S., Keeper of Mining Records. 3 vols. 8vo. £4.

Walford. — The Handybook of the Civil Service. By EDWARD WALFORD, M.A., late Scholar of Balliol College, Oxford. Fcp. 8vo. 4s. 6d.

"HERE is the very book which aspirants to Government situations are in search of. It explains the whole system from principles to details. One objection to it may be that it tends to open for the candidate a road rather too royal." ATHENÆUM.

Warburton. — Hunting Songs and Miscellaneous Verses. By R. E. EGERTON WARBURTON. *Second Edition*. Fcp. 8vo. 5s.

Waterton's Essays on Natural History, chiefly Ornithology: With Autobiography of the Author. THREE SERIES; with Portrait and 2 Vignettes. 3 vols. fcp. 8vo. price 16s.

Webb. — Celestial Objects for Common Telescopes. By the Rev. T. W. WEBB, M.A., F.R.A.S. With Map of the Moon, and Woodcuts. 16mo. 7s.

Webster and Parkes's Encyclopædia of Domestic Economy; comprising such subjects as are most immediately connected with Housekeeping; viz. The Construction of Domestic Edifices, with the Modes of Warming, Ventilating, and Lighting them — A description of the various Articles of Furniture, with the Nature of their Materials — Duties of Servants — &c. With nearly 1,000 Woodcuts. 8vo. 50s.

Weld.—Two Months in the Highlands, Orcadia, and Skye. By CHARLES RICHARD WELD, Barrister-at-Law. With 4 Illustrations in Chromo-lithography and 4 Woodcuts from Sketches by Mr. GEORGE BARNARD and the Author. Post 8vo. 12s. 6d.

Weld's Pyrenees, West and East. With 8 Illustrations in Chromo-xylography. Post 8vo. 12s. 6d.

Weld's Vacation Tour in the United States and Canada. 10s. 6d.

Weld's Vacations in Ireland. Post 8vo. 10s. 6d.

Dr. Charles West's Lectures on the Diseases of Infancy and Childhood. Fourth Edition, carefully revised throughout; with numerous additional Cases, and a copious INDEX. 8vo. 14s.

Dr. Charles West on Nursing Sick Children: Containing Directions which may be found of service to all who have the Charge of the Young. *Second Edition.* Fcp. 8vo. 1s. 6d.

White and Riddle.—A Latin-English Dictionary. By the Rev. J. T. WHITE, M.A., of Corpus Christi College, Oxford; and the Rev. J. E. RIDDLE, M.A., of St. Edmund Hall, Oxford. Founded on the larger Dictionary of Freund, revised by himself. Royal 8vo. [*Nearly ready.*

Whiteside.—Italy in the Nine-teenth Century. By the Right Hon. JAMES WHITESIDE, M.P., LL.D. *Third Edition*, abridged and revised; with a new Preface. Post 8vo. 12s. 6d.

Wilkins.—Political Ballads of the Seventeenth and Eighteenth Centuries, annotated. By W. WALKER WILKINS. 2 vols. post 8vo.

Willich's Popular Tables for ascertaining the Value of Lifehold, Leasehold, and Church Property, Renewal Fines, &c. With numerous additional Tables—Chemical, Astronomical, Trigonometrical, Common and Hyperbolic Logarithms; Constants, Squares, Cubes, Roots, Reciprocals, &c. Fourth Edition. Post 8vo. 10s.

Wills.—"The Eagle's Nest" in the Valley of Sixt; a Summer Home among the Alps: Together with some Excursions among the Great Glaciers. By ALFRED WILLS, of the Middle Temple, Esq. Barrister-at-Law. Second Edition, with 2 Maps and 12 Illustrations. Post 8vo. 12s. 6d.

Wilmot.—Lord Brougham's Law Reforms; or, an Analytical Review of Lord Brougham's Acts and Bills from 1811 to the Present Time. By Sir JOHN E. EARDLEY-WILMOT, Bart., Recorder of Warwick. Fcp. 8vo. 4s. 6d.

Wilmot's Abridgment of Black-stone's Commentaries on the Laws of England, in a series of Letters from a Father to his Daughter. 12mo. 6s. 6d.

Wilson's Bryologia Britannica: Containing the Mosses of Great Britain and Ireland systematically arranged and described according to the Method of *Bruch* and *Schimper;* with 61 illustrative Plates. Being a New Edition, enlarged and altered, of the *Muscologia Britannica* of Messrs. Hooker and Taylor. 8vo. 42s.; or, with the Plates coloured, price £4. 4s.

Yonge's New English-Greek Lexicon: Containing all the Greek Words used by Writers of good authority. *Second Edition.* Post 4to. 21s.

Yonge's New Latin Gradus: Containing Every Word used by the Poets of good authority. For the use of Eton, Westminster, Winchester, Harrow, and Rugby Schools; King's College, London; and Marlborough College. *Sixth Edition.* Post 8vo. 9s.; or, with APPENDIX of *Epithets*, 12s.

Youatt's Work on the Horse: With a Treatise on Draught. New Edition, revised and enlarged by E. N. GABRIEL, M.R.C.S., C.V.S. With numerous Woodcut Illustrations, chiefly from designs by W. Harvey. 8vo. price 10s. 6d. cloth.

Youatt.—The Dog. By William Youatt. A New Edition; with numerous Engravings, from Designs by W. Harvey. 8vo. 6s.

Zumpt's Grammar of the Latin Language. Translated and adapted for the use of English Students by Dr. L. SCHMITZ, F.R.S.E.: With numerous Additions and Corrections by the Author and Translator. 8vo. 14s.

[*October* 1860.

CPSIA information can be obtained
at www.ICGtesting.com
Printed in the USA
LVHW082133260520
656621LV00007B/20